NATURE ON THE EDGE

NATURE ON THE EDGE

Lessons for the Biosphere from the California Coast

BRUCE A. BYERS

Oregon State University Press   Corvallis

Oregon State University Press in Corvallis, Oregon, is located within the traditional homelands of the Marys River or Ampinefu Band of Kalapuya. Following the Willamette Valley Treaty of 1855, Kalapuya people were forcibly removed to reservations in Western Oregon. Today, living descendants of these people are a part of the Confederated Tribes of the Grand Ronde Community of Oregon (grandronde.org) and the Confederated Tribes of the Siletz Indians (ctsi.nsn.us).

Cataloging-in-publication data is available from the Library of Congress.

ISBN 978-1-962645-14-0 paperback; ISBN 978-1-962645-15-7ebook

∞ This paper meets the requirements of ANSI/NISO Z39.48-1992 (Permanence of Paper).

First published in 2024 by Oregon State University Press
Printed in the United States of America

Cover photograph by the author.
Frontispiece illustration by Robin L. Chandler.
Maps by Nora Sherwood.

Oregon State University
OSU Press

Oregon State University Press
121 The Valley Library
Corvallis OR 97331-4501
541-737-3166 • fax 541-737-3170
www.osupress.oregonstate.edu

Contents

Preface

OFF EARLY FROM THE Comfort Inn in Fillmore, Utah, and across the Nevada border on US Highway 50 West. Basin and range, basin and range, again and again, beautiful waves of the Earth's crust. Each range rises to nearly 12,000-foot peaks with snow fields, and one, Wheeler Peak, tops 13,500 feet. On the map, green stripes of national forests—the Toiyabe, Humboldt, and Shoshone—run north–south along the ranges. And the basins. Some bone dry, with alkali lakes, as if the planet here was drying up and turning into Mars. Let's hope it's not. In others, old hay farms, and a few modern hay farms. A wind farm in one valley, a place where I wouldn't have thought the wind density would be high, but it probably funnels through between the ranges on either side.

This landscape had a familiar feel, driving déjà vu. I'd driven the same route many times in my past, but not for decades. I drove it going back and forth from my hometown in New Mexico as an undergraduate at Stanford University, and again from Colorado while doing my PhD research on the ecology and behavior of a Pacific Coast snail. I was on my way in June 2021 to a writing residency at the Mesa Refuge in Point Reyes Station, California, a little town at the toe of Tomales Bay.

The Mesa Refuge website describes it as "a residency for writers, journalists, and other creatives . . . focusing on 'ideas at the edge' of the areas we value: nature, economic equity and social justice."[1] The phrase "ideas at the edge" immediately caught my imagination. I wanted to do some "edgy" thinking from the edge of the continent. The website description seemed slightly slanted toward *human* "economic equity and social justice." I agree with that in and of itself, but I wanted to expand that mission, à la Aldo Leopold, and explore some ideas about equity and justice for the whole biotic community, not just humans.

The town of Point Reyes Station sits virtually on top of the San Andreas Fault. To the north, Tomales Bay fills the drowned fault valley for fifteen miles to its mouth at Dillon Beach. To the south, the Olema Valley marks the fault line to Bolinas Lagoon, where it goes offshore until it hits and splits the San Francisco Peninsula. I was at the edge of two of Earth's great tectonic plates (the Pacific and North American), the edge of a continent, the edge of land and sea. Edges are dynamic places where change and movement, both social and ecological, happen. We talk about the "leading edge" or "cutting edge" of something, usually with a positive connotation. Ecologists call these dynamic edges "ecotones." That's where I wanted to be.

I wanted to explore ideas about the relationship between humans and nature at the edge of colliding worldviews: on the one hand, the human-centered Western worldview that sees the near-total human domination and exploitation of nature as proper and good; and on the other, an ecocentric worldview in which humans are seen as only one small part, an equal member, of Earth's biotic community. This trip, searching for evidence that the human-nature relationship is healing in the San Francisco Bay Area, was like making a big circle for me in time and space—a coming back, and looking back, after the experiences from my entire career so far.

So, where do we stand now? What progress have we made to develop the political will to implement what the science of ecology clearly says we must do? How much progress have we made toward an ecologically *and* socially sustainable society; an "ecotopia," as Ernest Callenbach called it in his 1975 eco-future-fiction novel with that title?[2] Those were my questions as I drove across the basins and ranges, up and over the passes, and out to the edge of our country and continent, where experiments to try to heal the human-nature relationship have been underway for a long time. Answering those questions was my quest; the essays that follow are my reports from the field.

Pepperwood
Preserve

Santa
Rosa

Bodega
Bay

Tomales
Point

Tomales Bay

Point
Reyes

Drakes
Bay

Mt.
Tamalpais

Muir
Woods
Green
Gulch

Berkeley

San
Francisco

San
Bruno
Mountain

San
Francisco
Bay

N

W   E

S

Jasper
Ridge
Preserve

San Jose

Mt.
Umunhum

Coyote
Ridge

Golden Gate
Biosphere Reserve
(Central Area)

Santa
Cruz

Elkhorn
Slough

Monterey
Bay

Monterey

Channel Islands
Biosphere Reserve

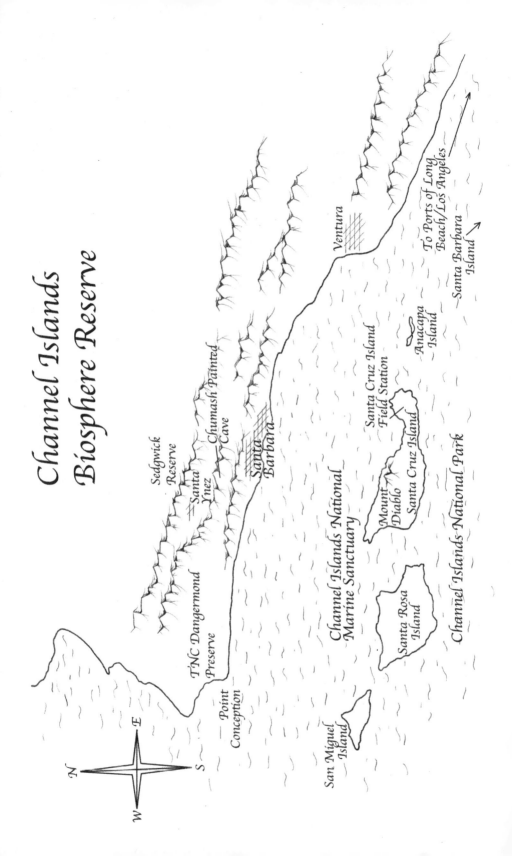

Introduction

There is a real situation, that can't be denied, but it is too big for any individual to know in full, and so we must create our understanding by way of an act of the imagination.
—Kim Stanley Robinson, *The Ministry for the Future*[1]

WE ARE IN THE MIDST of an inevitable transformation of the human-nature relationship. We must bring back some kind of resilience and sustainability to the ecology of our species before our actions destroy the ecology of the planet that sustains us. The transformation has been going on for at least half a century, very slowly—almost unrecognizably slowly to most people, busy living their own lives, caught in a kind of temporal nearsightedness that discounts the future, and more or less trapped in an unsustainable global political and economic system that is based on a fundamentally human-centered worldview.

The late 1960s and 1970s saw an exponential increase in attention to the emerging ecological crisis in the United States and worldwide. These essays explore the history and dimensions of the problem and response through the lens of one of the major programs of global cooperation invented to deal with it at that time, the Man and the Biosphere Programme (MAB) of the United Nations Educational, Scientific, and Cultural Organization (UNESCO), which set up an international network of biosphere reserves. The United States played a key role in the establishment of the program and network. But domestic politics forced the US MAB program underground in the 1990s and almost killed it completely in the 2000s. In about 2015, UNESCO issued an ultimatum: provide updated "periodic reviews" on the status of US biosphere reserves, or they would be dropped from the program. Twenty-eight of the forty-seven US biosphere reserves in existence at the time completed periodic reviews in 2016 and remain in the program; nineteen did not and withdrew.

Cutting-edge ideas from California were woven into the fabric of the program from the beginning, as I'll describe here. In part because of that, and in part because of the uniqueness, complexity, and scale of California's two coastal biosphere reserves (Golden Gate and Channel Islands), I wanted to compare them with Oregon's Cascade Head Biosphere Reserve, which I wrote about in a 2020 book of essays, *The View from Cascade Head: Lessons for the Biosphere from the Oregon Coast*.[2] I was curious to see how the conceptual framework of themes and lessons that I developed there might apply in California. It worked well, validating and extending some lessons from Cascade Head, and also led to new insights and inspiring stories that apply globally.

There are three main lessons. First, the history of human interaction with an ecological landscape can be seen centuries later, and it is important and often inspiring to understand the history of nature conservation in a place. That history is always full of individual "heroes" who model for us the effectiveness of individual action, and sometimes these catalytic individuals join to form groups that catalyze collective conservation action. The second lesson is that ecological mysteries still abound, despite all the scientific knowledge we've gained. That means that the need for research to inform sustainable ecological management is never-ending. Ecological research is needed to guide ecological restoration, and restoration often reveals unknown ecological relationships. Finally, how we think about our place in nature—our worldview—shapes our individual and collective behavior and thereby our effects on the biosphere that sustains us. A root cause of the multifaceted ecological crisis is the human-supremacist worldview that now dominates, and is used to justify, the current global economic and geopolitical system. A successful transformation to an ecologically sustainable human relationship with the planet will require a new, ecocentric worldview. Two sources could inform the development of such a worldview. One source is old worldviews of ecologically adapted cultures from around the world that have managed to survive the onslaught of Western colonization, or at least some surviving elements of them that could be revitalized. The other potential source of an ecocentric worldview is ecology and other systems sciences.

~

The biosphere is where the nonliving parts of our round planet, the lithosphere, hydrosphere, and atmosphere—rock, water, and air, in simple terms—meet and mingle and create the conditions in which life evolved. Each of these "spheres" is a highly dynamic system by itself. But add life to the mix, and the biosphere is more dynamic still, with its food webs, nutrient cycles, symbioses, ecosystems, and evolution. For us, or any species, the biosphere is it, our one and only home here on this far-flung lonely island Earth, circling an undistinguished star in an outer band of the Milky Way galaxy.

The biosphere is *thin*, very thin. From the depths of the deepest oceans, maybe six miles deep, to the tops of the tallest mountains, maybe six miles high, it's only about twelve miles thick. Compared to the diameter of the Earth, this living skin is not much more than one-thousandth as thick as the planet is wide, about as thick relative to the whole Earth as the skin of an apple is to the apple. If you look at the famous Apollo 17 photo of Earth, sometimes called the "blue marble" photo,[3] you can barely see the thin layer of atmosphere around the edges. That thinness screams fragility.

It took scientists quite a while to begin to imagine the Earth-ecosystem as a whole. The term "biosphere" was first used in something like its modern sense in 1885, and the term and concept were promoted by Ukrainian geochemist Vladimir Vernadsky in a 1926 book, *The Biosphere*. Ecological historian Frank Golley describes Vernadsky's book as "a scientific expression of a global system of man and nature."[4] The biosphere *concept* is a cutting-edge idea about why everything we do is interconnected and interdependent. It posits that the fate of humans and the nonhuman species of the planet cannot be disentangled, that human well-being requires the well-being of all species.

In 1968, with concern about human damage to the environment rising rapidly, UNESCO organized an international meeting called the "Biosphere Conference" in Paris.[5] It was the first time the word "biosphere" was used in international deliberations. The conference concluded that human development and nature protection had to be linked, and it was thus the first intergovernmental forum to discuss and promote what came to be called "sustainable development."

After this conference, in 1971, UNESCO launched the Man and the Biosphere Programme (using "man" to refer to all humans, both men and women). The program established sites called "biosphere reserves" within ecologically and culturally diverse regions of the biosphere where the human-nature relationship could be studied, monitored, and improved, working toward a goal of long-term sustainability and resilience for both humans and nature.

What are biosphere reserves? The UNESCO website provides this summary:

> Biosphere reserves are learning places for sustainable development. They are sites for testing interdisciplinary approaches to understanding and managing changes and interactions between social and ecological systems, including conflict prevention and management of biodiversity. They are places that provide local solutions to global challenges. Biosphere reserves include terrestrial, marine and coastal ecosystems. Each site promotes solutions reconciling the conservation of biodiversity with its sustainable use.[6]

I have always described biosphere reserves as laboratories and models for understanding and improving the human-nature relationship. A few people have challenged my use of the term "laboratory," saying that it's too scientific sounding, and we don't want to suggest that we are experimenting with people. But we *do* need to experiment, both socially and ecologically, because what we are doing now is having serious negative consequences in many places, and we don't really know what to do or what will work.

Biosphere reserves are not just another kind of "protected area," a term commonly used to refer to places like national parks, national forests, or nature preserves. All biosphere reserves are "multiple use" areas—where the anthropocentric term "use" refers to human activities and the kinds of ecological benefits that flow to people from them. Most biosphere reserves have one or more zones where human uses are strictly limited and nature is more or less allowed to take its own wild course without much human influence or impact. These could be wilderness areas, strict nature preserves, watersheds that are closed to public access, marine protected areas, or research natural areas, for example. The UNESCO MAB Programme calls these "core areas." It's not that these zones have *no* human uses—scientific research, outdoor education, and certain low-impact kinds of recreation can occur in them— but simply that they are protected from activities that would damage their biodiversity or ecological integrity.

All biosphere reserves also include zones with greater or lesser degrees of human influence, where the ecological effects of those activities can be observed and regulated. Areas with intermediate levels of human activity and influence are labeled "buffer zones" by UNESCO MAB, and usually called "managed use areas" in US biosphere reserves. Areas with the most human impact, in many cases urban areas or farmland where natural ecosystems have been mostly or completely replaced, are labeled "transition areas" by UNESCO MAB, and called "areas of partnership and cooperation" in US biosphere reserves. Most biosphere reserves encompass a mosaic of these three kinds of areas, sometimes without sharp boundaries between them, reflecting the existing land and water ownership patterns and the legal management authorities and responsibilities of those land and water owners. A simplistic "bull's-eye" pattern of zones, as depicted on the UNESCO MAB website,[7] almost never exists in reality.

Biosphere reserves are sometimes very large—the Golden Gate Biosphere Reserve is about twenty-eight thousand square miles of land and sea, for example—and are a mosaic of land and water uses and jurisdictional authorities. Because of their size and complexity, and because the term "reserve" is thought by some to suggest a strict limitation on human uses and activities, the collaborative network representing US biosphere reserves recently recommended that they be called "biosphere regions."[8] However, in order to reflect the history of the MAB Programme and to emphasize its international structure, I will use the official term "biosphere reserve" throughout these essays.

The challenge, which biosphere reserves are an attempt to solve, is that ecosystems function at relatively large scales and have porous boundaries, whereas human social and political boundaries now often, even usually, ignore natural ecological units. That wasn't always or usually the case, as I'll explore in later essays. The modern mismatch between ecological and social reality is a major reason for the environmental crisis we now face. Public lands and waters, managed for different goals (sometimes incompatible ones) by different public agencies at different scales—local, regional, state, national—are scattered among private lands, which are also subject to legal and management restrictions, but far fewer than public lands. Bottom line: it's a mess. Biosphere reserves may help us sort the mess and explore potential solutions. At least that's the idea.

∽

I was born into the post–World War II bust-out of optimism and baby-booming—the "Ike Era" maybe we could call it, after President Dwight Eisenhower, who presided over it from 1953 to 1961. Then, in the 1960s, there was a gradual waking up, a cultural "uh-oh" decade, the beginning of questioning where all of the booming was leading. Some people got a bit scared, especially on the countercultural and antiwar fringes of mainstream America.

In fact, some prescient ecologists had already been raising the alarm much earlier. In 1948, ecologist William Vogt had published *Road to Survival*, in which he concluded, "Unless, in short, man adjusts his way of living in the fullest sense—we may as well give up all hope of civilized life."[9] Conservationist Fairfield Osborn's book *Our Plundered Planet* was published the same year; the teaser on the cover of the first edition stated, "With disturbing clarity this book points out that we are more likely to destroy ourselves in our persistent and world-wide conflict with nature than in any war of weapons yet devised."[10] That was stark and apocalyptic language indeed, only three years after Hiroshima and Nagasaki. Both books called attention to the threat of exponential growth of the human population and our impact on the planet. But in 1948, "the world was not in a mood to be told of the limits to growth," said Raymond Dasmann, a California ecologist who was an architect of the UNESCO MAB Programme.[11] Both books were forerunners to Paul Ehrlich's *The Population Bomb*,[12] published in 1968 in an era much more ready to hear the message.

At the Biosphere Conference in Paris in 1968, prominent ecologists concerned about the human future presented their views. In the proceedings of the conference you can hear the struggles of those politically engaged ecologists from around the world trying to figure out what to do. "Holy shit! We are in a bad place!" I hear them thinking to themselves as they are writing and presenting their carefully crafted remarks. American ecologist Stanley Cain said that

> tinkering with the complex ecosystems as we have in the past, without realizing that they are in fact "systems," can no longer be warranted. We are now learning the cost of uncoordinated actions. We need to repair the biosphere, to the extent that we can, and act in harmony with it, as, in the long run, we must.[13]

Cain argued in his Biosphere Conference presentation that the solution would need to bring the natural and social sciences "into co-operative participation for planning, policy formulation, management and use" of the environment. He proposed the "formation of multidisciplinary, multiagency, approaches to a complex problem, and the design of social machinery (institutions)" for both nature conservation and human development. He pointed out "the inadequacy of governmental and social institutions for total, integrated planning and management of natural and human ecosystems."[14] His language is quite technical and managerial, emphasizing rational, science-based planning.

But Cain also raised a deeper issue when he stated that "behind this inadequacy lie ideological barriers to such planning."[15] He did not use the term "worldview," but the "ideological barriers" he referred to are the result of the anthropocentric Western worldview that was being used to justify the near-total human domination and exploitation of nature (as it still is).

Some socially attuned ecologists were well aware of the challenge to the dominant Western worldview posed by the science of ecology. In a 1964 article in the journal *BioScience*, provocatively titled "Ecology—a Subversive Subject," ecologist Paul Sears wondered: "Is ecology a phase of science of limited interest and utility? Or, if taken seriously as an instrument for the long-run welfare of mankind, would it endanger the assumptions and practices accepted by modern societies, whatever their doctrinal commitments?"[16] In 1967, historian Lynn White's article in *Science* magazine, "The Historical Roots of Our Ecological Crisis,"[17] drew widespread attention to the importance of worldviews.

At roughly the same time as the Biosphere Conference, thinking about the human-nature relationship was moving on a more grassroots, countercultural front, and California was where a lot of that was happening. Gary Snyder, a poet, anthropologist, and Zen practitioner with deep California ties, wrote "Four Changes,"[18] which has been called a "prophetic manifesto" for the environmental movement.[19] First published as a broadside in 1969, it was reprinted many times before the first Earth Day in 1970. Snyder lays out his eco-manifesto in four sections—"Population," "Pollution," "Consumption," and "Transformation"—and for each describes the "condition" as it is, and the "action" needed to change it. For me and many others at the time, this was a bold, brave vision, a recipe for change, and a call to action. Snyder says:

> If man is to remain on Earth, he must transform the five-millennia-long urbanizing civilization tradition into a new ecologically-sensitive harmony-oriented wild-minded scientific-spiritual tradition. Nothing short of total transformation will do much good. What we envision is a planet on which the human population lives harmoniously and dynamically by employing various sophisticated and unobtrusive technologies in a world environment which is left natural.[20]

≈

Then came the turbulent 1970s—should we call that decade the "Environmental Watershed–Watergate Era"? With a sudden and dramatic response of political and institutional action, the foundation of environmental laws and institutions that hadn't changed much up to that point was laid. President Nixon, a former California representative, senator, and vice president under Eisenhower, toured the beaches of the Santa Barbara Channel after the massive oil spill in early 1969. Environmental activists at the University of California, Santa Barbara, organized "Santa Barbara Environmental Rights Day" in January 1970, the one-year anniversary of the spill, and that catalyzed the first Earth Day in April 1970. The National Environmental Policy Act (NEPA) was enacted that year, and the Endangered Species Act three years later. In June 1972, the United Nations held a Conference on the Human Environment in Stockholm; that conference had first been proposed at the 1968 UNESCO Biosphere Conference. The UN Environment Programme (UNEP) was founded after the Stockholm Conference, with headquarters in Nairobi to please developing countries, which didn't want environmentalism to become another tool of colonialism and block their development.

At the 1972 Moscow Summit, President Nixon and USSR general secretary Leonid Brezhnev signed important arms control treaties but also pledged to improve relations through scientific cooperation. One aspect of that was to work together in the UNESCO MAB Programme to establish a network of biosphere reserves in the two countries. Planning and site selection began in 1974, and the first twenty-nine US biosphere reserves were designated in 1976. The Channel Islands Biosphere Reserve was one of that first group, included because of its unique biodiversity, for which it was known as "California's Galapagos." The Golden Gate Biosphere Reserve was not established until 1988, but a part of its foundation was laid when both the Golden Gate National Recreation Area and Point Reyes National Seashore were established in 1972.

∽

The 1970s seem, in retrospect, to have left everyone in eco-limbo, caught somewhere between despair at the perilous state of the global environment and hope grounded in a vision of science-based action and international cooperation. Raymond Dasmann wrote about his own views in his 1972 book, *Planet in Peril? Man and the Biosphere Today*, and said that Frank Fraser Darling, a leading British ecologist and conservationist, had summed up the situation as well as anyone could when he addressed the Biosphere Conference in 1968. He quoted Darling: "Ecologists can scarcely afford to be optimists. But an absolute pessimist is a defeatist, and that is no good either. We see there need not be complete disaster, and if our eyes were open wide enough, world-wide, we could do much toward rehabilitation."[21]

Is this a statement of hope? Nope. At least I don't think so. But it seems to be a call to action. If the biosphere is to be saved, Darling seemed to be saying, ecologically informed global action will be needed. Stanley Cain seemed to second Frank Darling's call to action at the Biosphere Conference:

> Although the vision may have been glimpsed, it is not a promised land that lies somewhere awaiting human enjoyment—a Utopia or Garden of Eden that could be moved into. It must be created by human effort from the rubble and confusion and inefficiencies that have accumulated from past actions—uses and abuses of the environment, uses and abuses of human powers.[22]

Cain's words "Utopia" and "Garden of Eden" immediately call to mind words from Ernest Callenbach's 1975 novel, *Ecotopia*—fictional, but well grounded in the zeitgeist of the times, especially in California:

> Ecotopia still poses a nagging challenge to the underlying national philosophy of America: ever-continuing progress, the fruits of industrialization for all, a rising Gross National Product. During the past two decades, we as a people have mostly tried to ignore what has been happening in Ecotopia—in the hope it will prove to be mere foolishness and go away.[23]

Cain and Callenbach were thinking about the same thing, I think. In a 2008 interview, Callenbach said, "It is so hard to imagine anything fundamentally different from what we have now. But without these alternate visions, we get stuck on dead center. And we'd better get ready. We need to know where we'd like to go."[24] At the Biosphere Conference in 1968, Cain was trying to imagine Callenbach's "Ecotopia," an ecologically sustainable society "created by human effort."

So am I. Join me on a journey to find out what progress we have made in the half century since the UNESCO Biosphere Conference tried to implement a vision of how to heal the human-nature relationship and save our species. It takes an act of the imagination. The essays that follow are my quest for that vision.

I
Evolutionary Ecology on California's Galapagos

The natural history of these islands is eminently curious, and well deserves attention. Most of the organic productions are aboriginal creations, found nowhere else; there is even a difference between the inhabitants of the different islands; yet all show a marked relationship with those of America.

—Charles Darwin, *The Voyage of the Beagle*, 1839[1]

SUNDAY, OCTOBER 24, 2021. Our reservations for the trip to Santa Cruz Island had been made months ago. But the weather during the past week had forced Island Packers, the commercial concessionaire that currently provides transportation for visitors to the four northern islands within Channel Islands National Park, to cancel its trips on several days because of rough seas and fierce northwest winds. We were packed and ready; would we go? At 5:30 a.m. we called the Island Packers trip-status number from our hotel room near Ventura Harbor: all trips were on today! Out to a nearby Starbucks to pick up breakfast sandwiches, almond croissants, and large coffees. I'm moderately prone to seasickness but figured it was better to have something in my stomach to come up, if the sea conditions on the crossing dictated that. And the coffee *was* a definite necessity. At 8:00 a.m. we were waiting at the dock to load our week's worth of food and gear onto the *Island Explorer* on a beautiful sunny morning, and we were off on schedule at 9:00 a.m. for the 25-mile, hour-and-a-half trip to the island.

The *Island Explorer*, a 65-foot catamaran-design vessel that can carry 145 passengers, was nearly full. Everyone was wearing masks because of California and company COVID protocols. Most passengers were going only for the day to Scorpion Anchorage on the east end of the island for hikes or kayaking trips. A few of us were going on to Prisoners Harbor on the north shore of the island, most for longer stays so with more gear stored below. Although there was some wind and exhilarating bow splash as we went west, the seas weren't such as to provoke seasickness. Anacapa Island and one of the still-pumping oil platforms in the oil-spill-infamous Santa Barbara Channel passed as silhouettes against a silver sea to the southeast. Most of the day-trippers got off at Scorpion, and we went on to Prisoners Harbor. Our gear was unloaded off the boat and into the back of an old black Toyota Tacoma pickup, and we were taken up a rocky road in a dry river valley to the field station of UC Santa Barbara's Santa Cruz Island Reserve by Dr. Lyndal Laughrin, the director emeritus, who still lives there.

Thanks to the calm seas, breakfast had stayed down. But it was lunchtime now—and apparently the island's time to introduce us to two of its most iconic nonhuman residents, one a bird, one a mammal.

The first self-introduction was by the island scrub-jay (*Aphelocoma insularis*). As soon as we sat down at the picnic table on the deck at the back of the main field station building and brought out our sandwiches, an aggressive jay appeared, hopping on the table and inviting a handout—or threatening theft. The crest and back of the head, shoulders, back, wings, and tail of this jay were a sharp turquoise blue. Its white breast and belly gave it a certain air of propriety, but a gray cheek patch like a robber's mask swept back from its long, bold bill, and its quick, dark eyes missed nothing. The island scrub-jay is now found only on Santa Cruz Island, and nowhere else on Earth.[2] Birders come from across the country and around the world to add this species to their life lists.

While we were shooing off the jay, a tiny, nonchalant island fox (*Urocyon littoralis*) came up on the deck nearby. It seemed to completely ignore us and settled down for a siesta in the sun a few feet away. The fox's coloration was as striking and beautiful as that of the jay, but patterned with a different palette: silver gray, rusty orange, and snow white. Its behavior was surprising and somewhat disconcerting; this was just how a pet cat or dog would claim its favorite spot in its owner's house. Was this really a wild fox?

The same jay—named "Jay-Jay" by the daughter of the current director of the reserve and research station, Dr. Jay Reti—was our constant companion at every outdoor happy hour or meal for the rest of our stay. Foxes would appear ephemerally around the station, seemingly oblivious to our presence. They claimed it as their territory according to standard island fox protocol by marking the picnic tables on the deck and certain other places around the buildings with their poop piles. We met many more jays and many more foxes on our forays around the island, and they continued to endear themselves throughout our stay.

The jay was big and aggressive, the fox small and demure. Both personalities were perfect emissaries from the island. The fox and the jay embody and illustrate here, on what have been called "California's Galapagos," some of the biogeographic patterns often seen most clearly on islands. These patterns struck Charles Darwin so forcefully on Ecuador's Galápagos Islands in 1835 that they seem to have led him to develop his theory of evolution by natural selection, which he laid out much later, in 1859, in *On the Origin of Species*.

One fact that the Galápagos archipelago thrust upon Darwin is that the relative isolation of populations of a species enables and encourages their ecological and evolutionary divergence and eventual speciation. A suite of closely related finches found there, now referred to as "Darwin's finches," was exhibit number one. After colonizing an island, a pair or small group of finches (or any other species) is more or less reproductively isolated, breeding among themselves in that isolated place. That allows the forces of natural selection to adaptively shape their population to that place, independently of the forces that shaped or constrained their mainland ancestors, or even their cousins on nearby islands. Santa Cruz Island and the seven other islands of "California's Galapagos" abound in examples as surprising and illuminating as the finches and other unique island species from the other Galápagos.

～

Before diving in, I want to explain why I think these stories of evolution and ecology on Santa Cruz Island are important.

First, they're fascinating and fun, and the science is fairly simple. You don't have to be a scientist of any kind to understand this stuff. They illustrate well one of the lessons that biosphere reserves have to teach, which is that despite all we have learned, there is still much we don't know. The need for ecological research is never-ending, and it can inform the restoration of damaged ecosystems and how we manage them into the future. But the examples I present here also speak to another lesson of biosphere reserves: worldviews—how we think about the human-nature relationship—matter, because they influence how we act. These examples of evolutionary ecology on Santa Cruz Island illustrate some key principles: adaptation, diversity, interdependence, symbiosis, mutualism, and resilience. These scientific principles must also be incorporated into the philosophy and ethics of the new ecological worldview we desperately need to save our imperiled planet.

Second, the history of how the Channel Islands came to be protected in a national park and biosphere reserve illustrates another main lesson that biosphere reserves can teach: the actions and efforts of individuals can have catalytic effects. These conservation heroes, as I called them in the introduction, can inspire us to action also.

In this case, one such hero is Theodore Dru Alison Cockerell (1866–1948), a British-born biologist whose fascinating biography can only be sketched here. Cockerell, who always used his initials T.D.A. instead of his name(s), studied at private schools but never earned a university degree. In his early twenties he contracted tuberculosis and moved for three years to Colorado, where the climate was thought at the time to be curative. When he returned to England, he worked at the British Museum as an assistant to Alfred Russel Wallace, codiscoverer of evolution with Charles Darwin, assisting Wallace with his research and writing about island biogeography. When his tuberculosis flared up again in 1892, he again came to the United States, and by 1904 he had settled into a teaching and research career at the University of Colorado Boulder. After his supposed "retirement" in 1934, he continued an active research program, and from 1937 to 1940 he focused his attention on the Channel Islands. He visited five of the islands, compiled scientific information on all eight of them, and published sixteen papers about the islands during that time. Cockerell was a noted expert in the taxonomy of bees and gave scientific names to fifty-one Channel Islands bee species, many found nowhere else and never previously described. His research on fossil stratigraphy contributed to understanding the evolutionary history of the Channel Islands pygmy mammoth.[3]

It took an observant, curious, and highly trained naturalist to recognize the scientific importance of the biogeographic patterns on the California Channel Islands. But Cockerell brought another critical quality not found in every scientist: his interest in public affairs and his willingness to engage with government agencies to bring a "science-based" (to use a currently popular phrase) perspective to the public policy process. That combination was the key to his catalytic role in gaining federal protection for some of the Channel Islands.

In 1932, the US Bureau of Lighthouses contacted the National Park Service and suggested that Santa Barbara and Anacapa Islands, over which it had federal jurisdiction, could be turned over to the NPS.[4] Decision-making was slow, but in 1937, Dr. Harold Bryant, assistant director of the Park Service, wrote to his NPS colleagues that "I am told that Prof. T.D.A. Cockerell of the University of Colorado has been making a careful biological survey of the whole island group," and that he had written to Cockerell to get his opinion of the scientific value of the islands and why and how they should be protected.[5]

Cockerell responded to Bryant's letter, saying:

> Although it is true that many zoologists and botanists have written on the biota of the islands, no one has assembled all the results together, and it is evident that few, even of the scientific men of California have any appreciation of the great value of the subject for the understanding of evolution and the biological phenomena. The more I work at the subject, the more impressed I become with the extraordinary importance of these islands for natural history studies. Having said this much, you can well believe that I am anxious to see the islands publicly owned, and preferably in the hands of the Park Service.[6]

Cockerell's letter seems to have tipped the balance of opinion toward National Park Service takeover, and in 1938 President Franklin D. Roosevelt signed a proclamation designating Channel Islands National Monument.

This history especially intrigued me because I have what feels like a personal, serendipitous connection with T.D.A. Cockerell. When I was teaching at the University of Colorado Boulder in the late 1980s, I became acquainted with a rare local moth, which, unlike most of the drab species in its family, was brightly colored. Its burgundy wings and yellow head and thorax gave it perfect camouflage when resting on the red-and-yellow blossoms of blanketflower (*Gaillardia aristata*). I was amazed and delighted, and I began to look into what was known about this species. I learned that it had no common name, only a scientific name, *Schinia masoni*. The type specimen was placed in the University of Colorado Museum (now the University of Colorado Museum of Natural History) by T.D.A. Cockerell. Cockerell first noted the distinctive camouflage of *Schinia masoni* in a 1910 paper[7] and wrote later, in 1927, that this species "was discovered by Mr J Mason, formerly of Denver, through the picking of a *Gaillardia* flower on which a moth happened to be resting."[8] My fascination with this moth led to research on its then-undescribed life history and the discovery that because blanketflower, its host plant, is a fire-following species, the moth—which I came to call the Colorado firemoth—is a sensitive indicator species for the fire history in its range. Its rarity is now probably a result of suppression of the historic fire regime in Colorado Front Range forests during the last century or so.[9]

∾

To understand why the term "California's Galapagos" is appropriate, we should first consider the geological history of these islands. I'll focus on the four northern Channel Islands, and only on relatively recent history. Sixteen thousand years ago—a relative eyeblink in evolutionary time—at the end of the most recent glacial episode of the Pleistocene Ice Age, when huge amounts of water were stored in continental ice sheets, the four now-separated northern Channel Islands of San Miguel, Santa Rosa, Santa Cruz, and Anacapa were a single large island, which has been called Santarosae Island (sometimes written as two words, Santa Rosae).[10] At that time, Santa Rosae was estimated to be only a handful of miles from the nearest point on the mainland, which would have been southwest of modern-day Oxnard. But the big island of Santa Rosae had been there much, much longer—it was the top of a mountain ridge thrust up by the tectonic tantrum that began around four million years ago and created the Transverse Ranges and the bend in the Southern California coast called the Southern California Bight. Plenty of time, in other words, for the island or islands to be colonized by plants and animals from the California mainland—whether they arrived by riding on intact pieces of it as those broke away, or whether they flew, blew, rafted, swam, or were brought there by people.

~

Perhaps a place to begin this evolutionary story is with the pygmy mammoth, *Mammuthus exilis*, a classic example of the evolution of small body size, or dwarfism, on islands. Island dwarfism is a relatively common evolutionary phenomenon worldwide. Skeletons of this tiny mammoth ("exiled" to the Channel Islands, as its scientific name suggests) were first excavated on Santa Rosa Island beginning in the 1920s.[11] These Ice Age elephants stood about as tall as a human, in contrast to their mainland cousins, Columbian mammoths (*Mammuthus columbi*), which were twice as tall, about the size of modern African elephants. Just think—mounting a pygmy mammoth for a ride would have been about the same as mounting a small horse, even a pony!

Somewhere between forty thousand and twenty thousand years ago, when the skyline of the superisland of Santa Rosae was only a few miles offshore and the smell of its vegetation may have wafted in on west winds, it is hypothesized that big Columbian mammoths swam over and colonized the island. Swimming elephants aren't a stretch of the imagination. African elephants are known to be good swimmers; they have been documented swimming fifteen miles across Lake Kariba, which flooded the Zambezi Valley between Zimbabwe and Zambia when the Kariba Dam was constructed in 1959, interrupting what must have been a common elephant migration route.

Island-evolved dwarfism is thought to result from selective pressure on isolated populations where food supplies and migratory ranges are limited and predators few. Smaller body size theoretically allows for larger populations, and larger populations are more resistant to extinction from random environmental events.

Mammoths—on both the mainland and the Channel Islands—disappeared by around thirteen thousand years ago. One hypothesis places the blame on overhunting by paleo-humans. On the islands, no direct evidence that people hunted or ate pygmy mammoths—such as spear points stuck in mammoth rib cages—has been found so far. Another explanation for their extinction focuses on the rapidly changing climate as the Ice Age faded. Some scientists speculate that climate change and human hunting combined to cause the extinction of mammoths and many other species of large Ice Age mammals, the so-called "Pleistocene megafauna."

∿

What about our little friend the island fox? It is now found on only six of the eight Channel Islands, but not on the California mainland. Its closest relative is the gray fox (*Urocyon cinereoargenteus*), which is found throughout the southern United States, Mexico, and Central America. But the island fox is one-third smaller than the gray fox; standing about a foot high and weighing only four or five pounds, it's about the size of a house cat.

The question of when and how foxes got to the Channel Islands has been the subject of scientific controversy. New methods of determining the age of the oldest fox bones from Santa Rosa Island date them to around 6,500 years ago, thousands of years after the first humans arrived, rather than to 16,000 years old, as reported in an earlier study.[12] All of the extensive recent paleontological research on the northern Channel Islands has dated fox bones only to the time after humans got there, and that coincidence has convinced almost all archaeologists that people brought foxes to the islands.[13] Foxes showed up much later in the archaeological record on three of the four southern Channel Islands where they were found, first San Clemente Island about 3,400 years ago, and even later on San Nicolas and Santa Catalina. It seems clear that those foxes were transported to the southern islands by humans.[14]

The fact that island foxes were almost surely introduced to the islands by people, who also had dogs, raises the interesting question of how foxes were treated. Were they "domesticated" and kept as pets, or for their fur, or for spiritual reasons? Fox skulls have been found with several human burials on Santa Cruz and Santa Rosa Islands, indicating that they may have been seen as the "spirit guides" or "dream helpers" of those individuals.[15] And even if tamed and domesticated, did some foxes also escape and establish feral, "wild" populations on various islands? The behavior of the fox who appeared at lunch on our arrival at the research station at least shows that the supposedly wild island foxes of today are quite tame and unafraid of people. The explanation could be that they were once tame and then became feral again on the islands. Interesting experiments on the genetics of tameness and fear of humans in the European red fox (*Vulpes vulpes*) are likely to be relevant in answering this question about the island fox,[16] but that's another story that's too long to go into here.

The fact that people probably brought the first foxes to the Channel Islands also complicates the explanation for their small size. Is this another case of the evolution of island dwarfism like the pygmy mammoth, caused by ecological factors in feral fox populations? Island foxes eat mice, lizards, insects, and fruits such as those of manzanitas. Even the largest of the islands, Santa Cruz, seems able to support a population of only a few thousand foxes at most. These ecological factors may explain why evolution favored smaller size in island foxes.

An alternative explanation is that the small size of island foxes is an example of selective breeding by humans. Such selection could easily, over a few thousand years or less, have reduced their size. Foxes belong to the same mammalian family (Canidae) as the domestic dog, *Canis familiaris*. Dogs exhibit a greater diversity of body size than any other species of terrestrial vertebrate. They range from six-inch-long Chihuahuas to eight-foot-long Irish wolfhounds. Dogs have been domesticated, originally from wolves, for only around fourteen thousand years, and the diversity seen in the more than four hundred genetically distinct breeds has been the result of selection by humans over a much shorter time span.[17] Research on the genetics of body size in dogs has shown that a single genetic variant in the insulin-like-growth-factor-1 gene is found in all small breeds and is nearly absent in large breeds, suggesting that it alone is a major determinant of size.[18]

The actual explanation for why island foxes are tiny may be a combination of both artificial selection by their human owners and natural selection in feral (or perhaps even food-limited domestic) populations. Future fox scientists should have a fun time trying to sort that out!

~

The island scrub-jay is related to the California scrub-jay (*Aphelocoma californica*), common and widely distributed on the mainland. But the island scrub-jay is about one-third larger, illustrating a fairly common phenomenon of the evolution of "giantism," or large size, on islands—the opposite of the dwarfism seen in the pygmy mammoth and island fox. Genetic analysis indicates that this species diverged from its mainland relative, the California scrub-jay, about 150,000 years ago.[19]

One morning as we hiked up Mount Diablo, the highest point on Santa Cruz Island, we came to a windswept cluster of oaks along the mostly treeless ridge. The trees were bustling with island scrub-jays harvesting the just-ripe acorns. Gangs of jays seemed to be competing here. We watched several tussles between jays when an acorn being plucked above dropped to the ground. When a jay had an acorn in its beak, it sailed off downslope in one of two directions: some jays glided down to the northeast, but others decidedly northwest. Were these two extended-family groups working together but competing with each other for acorns, I wondered?

The sociobiology of island scrub-jays is interesting. They are relatively long-lived, living up to twenty years; they are monogamous and may stay with the same mate for life; and they maintain year-round territories in island chaparral vegetation dominated by oaks. The jays depend on acorns for food, and when acorns are ripe, they harvest them, transport them in their bills for varying distances, and hide them for later consumption in spatially dispersed caches. Despite the jays' incredible spatial memory, some caches are never consumed—either because they are forgotten or because of the demise of the jay that cached them—and the acorns germinate, starting a new tree or cluster of trees. Thus, a mutually beneficial symbiosis has evolved.

But the system is a delicate coevolutionary dance, favorable when in balance, but risky for either species when out of balance. The oaks' strategy for keeping the balance is to "mast"—that is, to produce large crops of acorns one year and hardly any for the next year or two. Masting means jay populations can't grow so big that they could consume so many acorns that oak recruitment would be suppressed. The jays' strategy for keeping the balance is to defend territories where oaks are producing acorns, or where acorns from previous-year crops are cached all year long against their fellow jays. This territorial behavior helps limit population growth in island scrub-jays to the carrying capacity of the territory. Large body size and longevity in the jays may both have been positively selected to facilitate territorial defense.

The oaks on the Mount Diablo ridge were island live oaks, *Quercus tomentella*. This species is found on only three of the northern Channel Islands (all except San Miguel) and two of the southern islands (Santa Catalina and San Clemente). It is closely related to canyon live oak (*Quercus chrysolepis*), which is widely distributed on the California mainland and also found on Santa Cruz Island in some places. Fossils show that the island live oak was once also found on the mainland, so some botanists might call it a "relict" species—that is, the last small populations of a formerly more abundant species now hanging out and hanging on in isolated backwater ecosystems like the Channel Islands. But hey—if you are an island oak thriving on a north-facing ridge below Mount Diablo on Santa Cruz Island, with island jays going crazy harvesting and caching your crop of acorns—some of which will get forgotten and seed your descendants nearby—life is good!

Evolution is a creative, flexible, ongoing process. California is the center of biological diversity of oaks in North America, and the palette of oak genotypes painted over this part of the continent over the past tens of millions of years has adapted, diversified, speciated, evolved, hybridized, and thereby survived all of the geological, geographic, and climatic changes our dynamic old Earth could throw at it. Life is good as long as the creativity of evolution and symbiosis can outrun the challenges posed by our dynamic planet.

Ranching activities began on Santa Cruz Island in the 1850s, and large flocks of sheep, herds of feral pigs, and grazing by horses and cattle destroyed oak chaparral and suppressed oak reproduction. After the removal of these introduced, exotic species from the island beginning in the mid-1980s, native vegetation rebounded dramatically. Oak recovery has enabled the island scrub-jay population to increase by an estimated 20 to 30 percent in a positive feedback process.[20] Maybe we could think of the jays as oak "farmers," lured by the oaks' abundant acorns in mast years into propagating and spreading them. It's not really that different from the evolutionary game played by wheat, rice, maize, potatoes, and other domesticated crops, which have tricked one familiar animal species into eating and spreading them, dramatically increasing the evolutionary success of those plants.

And the future of the jays? There are fewer than three thousand individuals of this isolated species, and its small range and population size make it vulnerable to natural disasters and vegetation shifts caused by climate change.[21] Research on the symbiotic mutualism of endemic oaks and the endemic island scrub-jay provides an example of the link between research and restoration that was so obvious at Cascade Head in Oregon, where estuarine restoration enabled discoveries about salmon life history and ecology that would not have been possible otherwise.[22] There, restoring salt marsh habitat had a positive feedback effect on salmon populations. On Santa Cruz Island, oak restoration had a synergistic effect on jay numbers.

Research on Santa Rosa Island is beginning to show how restoring oaks affects ecosystem functioning and the ecosystem services it creates. There, island oak groves on highland ridges capture fog and increase water inputs to soils and watersheds—essentially functioning as cloud forests. Between 1994 and 2015, fourteen oak groves on the island expanded by an average of about 37 percent.[23] The restoration of oaks must be a result of the elimination of herbivory by sheep, pigs, and cattle, rather than the assistance of island jays, which no longer exist on Santa Rosa Island—although they once were found there, and also on San Miguel Island, until the late nineteenth century.[24] The restoration of vegetation and the ecohydrological role it plays raises intriguing questions about the old view of the "marginality" of the islands for human habitation. Before their ecosystems were damaged by overgrazing, the islands probably had more water and vegetation than we can guess, having seen them only in a degraded state.[25]

≈

Some recent research that I can't resist summarizing here takes the evolutionary story of island scrub-jays to a new level. In a paper titled "Islands within an Island: Repeated Adaptive Divergence in a Single Population," published in the journal *Evolution* in 2015, Kathryn Langin and her coauthors report that the jays on Santa Cruz Island have evolved adaptations to different vegetation communities on the island, as if those habitats were "islands" themselves.[26] Jays from the three separate areas where bishop pine (*Pinus muricata*) is found on the island had beaks that differed in size and shape from those from surrounding areas of oak chaparral vegetation. Jays from bishop pine stands had long, shallow bills, more efficient for extracting seeds from pine cones but probably less efficient for hammering and prying open acorns. Bill morphology is inherited, so this is a kind of microevolution and microadaptation to local conditions at a small spatial scale. The social behavior of the island scrub-jays must enable such microevolution and adaptation. Their food resources are limited, they are competitive and territorial, and viable breeding territories are scarce. Consequently, the offspring of a pair holding a breeding territory (remember, they are long-lived and monogamous) don't have much of anywhere else to go. They hang around "home" until they can inherit the property, so dispersal and gene flow are limited, making home territory a kind of island.

Bishop pine is considered a relict species on Santa Cruz Island. Still hanging on in the face of a changing climate, it was much more common in the wetter and cooler Pleistocene, and the sparse stands that remain seem to be tough survivors. Although still reproducing—we saw lots of baby pines in the central stand on our hike to Pelican Harbor, for example—they were poor cousins to the rich, fog-nourished bishop pine forests I'd seen on Inverness Ridge at Point Reyes in the Golden Gate Biosphere Reserve. Bishop pines are fire adapted, with woody "serotinous" cones whose scales are sealed shut with resin that melts with the heat of a fire, opening the cones and seeding a new generation of pines onto a burned landscape. Sometimes, though, hot weather causes the cones to open without fire, as it does on Santa Cruz Island, where at least now fires are not common. Island scrub-jays living in the remaining pine habitats on the island have been observed patrolling the pines for open cones and harvesting their pine nuts, and probably caching them as they do with acorns, helping the pines hang on here.

2

The Art of Ecological Restoration on Santa Cruz Island

The last word in ignorance is the man who says of an animal or plant,
"What good is it?"
  —Aldo Leopold, "The Round River," 1949[1]

THE LARGE FABRIC PRINT hanging on the west wall of the dining room of the Santa Cruz Island Reserve research station caught my eye immediately. A tangle of creatures drawn in detailed black covered the white background, intertwining in almost Escher-like fashion. There were sheep and foxes, eagles and jays, oaks and mallows, skunks and abalone, and as I got closer and began to really see the detail, my head was spinning. What was this piece, and who had done it?

After some quick inquiries and online searching, the story of this eco-logical art emerged. Titled *Limuw | Santa Cruz Island*, this pencil drawing by Zoe Keller is seven and a half feet wide and four feet tall and includes over sixty species found on Santa Cruz Island.[2] Why does this deserve to be called "ecological art" rather than just nature art or scientific illustration? Because Keller is ambitiously telling an ecological story here, not just using plants and animals as pretty subjects. As you move across the drawing from left to right, species that were important to the Indigenous inhabitants of the island are shown; then we see the gradual mixing in of the nonnative species introduced by Euro-Americans and their ecological effects on the unique biodiversity of the island. This is a tour de force of ecological art.[3]

What a story Zoe Keller's ambitious work tries to capture in a visual canvas of only seven and a half by four feet! Indigenous Americans lived on Santa Cruz Island—the name in the language of the most recent of them, the Chumash, is *limuw*—for more than thirteen thousand years (note that Chumash place names are deliberately not capitalized, as such names are in English). They must have come by boat, because even then, at the end of the last glacial maximum when sea level was hundreds of feet lower, the Channel Islands were still a few miles from the mainland of what would much later come to be called "California" by the Spanish.[4]

~

This essay concerns the ongoing story of the efforts to undo the ecological impacts from more than 150 years of assault by introduced European livestock—sheep, pigs, cattle, and horses—on an island with no native large herbivorous mammals. By the early 2000s, nine species of plants and one animal, the island fox, were listed under the Endangered Species Act as either threatened or endangered. Several decades of efforts to undo the damage done to the Santa Cruz Island ecosystem have produced some remarkable successes but also highlight ongoing challenges. Biosphere reserves in UNESCO's Man and the Biosphere Programme are meant to be laboratories for learning how to heal the human-nature relationship, and perhaps models to be replicated elsewhere. Santa Cruz Island, as a core site in the Channel Islands Biosphere Reserve, is a rich and fascinating case to study. Before discussing some successes and remaining challenges, we need to set the stage with a summary of the recent history of people and nature here.

By 1800, more than 250 years since their first encounter with Spanish explorers, the Chumash population on limuw had been devastated by introduced European diseases, and the last inhabitants were removed from the island by 1814 and taken to the San Buenaventura and Santa Barbara Missions on the mainland. In 1839, the Mexican government gave the entire island as a land grant to an army captain, Andres Castillero, who began ranching operations there; by 1853, historical records document large numbers of sheep, pigs, and horses on the island. Castillero sold the island to American investors in 1857. By the time of the Civil War, which increased the demand for wool for military clothing, twenty-four thousand sheep roamed the island, and it was known for the quality of the wool it produced. In 1869 the island was sold again, to a group of San Francisco–based investors. By 1880, one of them, French immigrant Justinian Caire, had become the sole owner. Caire expanded ranching operations and planted vineyards and fruit and nut orchards. He also brought in other nonnative species such as Australian eucalyptus trees and European sweet fennel. The fennel soon became naturalized and spread enough that it now dominates large areas on the island, overwhelming native vegetation. By 1890 there were more than fifty thousand sheep on the island. Wine and wool were the main products of Caire's Santa Cruz Island Company; it produced what was reputed to be one of the best Zinfandel vintages in California at that time, until Prohibition closed the wine-making operation in 1920.[5]

In 1937, Caire's descendants sold 90 percent of the island to Los Angeles oilman Edwin Stanton, who soon switched the ranching program from sheep to beef cattle. When he died in 1964, his son Carey, a physician, moved to the island and continued the cattle ranching operation. Both the elder and younger Stanton recognized the geological, ecological, and anthropological uniqueness and importance of the island, and they welcomed scientists. Carey Stanton began his relationship with UC Santa Barbara in 1964, when a summer field geology class was held on the island for the first time. By 1966 a rudimentary field station of what would become UC Santa Barbara's Santa Cruz Island Reserve was established. In order to protect the island from future development, Dr. Stanton sold his part of the island to The Nature Conservancy (TNC) in 1978 for a fraction of its market value, and TNC's Santa Cruz Island Preserve was established. In 1980, Channel Islands National Park expanded Channel Islands National Monument (established in 1938 by Franklin D. Roosevelt, which then included only Anacapa and Santa Barbara Islands) to encompass Santa Cruz Island and its northern siblings, Santa Rosa and San Miguel Islands.[6] Although Santa Cruz Island is included within the boundaries of Channel Islands National Park, TNC's portion of the island—the western 76 percent—does not belong to the National Park Service.[7] Today, the national park, TNC, UC Santa Barbara's Santa Cruz Island Reserve, and the Santa Cruz Island Foundation[8] work together to protect the island's natural, cultural, and historic resources. The Santa Cruz Island Reserve continues to provide facilities and access to the island for education and research through an agreement with TNC.

～

I love hollyhocks, especially the pink ones. That's because of their emotional connection with New Mexico for me. Pink hollyhocks leaned over fences around old adobe houses in Santa Fe, grew in my mom's garden in Los Alamos, and embedded themselves in my memory of delight. Hollyhocks are members of the plant family Malvaceae, whose unique pink colors carry throughout the blossoms of the family. So, when I first saw a photo of the federally endangered Santa Cruz Island bush mallow (*Malacothamnus fasciculatus* var. *nesioticus*), how could I not be enamored?

Karen Flagg, Don Hartley, and Steve Barilotti, plant-restoration specialists who have worked for decades to restore this endemic species to the island through their nonprofit organization Growing Solutions, arrived at the field station midway through our week there for an end-of-season monitoring visit. By this time of year, the bush mallows were going into dormancy, so I didn't get to see their seductive pink blossoms.

The island bush mallow is "a long-lived, clonal shrub"[9] that "reproduces vegetatively by rhizomes, the primary means of establishment and persistence in natural populations."[10] In less technical words, a bush mallow can send out roots, which can then send up new shoots away from the mother plant, but those shoots are genetically the same as—clones of—their mother plant. The bush mallow is typically found growing in island chaparral vegetation among other chaparral species like island scrub oak (*Quercus pacifica*) and manzanitas. Chaparral is a fire-adapted plant community, and the bush mallow's underground mode of vegetative reproduction fits right in as a strategy for surviving periodic fires.

The Santa Cruz Island bush mallow was first described scientifically in 1886. In the late 1990s, after more than a century of overgrazing by sheep and cattle, erosion and soil loss from rooting by feral pigs, suppression of fires, and other habitat alteration, a search for the last survivors was mounted. According to Karen, Don, and Steve, they finally found a thriving plant among the splintered boards of an old outhouse that had blown down long ago at the Christy Ranch on the western end of the island, where the last bush mallows had been reported by botanists in 1927 and 1930. Apparently the sharp, splintered lumber of the outhouse, like a fence of archers' stakes on a medieval battlefield, saved that single plant from the sheep and cattle that had grazed there until the late 1970s. The outhouse was on top of a narrow rocky ridge, "a weird spot for an outhouse, but it certainly had outstanding views of the coastline and beach," Karen recalled.

When it was federally listed as endangered under the Endangered Species Act (ESA) in 1997, further surveys had found more plants at Christy Ranch, and a small population on a steep, south-facing slope near the UC Santa Barbara field station. Only forty-two plants were counted in these two widely separated populations. An ESA recovery plan for the species "called for studies of life history and seed germination, development of propagation protocols and outplanting techniques, and subsequent establishment of viable populations."[11] Two additional surviving populations were discovered through surveys after ESA listing, one on the south side of the island, and one that appeared on Cebada Ridge near Christy Ranch after a controlled burn in 2000—a nice demonstration of the fire-following ecology of the species.[12] That population probably resprouted from long-suppressed underground roots, or perhaps even grew from seeds that had been waiting in the soil "seed bank" for release by the heat or leachate from charcoal from the fire, both known to stimulate germination in other chaparral species.

To implement the ESA recovery plan, Karen, Don, Steve, and volunteers from Growing Solutions located plants in the surviving populations, took cuttings from them beginning in 2011, and propagated over five hundred plants in a nursery-like shade structure not far from the research station. In 2016, these nursery-raised plants were planted out at suitable sites across the island and were reported to be surviving and sending out roots that would eventually give rise to new plants. It was these outplantings that Karen, Don, and Steve were here to monitor when our visits to the island overlapped.

Studies have shown that *Malacothamnus fasciculatus* var. *nesioticus* is genetically distinct from the other, mainland subspecies of bush mallow. That research has also shown that it has low levels of genetic variability,[13] which could potentially harm its adaptive potential and long-term survival. Two things could explain its low genetic diversity. One is that small populations retain less diversity than larger populations can—and the island bush mallow has certainly experienced what biologists call a population "bottleneck" because of its small numbers. The other explanation might be the lack of genetic mixing through sexual reproduction (pollen, seeds, etc.) and the predominance of vegetative reproduction in today's widely separated populations. Bush mallow populations must have been much more contiguous before their devastation by the hungry mouths of sheep and cattle.

The island bush mallow can reproduce sexually through seed production; it is even "self-compatible," meaning that flowers from a single plant can produce seeds, although that requires visits by pollinating insects. Research on Santa Cruz Island by entomologist Dr. Robbin Thorp of the University of California, Davis, reported few native bush mallow pollinators, and "therefore, pollinator limitation may be a factor in poor seed set at one or more sites."[14] Hand pollination—mimicking natural insect pollination by using tiny paintbrushes to move pollen from one flower to another—was shown to increase seed production, but this attempt to replace natural pollinators with human labor was a costly exercise, not sustainable in a field setting.

Some interesting research has investigated the ecological interaction between the nonnative honeybee and native pollinators. European varieties of the honeybee *Apis mellifera* were deliberately introduced on the Caire ranch in the 1800s, supposedly to assist with pollination of his orchards and vineyards and also to produce honey. The honeybees escaped and established feral colonies, aggressively competing with the native pollinators with which native plant species, like the island bush mallow, had evolved. Research by the aforementioned Dr. Thorp and Dr. Adrian Wenner of UC Santa Barbara compared the frequency of visits from native bees and introduced honeybees on the island to try to determine whether they were competing for pollen and nectar from native plants. After two years of documenting plant visitation by both wild native bees and honeybees, the researchers located and removed feral honeybee colonies on the eastern half of the island. Subsequent data showed that after removal of honeybees, native bees were by far the most common visitors to manzanita flowers on the eastern half of the island. But on the western side, feral honeybees still dominated such pollination visits.[15] Whether honeybees pollinate bush mallows or whether their competition is suppressing the native pollinators that do pollinate them is a question that research so far has not answered. |

~

This vignette of the near demise and potential restoration of the Santa Cruz Island bush mallow is a bit bittersweet. In his essay "The Round River," Aldo Leopold wrote:

> The last word in ignorance is the man who says of an animal or plant, "What good is it?" If the land mechanism as a whole is good, then every part is good, whether we understand it or not. If the biota, in the course of aeons, has built something we like but do not understand, then who but a fool would discard seemingly useless parts? To keep every cog and wheel is the first precaution of intelligent tinkering.[16]

It seems that some relatively heroic efforts have saved the island bush mallow for the time being. But they have not restored its former range and ecology, part of which may depend on the restoration of a suite of native pollinators that were affected by the introduction and partial naturalization of European honeybees. As the old English nursery rhyme warns, "All the king's horses and all the king's men couldn't put Humpty together again." We are trying, still hoping, but we don't yet know whether it is even possible to put an ecosystem together again once it has experienced such a great fall. There is a lot more to the ecological story of putting Humpty together again on Santa Cruz Island. In many ways it can be held up as a model of complex but generally successful ecological restoration, with many lessons learned.

Let's start with an important but relatively easy part of the restoration effort: sheep and cattle removal. Between 1981 and 1989, The Nature Conservancy removed approximately thirty-seven thousand sheep and the last two thousand cattle from its part of the island. The National Park Service continued the process on the eastern end of the island between 1997 and 2000, removing about ten thousand more sheep. Native vegetation began to recover, but nonnative weeds took advantage of the relaxed grazing pressure and began to expand too. European sweet fennel (*Foeniculum vulgare*) responded strongly, especially in overgrazed areas, and by 1991 was estimated to occur on 10 percent of the island, often crowding out native vegetation.[17]

And now, on to the pig story. Pigs, like sheep, were brought to the island in the early ranching days in the mid-1800s and escaped into the wild. Although they were not nearly as numerous as feral sheep, their ecological impact was more devasting: they ate the acorns of native oaks and rooted for underground bulbs and roots of native plants, causing soil erosion (not to mention also damaging invaluable archaeological sites). By 2004, it was clear from the recovery plans for a number of ESA-listed species on the island that the pigs had to go.

The contract to eliminate pigs went to a New Zealand company, Prohunt Inc., a "professional vertebrate eradication contractor," which fielded an eight-man team for the job.[18] Pig-proof fences divided the island into five pig-removal zones. A tiny doorless helicopter, from which a hunter in the passenger seat could shoot pigs from the air, was used. Animal rights organizations squealed, and sued to stop the process, but the NPS and TNC prevailed with the argument that they had a legal obligation under the Endangered Species Act to save the island's endangered species, and that there were no other effective alternatives that could quickly eliminate the nonnative feral pigs, a main threat to those listed species. Radio-collared female pigs, reportedly called "Judas pigs," helped the hunters find and eliminate the last sneaky male porcine holdouts. The pig eradication effort worked well and finished ahead of schedule. After a fifteen-month campaign, approximately five thousand pigs were killed, and the island was pig-free for the first time in a century and a half by 2006.[19] The fences still span the island; the pig-removal budget of approximately $5 million apparently covered their installation but not their removal.

All reports were that the Kiwi pig hunters were well liked, and once the pigs were gone, they did various other useful projects around the island until their contract ended, such as using their helicopter to haul away junk that had accumulated on top of Mount Diablo as communication equipment was being installed. I joked with Dr. Lyndal Laughrin, who was the director of the research station at the time,[20] that they should have set up a smokehouse to produce and market conservation-friendly "Save Santa Cruz Island" bacon and ham made from the culled pigs.

Ecologically sustainable economic benefits are one of the three key planks of the biosphere reserve model in UNESCO's formulation, after all (the others being biodiversity conservation, and research and education). In my international consulting work, I've had the opportunity to visit thirty-five biosphere reserves in seventeen countries so far, and I've seen many examples of local eco-enterprises. In the Golija-Studenica Biosphere Reserve in Serbia,[21] for example, I tasted and purchased jams and liquors made from wild berries, herbal teas from wild plants, wildflower honey, and dried wild mushrooms. So why not Santa Cruz Island pork products? Lyndal didn't smile; his face was serious as he remembered those days: "We tried some of that pork," he said, almost scowling, "but the pigs had been eating a lot of fennel weed, and the meat tasted like . . ." I won't quote his exact description of the flavor, but "unpalatable" was the gist of it.

≈

And now, on to the story of the near extinction and successful recovery of the island fox on Santa Cruz Island (I wrote about the evolution of this species in the previous essay). To begin, we have to step back seventy years and start with bald eagles. Bald eagles, which are highly territorial, apparently chased away any golden eagles that strayed over to the Channel Islands from the mainland until their local extinction on the islands because of DDT contamination in the 1950s. Bald eagles feed along the shoreline on fish and other marine foods, often scavenging already-dead fish and marine mammals, and don't hunt terrestrial animals.

DDT (dichloro-diphenyl-trichloroethane) was developed as the first of the modern synthetic insecticides in the 1940s and was widely used in agriculture, livestock production, and even homes and gardens at the time. The Montrose Chemical Corporation, whose main plant was near Los Angeles Harbor, was the largest producer of DDT in the United States from 1947 to 1982 (DDT was banned in the United States in 1972, but still produced for export). The company was allowed to discharge an estimated 1,800 metric tons of DDT from an ocean sewage outfall about two miles offshore (listed as a Superfund site by the EPA in 1996), and to dump hundreds of thousands of barrels of DDT-containing chemical waste at an ocean dumping site about ten miles northwest of Santa Catalina Island.[22] Some of the barrels were reportedly punctured before dumping to make sure they sank. It is little wonder that the marine ecosystem of the entire Southern California Bight was contaminated. DDT infiltrated marine food chains around the Channel Islands, concentrating in top predators like bald eagles and causing their eggshells to become so thin that they were crushed by incubating parents. Rachel Carson called everyone's attention to this problem in her book *Silent Spring*, published in 1962, and federal regulatory actions reduced and eventually banned DDT in 1972. In the meantime, the local extinction of bald eagles left a "hole" in the defenses of island ecosystems. Golden eagles from the mainland colonized Santa Cruz Island around 1990. Lambs and piglets from the large populations of sheep and pigs on the island provided a good food supply for the golden eagles, and their population grew.

But when the sheep and pigs were removed as part of the ecological restoration of the island, and with the bald eagles gone and the golden eagles established, the golden eagles began hunting island foxes, which had no evolutionary fear of aerial predators. The fox population plummeted rapidly in the late 1990s, until by 2004 there were only about one hundred island foxes left on Santa Cruz Island, and the fox was federally listed as endangered under the Endangered Species Act. That listing required a recovery plan, which had two planks: one, to remove the threat factor—golden eagles; and two, to protect and expand the population of the remaining foxes. The two activities were instituted simultaneously.

Approximately three dozen golden eagles were trapped and removed by 2006. Ten pairs of island foxes were brought into captivity in 2002 to protect them from golden eagle predation.[23] The foxes were quite cooperative when taken into captive-breeding enclosures, producing tiny, cute kits that were later released across the island once the golden eagles were gone. The fox population has now rebounded to more than two thousand, probably close to the natural carrying capacity of the island, according to Lyndal Laughrin. In 2016, the Santa Cruz Island fox subspecies and those on Santa Rosa and San Miguel Islands were taken off the endangered list (the Santa Catalina Island subspecies is still listed as threatened).[24] This was "the fastest successful recovery for any ESA-listed mammal in the United States" according to the US Fish and Wildlife Service.

And our national bird, the bald eagle, is back, defending the island's shores from its golden eagle cousin. Between 2002 and 2006, sixty-one bald eagles were released on Santa Cruz Island, and in 2006 a nesting pair successfully hatched two chicks, the first successful nesting in over fifty years.[25]

The art—and science—of ecological restoration on Santa Cruz Island, or anywhere else, of course, is sort of like the game of "pick-up sticks" (or "jackstraws," if you prefer the British name of the game). After a century and a half of both deliberate and inadvertent attack on the island's ecosystem, if you pull out one "stick"—one introduced species, for example—chances are it will influence the whole ecological "pile" of sticks and rearrange the pattern, and you will have another problem on your hands. Everything is connected to everything else. You can't do just one thing. Conservation biologists and ecosystem managers on the islands are still dealing with the complexities of trying to undo and reverse the ecological damage done, and to restore an ecological balance that can sustain the islands' unique endemic species.

3
Black Helicopters over Mount Tamalpais

*I have never seen them. But enough people in my district have become
concerned that I can't just ignore it. We do have some proof.*
—Helen Chenoweth, Republican representative from Idaho,
1995[1]

THE GOLDEN GATE BIOSPHERE RESERVE, part of an international network
of biosphere reserves designated by UNESCO, the United Nations Educational, Scientific, and Cultural Organization, is huge. Its 28,000-square-mile
area, which includes both terrestrial and marine zones, stretches approximately 150 miles along the coast, from Point Arena to Point Año Nuevo.
Established in 1988, it is one of the most complex, sprawling, diverse, and
ambitious of any of the twenty-eight biosphere reserves in the United States.
Its fifteen or more partner organizations include various federal, state, and
local agencies and nonprofit organizations, including the National Park Service, US Fish and Wildlife Service, California State Parks, and San Francisco
Peninsula Watershed, which conserve and manage its terrestrial areas, and
two large national marine sanctuaries, Greater Farallones and Cordell Bank,
which protect the marine zone. Some people prefer to call it a biosphere "region" rather than "reserve" because of its size and complexity, but UNESCO
still calls it a biosphere reserve. The World Network of Biosphere Reserves,
to which it belongs, now includes 748 sites in 134 countries.[2]

Among US biosphere reserves, Golden Gate is the only one to encompass a major metropolitan area. More than two million people live in its designated "zone of partnership and cooperation," which includes San Francisco, San Mateo, Marin, and Sonoma Counties, and almost eight million in the nine-county San Francisco Bay Area.

During my research and travel in the Bay Area as I was gathering information and stories for this book, I asked everyone I met what they knew about the Golden Gate Biosphere Reserve. The usual response was "The *what*?" or "What's a biosphere reserve?" Based on my informal polling, I'm guessing that the Golden Gate Biosphere Reserve holds the world record for the most people living in one who have never heard of it. Part of the reason for its obscurity is US politics, in which a Bay Area congressman, Richard Pombo, played a leading role. But before I explain that, I want to first feature a couple of local heroes, without whom neither the UNESCO Man and the Biosphere Programme nor the Golden Gate Biosphere Reserve would exist.

~

A native son of San Francisco, Raymond Dasmann was an architect of the Man and the Biosphere (MAB) Programme. Born in 1919, Ray grew up birding in Golden Gate Park, got a PhD in wildlife management at UC Berkeley, and taught at Humboldt State from 1954 to 1966.[3] Concerns about the impact humans were having on the biosphere were rising rapidly in the 1960s; Rachel Carson's *Silent Spring* was published in 1962, Paul Ehrlich's *The Population Bomb* in 1968, and Gary Snyder weighed in with "Four Changes," his prescription for what we needed to do about it, in 1969. Ray Dasmann was riding the wave too, and his 1965 book, *The Destruction of California*, brought the environmental message home to his home state.[4]

In 1966, Dasmann launched into an international conservation career. He and his family moved to Washington, DC, where he worked for the Conservation Foundation, and then in 1970 to Morges, Switzerland, headquarters of the International Union for Conservation of Nature and Natural Resources (IUCN), where Ray was the senior ecologist. IUCN worked closely with UNESCO to organize the 1968 Biosphere Conference in Paris and played a major role in designing the MAB Programme and network of biosphere reserves, and Dasmann had a strong influence on all of it. For example, his 1974 IUCN report, "Biotic Provinces of the World," was used as a general scheme to identify where biosphere reserves should be situated to represent the ecological diversity of the planet.[5]

Dasmann's idea that every bioregion needed a biosphere reserve so that the human-nature relationship could be studied in each unique ecological and social situation undoubtedly had California roots. Over the years Ray had been engaged in what has been called a "trialogue" with Peter Berg and Gary Snyder. Berg is noted for promoting "bioregionalism." In a pathbreaking essay titled "Reinhabiting California," published in 1977, Berg and Dasmann teamed up to explain how a bioregional paradigm might be applied to their home state. The essay begins with this explanation of their ecocentric vision:

> Living-in-place means following the necessities and pleasures of life as they are uniquely presented by a particular site, and evolving ways to ensure long-term occupancy of that site. A society which practises living-in-place keeps a balance with its region of support through links between human lives, other living things, and the processes of the planet—seasons, weather, water cycles—as revealed by the place itself.[6]

These ideas were very much in the air in the Bay Area in the 1970s. Ernest Callenbach's 1975 novel, *Ecotopia: The Notebooks and Reports of William Weston*, was an imaginative future-fiction portrait of the ecologically sustainable bioregional nation formed when northern California, Oregon, and Washington seceded from the United States. Gary Snyder, who moved with his family to San Juan Ridge in Nevada County around 1970, was experimenting personally with "reinhabitation" of a place. Ray Dasmann bought land on San Juan Ridge near Snyder in 1973 and built a cabin there in 1976. In his autobiography, *Called by the Wild* (2002), Dasmann tried to explain why he built the cabin, and why he left IUCN for a teaching job at UC Santa Cruz in 1977, where he taught until his retirement in 1989:

I was fed up with being a California expatriate at a time when
all the social turmoil and possible hope for the future seemed to
be centered in my home state. I was based in Switzerland, where
nothing ever appeared to interfere with the orderly pursuit of
money. I wanted to get away from the manicured Alpine scenery
to the raw brush fields of home, where I might still encounter
mountain lions and bears. I was beginning to have nightmares
about being caught forever in an endless UN conference in a city I
did not know.[7]

~

The Golden Gate Biosphere Reserve (at first called the Central California
Coast Biosphere Reserve) was officially established in 1988, one of the last
of what would eventually be a network of forty-seven UNESCO biosphere
reserves in the United States. It wouldn't have happened without the leadership of a native daughter of San Francisco, Laurie Wayburn. "It was her baby,
she grabbed this and ran with it," said Terri Thomas, who was the chief of
natural resources and science at the Golden Gate National Recreation Area
(GGNRA) at the time.[8]

Born in San Francisco in 1954, Laurie was the youngest child of a conservation power couple, Dr. Edgar Wayburn and his wife, Peggy. Ed, a physician,
was president of the Sierra Club from 1961 to 1964 and again from 1967 to
1969, during the end of David Brower's long service as the club's executive
director. Together Ed and Peggy Wayburn contributed to many notable conservation achievements in the Bay Area and beyond, including the creation
of GGNRA, Point Reyes National Seashore, and Redwood National Park,
and the expansion of Mount Tamalpais State Park.[9] Laurie grew up among
big ideas about conservation and explored the realm of international conservation when she took a job at the headquarters of the United Nations Environment Programme in Nairobi, Kenya, in 1978. After a few years there, she
moved to the UNESCO MAB Programme in Paris, where she worked from
1982 to 1987.

Laurie returned to the Bay Area in 1987. She soon became executive director of the Point Reyes Bird Observatory (now called Point Blue). But a seed had been planted during her time with the MAB Programme, and she saw both a big need and a great opportunity for a biosphere reserve in the Bay Area, Laurie told me in an interview.[10]

"What were the needs?" I asked. It was "a turf-ridden federal and state situation," Laurie said, with "siloed management and funding," and yet "completely shared and permeable borders" between management units, although there were "small nuggets of cooperation," such as around Mount Tamalpais. She organized a group that wanted to build collaboration to solve common problems, starting at the federal level and then involving state agencies, county and municipal actors, and universities.

And the opportunities? First, Laurie said, the ecological diversity of the area is exceptional, "an unbroken suite of ecosystems from deep marine to mountaintops, and a lot of biodiversity and endemism." And overlaid on the ecological diversity was the social diversity, "from a dense urban center to de facto wilderness" in a relatively small area. What was compelling to her about the biosphere reserves model, Laurie told me, was that it integrated ecological and social dimensions. Long-term ecological research sites were being established, but she wanted to see sites to examine and monitor the social-ecological interactions over the long term as well. Everyone was in favor of bragging that the Bay Area is a very special place in the biosphere, she said, and they thought it had a unique combination of ecological and social circumstances that would make it a laboratory and a model for the rest of the world, through the MAB Programme.

She came up with the concept and proposal and got funding from the San Francisco Foundation to convene meetings and hire an assistant. Brian O'Neill, superintendent of GGNRA at the time, was the "convening power" for the group. Ed Ueber, director of NOAA's Greater Farallones and Cordell Bank National Marine Sanctuaries, was also highly supportive.[11] Both Brian and Ed were very open to collaboration among agencies, a big factor in overcoming interagency "turf" battles and siloed management. Nona Chiariello of Stanford's Jasper Ridge Biological Preserve brought in the science and research perspective,[12] and Ray Dasmann, then at UC Santa Cruz, was a strong supporter of the effort.

The MAB Programme adopted the proposed biosphere reserve in 1988, a year after Laurie returned to California. "How did you manage to get the proposal together and approved in only *one year*?" I asked. "I knew what I was doing," Laurie said. And it's true; she knew what should be said and how the proposal should be written because of her time in the UNESCO MAB office. I suspect her personal connections also helped expedite the process, although Laurie downplayed that.

In 1990, the Golden Gate Biosphere Reserve Association, a nonprofit "friends of" and coordinating group, was formed under Laurie's leadership. Nona Chiariello and Philippe Cohen, from the Jasper Ridge Preserve, took on leading roles in coordination of the organization.[13] When Ray Dasmann retired from UC Santa Cruz in 1989, he served as president of the board of trustees of the biosphere reserve association for about seven years. By then, the headwinds from Washington were beginning to blow more strongly against international cooperation in general, and biosphere reserves in particular.

In fact, they had been blowing for years. "When Reagan was elected, everything had to go underground," Tom Gilbert, a National Park Service scientist who played a central role in US participation in the UNESCO MAB Programme from the beginning, told me.[14] In 1984, the United States withdrew from UNESCO, supposedly because it had become highly politicized, anti-Western, anti-Israel, and pro–Soviet Union. It's remarkable that the Golden Gate Biosphere Reserve made it through the gauntlet of US scrutiny four years later. The explanation, I think, has to do with the professional integrity of federal civil servants, especially scientists in federal agencies, which created an institutional inertia that allowed US participation in the MAB Programme to continue in spite of the political posturing at higher levels.

~

Good stories need heroes and heroines, of course, but a homegrown villain helps spice up the plot. For that, we don't have to look far. Richard Pombo, who represented California's northeast Bay Area eleventh district from 1993 to 2007, fits the role perfectly. Representative Pombo was part of the "Republican Revolution" that flipped control of the House of Representatives during the Clinton administration, and he quickly made his mark as an extreme private property rights advocate and critic of the Department of the Interior, the Endangered Species Act, and all things environmental. *Rolling Stone* magazine called him an "Enemy of the Earth."[15] He chaired the House Natural Resources Committee from 2003 to 2007 during the George W. Bush administration, and in that capacity he almost undermined *all* US participation in the UNESCO MAB Programme. Here's where the "black helicopters" appear, for those who were intrigued by my title!

Black helicopters? I'd somehow missed this story at the time, but I've since learned that "black helicopters" were a common element of an old conspiracy theory that claimed there was a secret plot by UN-loving internationalists to take over the United States. The "New World Order theory," originally promoted by the far-right John Birch Society, claimed that a United Nations force would arrive in black helicopters to bring the United States under UN control. Foreshadowing the QAnon conspiracy theories and antigovernment extremist militias of today, a 1994 book by Jim Keith, *Black Helicopters over America: Strikeforce for the New World Order*, inflamed the fans of this claim. It gained more attention when Helen Chenoweth, a first-term Republican representative from northern Idaho, charged in 1995 that armed federal agents were landing black helicopters on ranchers' property in her state to enforce the Endangered Species Act.[16]

But back to the thread of the narrative and the role of the local villain. In 1995 the MAB Programme held a major conference in Seville, Spain, and issued a set of new, relatively strict criteria for sites to qualify as biosphere reserves. Some of the guidelines were related to the zonation of these areas, presenting a simplistic scheme of core, buffer, and surrounding zones.[17] A faction of the anti-UNESCO movement in the United States seized on this opportunity to claim that the MAB Programme was trying to use biosphere reserves to impose its control over US territory. An organization calling itself "Sovereignty International" was formed in 1997 to promote this anti-MAB version of the story, and it found an ally in California representative Pombo. At that point, US biosphere reserves went into "hibernation," to use Laurie Wayburn's term,[18] trying to fly below the radar and stay invisible.

But it only got worse. Around 2000, "we almost lost the program after the 'wise use' crowd got wind of it," a senior scientist in the Department of the

Interior, who had been the coordinator of the US MAB Programme for most of his career, told me in an interview.[19] ("Wise use" was the self-chosen term used at the time by people like Pombo to camouflage their antienvironmental policies.) When George W. Bush took office in 2001, the US MAB Programme was transferred from the Department of State, where it had resided, to the US Forest Service, significantly degrading its profile and responsibilities. Mark Rey, a former timber industry lobbyist, became undersecretary for agriculture and natural resources in the Bush administration, thus in charge of the US Forest Service. Pombo could not have found a more sympathetic accomplice in the executive branch. The United States rejoined UNESCO in 2003, but that didn't help rescue the US MAB Programme from Representative Pombo and Undersecretary Rey.

In 2005, Pombo, then chair of the House Natural Resources Committee, started an official congressional investigation of US participation in MAB and asked for all MAB records, including emails and phone records. According to my sources—key individuals involved in the US MAB Programme at the time—hundreds of documents were provided to Congress, but then word apparently came down that the Forest Service should destroy all MAB records. The Forest Service scientist then in charge of the US MAB Programme refused to carry out the order, I was told, and instead put the materials in unlabeled boxes and sent them to another federal scientist, who stored them in his garage. When that scientist retired, he sorted out the most important documents and worked with an archivist at the National Park Service and Clemson University to digitize them. They are now in an online archive of the George Wright Society, called "BRInfo."[20] I somehow feel a sense of deep appreciation for the "deep state": for principled, professional civil servants who know what is right, are dedicated to their science, and fight the political headwinds, flying below the radar, and against the prop wash of the black helicopter conspiracy stories.

∼

In 2016, after about twenty years of hibernation, and under pressure from the UNESCO MAB Programme, about half of the former forty-seven US biosphere reserves submitted the "periodic review" report required to remain in the program. The Golden Gate and Channel Islands Biosphere Reserves were among them. Since then, the headwinds have slackened and a tentative tailwind has begun to blow. President Biden has proposed to rejoin UNESCO, although that promises to be an arduous, politically charged process, so I'm not holding my breath.

In the Golden Gate Biosphere Reserve, fifteen key partner agencies and organizations held a three-session virtual retreat in 2021. They organized the "Golden Gate Biosphere Network,"[21] using the name to emphasize the institutional collaboration, coordination, and communication aspects of their relationship, rather than the geographic land and seascape they work in (i.e., the biosphere reserve or region itself). This biosphere reserve is coming out of its long hibernation and revitalizing communication and collaboration among its federal, state, local, and nongovernmental partners.

California condors once soared over all the hills and shores of the bioregion. Maybe someday those large black living objects will once again be sighted over Mount Tam, and the black helicopters will be remembered only as a bad dream.

4
Serpentine and Manzanita

Look like the innocent flower, but be the serpent under it.
—William Shakespeare, *Macbeth*[1]

MANZANITAS BELONG TO THE GENUS *Arctostaphylos* in the heath family, Ericaceae, the same family to which many familiar edible berries belong, such as blueberries, cranberries, and huckleberries. Like many other species in their family, manzanitas have delicate flowers shaped like narrow-mouthed bells, white and often tinged with pink. When their tiny fruits develop, their shape is like a little apple, from which the genus takes its common name; *manzanita* means "little apple" in Spanish. Many manzanita species are low-growing shrubs, some almost ground-hugging mats; a few species grow into small trees that can be more than twenty feet tall and a foot in diameter. They typically have smooth bark—often red, orange, chocolate brown, or even purplish—and tough, twisting trunks and branches. Of the roughly sixty species and more than forty recognized subspecies of *Arctostaphylos*, 98 percent (106 of 108) are found in California,[2] from foggy coasts and Mediterranean-climate chaparral to the alpine of the Sierra Nevada. California is their evolutionary home territory.

The diversity of manzanitas illustrates some fundamental principles of evolutionary ecology, in particular because of the intimate relationship between some species and toxic serpentine soils. Manzanitas also have fascinating and intricate ecological relationships with fire. They showcase the creativity of evolution and ecological adaptation to specific local circumstances and therefore perhaps have some lessons for us—yes, *us*, the human species. Let's have a look at what manzanitas can teach us.

~

Let's start with the "serpentine" part of this story, the "snaky" rocks and the soils derived from them. What's in a name? Sources generally say that the name comes from the similarity of the texture and color of the rock to that of the skin of a snake. When you touch a snake, the immediate impression is the unique feel of its skin, at least for me. This is slick, this is smooth, this is slippery, this is . . . like nothing else. Except when you touch a slip face of serpentine, your fingers feel slickness, smoothness, slipperiness . . . and you may just think "snake"! Serpentine rock is often shiny and greenish or bluish gray, reminiscent of some familiar snakes.

Geologists sometimes make a technical distinction between "serpentine" and "serpentinite," saying that rock composed of any of a group of minerals called serpentine should be called "serpentinite."[3] But it's an arcane distinction that even geologists often don't make, and in common usage this kind of rock is usually just called serpentine. I'll follow that common usage here—and that of the state of California, which officially designated "serpentine" as "California's state rock" in 1965, the first state to adopt a state rock and mineral.[4]

Serpentine is created in undersea subduction zones where two tectonic plates collide and one slides under the other. The intense pressure and mineral-rich water transform rock from the Earth's mantle and oceanic crust into serpentine in a process called hydrothermal metamorphism.[5] The serpentine exposed along the California coast was formed around one hundred million years ago when the Pacific Plate was pushed under the North American Plate.[6] Uplift and faulting along the San Andreas Fault, where these plates are now sliding past each other rather than subducting, have brought this serpentine to the surface in a coastal region stretching from Santa Barbara to southern Oregon.

Because serpentine was formed from Earth's mantle, its chemistry is quite different from that of most other surface rocks made from continental crust. It contains high levels of magnesium, nickel, cobalt, and chromium, which are toxic for many plants, and low amounts of important plant nutrients like potassium, calcium, nitrogen, and phosphorus. And because of its unusual chemistry, soils derived from serpentine present unusual ecological and evolutionary challenges to plants; many species won't grow on them at all. Serpentine soils are often shallow, rocky, and dry, in part because they support less soil-creating vegetation in the first place. Plant communities growing on serpentine are often sparser and more stunted than those on nonserpentine soils; grasslands often replace woodlands in these environments. A high proportion of serpentine plants have evolved biochemical tricks that enable them to grow on such toxic soils. Many such species are found only on serpentine, and many therefore have limited geographic ranges, restricted to the geological "islands" where serpentine rocks outcrop. Biologists call species that have a limited range and are found nowhere else "endemic" species, and those with very small ranges "narrow endemics."

California's comparatively extensive exposure of serpentine is a key reason for its botanical diversity. Although serpentine rocks and soils make up only about 1 percent of California's land area, about 10 percent of the state's endemic plants grow on them.[7] Only a few other places on Earth—Anatolia, Cuba, and New Caledonia—rival the richness of California's unique serpentine flora.[8]

~

On the traditional Mount Tamalpais circumambulation route[9] on the summer solstice, the trail snaked over serpentine ridges raked by fog to "Serpentine Power Point," a sprawl of rock almost barren of plants that looked down on Rock Spring from a hump on the ridge, one of the sites along the route for chants and prayers. Slick, shiny, slip-polished serpentine faces shone sky blue, turquoise, jade green. It was easy to feel the geological power of the planet here. This rock slithered out of undersea ridges at sprawling tectonic plate boundaries as pillow basalt and got subducted and serpentinized and faulted and thrust up here, the bones of Mount Tam. Ah, I love serpentine!

Winding around to the north side of the ridge above Rifle Camp, the Northside Trail crossed a large exposure of serpentine covered in a thriving thicket of *Arctostaphylos montana*, the Mount Tamalpais manzanita.[10]

The gnarly red-stemmed bushes reminded me of the dwarfed, wind-blasted "krummholz" trees found on mountaintops. The twisted old stems of some looked like snakes themselves, slithering over the rocky ground, spiraled with patches of bright red bark and weathered-gray barkless wood. Another California serpentine endemic, Sargent cypress (*Hesperocyparis sargentii*),[11] shared this habitat. In some places the cypress too was dwarfed to krummholz size.

A nonprofit organization called "One Tam" provides a communication and coordination service involving a number of the landowners and management authorities on and around Mount Tamalpais, including the National Park Service, California State Parks, Marin Municipal Water District, Marin County Parks, and Golden Gate National Parks Conservancy. Its mission is "to ensure a vibrant future for Mt. Tamalpais," according to its website.[12] In 2016, One Tam started the "Serpentine Endemic Occupancy Project," which set out to identify distinct patches of serpentine rocks and soils and their associated "serpentine barren" plant communities across the Mount Tam landscape. By 2019 the project had completed plant surveys at twenty-seven sites.[13] "There may be over 30 acres of serpentine barren habitat across more than 85 discrete patches" on the more than thirty-nine thousand acres of protected lands in the Mount Tamalpais landscape, according to the project report. Mount Tam is an archipelago of serpentine islands in a sea of nonserpentine habitat. The survey found that the Mount Tamalpais manzanita was the most common perennial plant on these serpentine barrens, present on twenty-five of the twenty-seven surveyed.[14]

≈

The remarkable evolutionary diversification of manzanitas began, according to the fossil record, only about 1.5 million years ago.[15] It was in part an evolutionary response to the legacy of geological changes in California created by its position between two colliding and slip-sliding tectonic plates. At the tectonic boundary, rocks slipped and slid, folded and faulted, mumbled and jumbled, and were pushed up and eroded down, creating lots of topographic and geological variation. Mountains, valleys, ridges, and slopes facing different directions resulted in a mosaic of microclimates. The underlying geology also produced an incredible diversity of rock and soil structure and composition, or "edaphic" variation.[16]

Over that period, the climate dried out and California's wet-winter, dry-summer "Mediterranean" climate became established. Some old species that were adapted to an earlier, wetter, more temperate climate went extinct, and opportunities were created for new ones to evolve. Glacial cycles, when the climate became alternately wetter and colder or drier and warmer, forced species to move around on the landscape to track the microclimates they needed to survive. This process led to the shrinking and fragmenting of populations of some species, leaving relict populations on islands of suitable habitat where local adaptation could occur and genetic differences could accumulate. Then, with another climate shift, populations could expand again.

This pulsing contraction and expansion of species ranges sometimes brought related but formerly isolated populations together, where they could—perhaps—hybridize and share their unique genetic adaptations, if speciation hadn't progressed so far as to make them unable to interbreed. Hybridization has played an important role in adaptation and speciation in *Arctostaphylos*. One study reported that among a group of forty-six endemic manzanitas found on a particular type of soil (such as serpentine), thirty-seven evolved from hybrids between their ancestral parent species.[17]

Hybridization in manzanitas appears to be facilitated by a process called "polyploidy," in which the number of chromosomes (the packages of DNA in the cell nuclei inherited from the mother and father plants) in the species is doubled. Most manzanitas have thirteen pairs of chromosomes, but almost one-third of the species and subspecies have double that number—four, rather than two, of each of the thirteen chromosomes. That genetic trick allows hybrids from more distantly related lineages to regain complete fertility even after significant evolutionary changes have occurred in the parent lineages.[18]

The geological diversity, climatic fluctuations, ecological adaptations, and genetic hybridization and polyploidy created perfect conditions for manzanitas to pump out new species and subspecies; 108 species and subspecies are currently recognized, making *Arctostaphylos* the most species-rich genus in its subfamily. The center of diversity for manzanitas is roughly San Francisco; the coastal areas and Coast Ranges of California, from Mendocino County to Santa Barbara County, are particularly rich in taxa. Nearly half of all California manzanita species or subspecies are considered rare, threatened, or endangered.[19]

The polyploidy and hybridization that enabled the extensive and rapid evolution of manzanitas is responsible for the headaches they give taxonomists trying to describe and name them. In species of hybrid origin, morphological characters observed by taxonomists—fruit size and shape, leaf size and shape, and so on—aren't necessarily intermediate between those of each parental species. Determining evolutionary and phylogenetic relationships in *Arctostaphylos* has long been, and remains, a challenge for botanists.[20] But as we will see in considering these relationships among several rare, narrowly endemic, and endangered serpentine specialist species, understanding the evolutionary relationships among them is essential for their conservation.

~

I couldn't write about manzanitas without mentioning Alice Eastwood, a pathbreaking California botanist and another example of one of the main themes of these essays—individuals sometimes play a key role in science and conservation. Eastwood is a heroine in the story of California botany, and I'm especially fond of her because we share a connection to Colorado. She was born in Toronto, Canada, in 1859 but moved to Denver, Colorado, in 1873. After graduating from high school in 1879, she taught at the same school for ten years. During that time, she taught herself botany and learned to ride horses so she could make botanical expeditions to more remote parts of the state. Her knowledge of Colorado plants became so widely recognized that in 1887 she was asked to guide Alfred Russel Wallace, codiscoverer with Charles Darwin of the theory of evolution, on a botanical trip up 14,278-foot Grays Peak, the highest summit of the Colorado Front Range, west of Denver.[21]

Eastwood and T.D.A. Cockerell, who was mentioned in the essay on the Channel Islands, must have known each other, but it is hard to dig out the details. Cockerell was living in Westcliffe, Colorado, south of Colorado Springs, from 1887 to 1890, and he was even then an avid botanist. After returning to England, he was a research assistant for Alfred Russel Wallace at the British Museum. When and how Cockerell and Eastwood met is not clear, but it was Eastwood's plant collection of 1,400 specimens that became the foundation of the herbarium at the University of Colorado Boulder, which was established by Cockerell after he settled there in 1904.[22]

Meanwhile, Eastwood was moving on, moving west. In 1892 she left Colorado for San Francisco to take a position as the joint curator of botany at the California Academy of Sciences. She became curator the following year and held that position until she retired in 1949 at the age of ninety. Eastwood is justly acclaimed for her heroic efforts to save the collection of more than one thousand original, irreplaceable type specimens and records from the Cal Academy herbarium after the great San Francisco earthquake of April 1906. She entered the damaged building as fires raged in the surrounding neighborhood, climbed broken staircases, quickly gathered the most valuable specimens, lowered them with improvised pulleys and ropes, and took them to her home for safekeeping.[23]

Manzanitas were one of Eastwood's favorite groups of plants. She described and named a rare manzanita, *Arctostaphylos virgata*, commonly called the Bolinas or Marin manzanita, which is found in only a few places near Bolinas and Point Reyes in Marin County; and a widespread species commonly called Eastwood's manzanita, *Arctostaphylos glandulosa*, found in coastal hills from southern Oregon to Baja California. And then there is the San Bruno Mountain manzanita, *Arctostaphylos imbricata*, also named by her, found only on that mountain just south of San Francisco.[24]

In 1897 she described a new species from serpentine areas around Mount Tamalpais, *Arctostaphylos montana*, the Mount Tamalpais manzanita. And in 1905, she described another manzanita found on serpentine only in San Francisco, naming it *Arctostaphylos franciscana*. As mentioned earlier, manzanitas have always been a difficult genus for taxonomists, and a taxonomic revision in 1968 proposed to lump Eastwood's two serpentine-associated species, the Franciscan and Mount Tamalpais manzanitas, as subspecies of Hooker's manzanita, *Arctostaphylos hookeri*. But in 1998, taxonomists using new genetic evidence such as chromosome counts and genomic sequences concluded that Eastwood had been right, and that the Franciscan and Mount Tamalpais manzanitas aren't close relatives. It turns out that the Franciscan manzanita is a diploid, with two of each chromosome, and the Mount Tamalpais manzanita (and its subspecies *ravenii*, Raven's manzanita) is tetraploid, with twice as many chromosomes—good evidence that these are separate species.[25]

In 1934, Eastwood—then seventy-five years old—published a 22-page article titled "A Revision of *Arctostaphylos* with Key Descriptions" in *Leaflets of Western Botany*, in which she paid keen attention to the relationship of manzanitas and serpentine. All told, she published over 310 scientific articles and described and named 395 plant species. There are seventeen currently recognized species named for her, as well as the genera *Eastwoodia* (in the aster family, with only one species) and *Aliciella* (in the phlox family, with a number of currently recognized species).[26]

Eastwood was a passionate advocate for native plant conservation. In 1904 she spoke at a women's garden club meeting in San Francisco to promote the conservation of the redwoods in Redwood Canyon on the southwest side of Mount Tamalpais, saying, "There is only one reason why I wish I had a million dollars. The only thing I want that amount of money for is to buy Redwood Park and Mount Tamalpais and present them to the State of California for a public reserve."[27] It turned out that San Francisco businessman, philanthropist, and politician William Kent and his wife, Elizabeth— who may well have been at that garden club meeting—*did* have the money, motivation, and political connections to protect Redwood Canyon. They acquired it and donated it to the federal government in 1908 to become Muir Woods National Monument, and they were also instrumental in the creation of Mount Tamalpais State Park.

There are some striking pictures of Alice Eastwood. One, from the California Academy of Sciences, dated 1910, a perfectly composed portrait by an unattributed photographer, shows her resolute face, perfectly lighted from her lower right, under a dark hat with the brim laden with white blossoms, and tied under her chin with a white scarf. She is wearing what appears to be a heavy dress of shiny black fabric with a high, tight collar and puffy shoulders; a spry sprig of white flowers tucked into the dress below the scarf combines with her bright eyes to let us know that she was one self-assured and spunky woman.

Another of my favorite photos of her was taken when she accompanied G. K. Gilbert, an eminent California geologist, to survey the effects of the 1906 San Francisco earthquake in the Olema Valley between Bolinas and Tomales Bay. In it she is standing beside a huge, jagged, sinuous fissure where the ground had been ripped apart, like a giant snake lying across the grassy slope. She is overweighted in the expected women's clothing of the era: a puffy white blouse with sleeves to the wrists and a heavy dark dress dragging the grass, wearing a black broad-brimmed hat with a pile of ribbons around its crown. In another photo taken by Gilbert she appears to be standing right on the fissure created by the quake. The caption for that photo, displayed along the Earthquake Trail near the Point Reyes National Seashore head-quarters, says that Eastwood was "more than just an ordinary field assistant. In a world of science dominated by men, her accomplishments conveyed her love of science and the geology that shapes California." They meant to em-phasize her importance as a pioneering woman scientist, but she was indeed more than just an ordinary field assistant. After the death of Gilbert's wife in 1898, Eastwood and Gilbert apparently enjoyed a romantic, as well as a scientific, relationship until his own death in 1918.[28]

⁓

The drying climate and establishment of a strong wet-dry seasonal cli-mate in California over the past 1.5 million years increased the frequency of fire in the ecosystems into which manzanitas were rapidly evolving, present-ing another environmental challenge, but also adaptive opportunities. Man-zanitas took on the challenge, as they had with serpentine soils, by making friends with fire. The suppression of vegetation on serpentine makes those areas drier than surrounding areas and therefore more prone to fire, so there is a natural association between serpentine and fire-adapted plant species like manzanitas.

Two strategies evolved in the genus *Arctostaphylos* to respond to fire. Some manzanita species can resprout after a fire from burls, called lignotu-bers, at the base of the plant, which are protected from fire by the soil. They can also produce seeds and are called "facultative" seeders. Most manzanitas are "obligate" seeders, however; they do not resprout after a fire but reproduce only from seeds that have accumulated over the years in the soil seed bank, where germination is stimulated by heat and/or compounds found in smoke or leached from charcoal and ash produced by fires.[29] About two-thirds of manzanita species are obligate seeders, and one-third resprouters (which also produce dormant, fire-stimulated seeds).[30] Why the difference, since both strategies help manzanitas hold territory in fire-prone environments?

The answer seems to be sex. Resprouting involves asexual reproduction, and the new generation of resprouted manzanitas are clones of their parents with exactly the same genetic makeup. Producing seeds involves sexual reproduction, which mixes and reassorts genes from the previous generation. In changing, disturbance-prone environments, it appears that sexual reproduction holds the advantage, leading to the somewhat counterintuitive result that in highly fire-prone California chaparral, for example, the majority of species lack the capacity for resprouting.

Obligate seeders, even the fire-adapted species, are not especially tolerant of frequent fires. They require a substantial length of time between fires for seedlings to establish, mature, reproduce, and get a load of seeds into the soil seed bank. Prescribed burns in chaparral habitats that are meant to reduce fire risk to people and their structures could end up killing stands of obligate seeders.[31] I hope Cal Fire, the California Department of Forestry and Fire Protection, which oversees wildfire response and prescribed mitigation of wildfire risk in the state, is getting the advice of manzanita ecologists to formulate their policies.

Walking the trails along Inverness Ridge in Point Reyes National Seashore where the Vision Fire burned in 1995, I got a firsthand look at the manzanitas found there, and their strategies for dealing with fire. The Marin manzanita (*Arctostaphylos virgata*), a fire-dependent obligate seeder, had hardly ever been seen recently until the Vision Fire triggered the germination of thousands of dormant seeds.[32] This manzanita is very rare according to the California Native Plant Society: "Known from only about 20 occurrences in the forests and maritime chaparral . . . it is dependent on wildfire and its survival is threatened by fire suppression."[33] But at other places along the same trails I saw Eastwood's manzanita, *Arctostaphylos glandulosa*, a postfire resprouter, which was also happy.

Other plants besides manzanitas have learned the evolutionary trick of making friends with fire through obligate-seeding life cycles. Sargent cypress, which shares its serpentine habitat on Mount Tam with the Mount Tamalpais manzanita, has cones that remain closed and attached to the branches until a fire sweeps through and opens them. The waiting seeds scatter, mixing with those of the manzanita, to begin reconquering the habitat after the next rains. On Inverness Ridge at Point Reyes, where the Vision Fire burned through maritime chaparral and bishop pine forest in 1995, the serotinous pines scattered their seed to mix with that of the Marin manzanita, waiting in the soil to rise from the ashes.

≈

The germination of manzanita seeds from both facultative and obligate seeders can be stimulated by heat or chemicals in smoke and charcoal following wildfires, but their dormancy can be broken by other means. Being passed through the digestive tract of an animal that ate the fruit containing them is one such means. Bears are prime suspects. In fact, the scientific genus name *Arctostaphylos* is taken from the Greek roots for "bear-grape," and the species name of a widespread and common species, *Arctostaphylos uva-ursi*, essentially translates as "bear-grape grape-for-bear." Call them grapes or little apples, no problem—bears like manzanita fruits. In his poem "Control Burn," Gary Snyder noted that

> manzanita seeds will only open
> after a fire passes over
> or once passed through a bear[34]

Two treelike species of manzanita are found only on Santa Cruz Island: the Santa Cruz Island manzanita, *Arctostaphylos insularis*, and McMinn's manzanita, *Arctostaphylos viridissima* (also called white-haired manzanita). Both are obligate seeders and cannot resprout following a fire. A third species, *Arctostaphylos tomentosa*, the island manzanita, is a resprouter and facultative seeder found on Santa Cruz and Santa Rosa Islands.[35]

Wildfires occur occasionally on the Channel Islands now, although, as elsewhere in California, they were probably more common before Euro-American settlement because of deliberate ecological use of fire by Native Americans. How dependent are the narrow-endemic Channel Island manzanitas on fire to regenerate their populations? I wondered.

There are no bears on the Channel Islands, but I mentioned in an earlier essay that island foxes mark their territory with scat piles—such as on the pic-nic tables at the Santa Cruz Island Reserve field station. Their territorial mark-ings were common everywhere one of their distinctive tiny trails crossed a human road or trail, and these scat cairns were often full of manzanita seeds. If passing through the gut of a bear can stimulate manzanitas to germinate, a trip through an island fox probably can also.[36] If so, there may be a still-unstudied seed-dispersal symbiosis between island foxes and the several endemic man-zanitas on the Channel Islands, perhaps similar to that of the mutualism of the island scrub-jays and island live oaks described in an earlier essay.

≈

I had arranged to meet Michael Chassé at the Langdon Court parking area in the San Francisco Presidio at 3:00 p.m. for a tour of his efforts to conserve two extremely rare manzanitas found only in this area. Michael is a plant ecologist with the National Park Service who has been involved in many initiatives to restore native plants in the Golden Gate National Recreation Area. It was only April 7, but it was a record-hot day for that date—eighty degrees or a little above. The Langdon Court parking was jammed with San Franciscans heading down the steep trail to Marshall Beach, delighted for this uncommon chance to shed some layers of clothing the climate usually requires. I found Michael supervising a group of volunteers who were pulling up nonnative invasive species in an area with an abundant colony of native Douglas iris in full, beautiful bloom.

Michael was the perfect guide for understanding these native manzanita restoration efforts. The title of his master's thesis from San Francisco State University was "San Francisco's Rare Endemic Manzanitas: Prospects for Recovery through Restoration." Slumping cliffs of blue-gray serpentine are exposed along the Presidio Bluffs here, above Marshall Beach and south to-ward Baker Beach, and the soils along the bluffs are derived from that rock. Michael pointed out recent plantings of four different clones of the Francis-can manzanita, the serpentine-specialist species found only on the San Fran-cisco Peninsula and first described by Alice Eastwood. Remember Alice?

Each of the tiny plants beside the busy public trail was labeled to indi-cate where it came from originally. Three of the four types were derived from cuttings taken from wild individuals that originally grew at the Laurel Hill Cemetery, a former cemetery on a large hill of serpentine in the city's Richmond District. In the late 1800s the area was described as one of "delightful dells, scooped out among the hills, with the evergreen oaks bordering and fringing their quiet beauty; valleys smiling all over with flowers, of every hue, and knolls covered with shrubs."[37] As San Francisco grew and the value of land went up, the cemetery was closed; in the late 1930s, thirty-five thousand bodies were removed and reinterred at another cemetery and the land was bulldozed and converted to houses.[38] Some dedicated plant conservationists saw the demise of Laurel Hill coming and brought specimens of native plants, including the Franciscan manzanita, into cultivation in local botanical gardens—the San Francisco Botanical Garden, the University of California Botanical Garden, and the Tilden Regional Parks Botanic Garden in the hills above Berkeley.

The fourth type planted here along the Presidio Bluffs, labeled "DD" for Doyle Drive, has a fun backstory. It was long thought that since the Laurel Hill Cemetery was converted to houses, the Franciscan manzanita was extinct in the wild and had survived only in botanical gardens. Then, in October 2009, a botanist working for Audubon Canyon Ranch, trained to scan roadsides for invasive plants, spotted something out of the corner of his eye along the highway at the southern end of the Golden Gate Bridge, at Doyle Drive. When he checked it out on foot, it was a giant old manzanita bush at least fifteen feet across, growing on a patch of serpentine—right in the path of a billion-dollar freeway expansion project at the end of the bridge. Local manzanita experts quickly investigated and decided that it was a Franciscan manzanita. Although it appeared to have a few mysterious characteristics that suggested an episode of hybridization sometime in its past, it was similar to some old specimens collected by Alice Eastwood from Laurel Hill and preserved in the California Academy of Sciences. Then began the heroic saga of rescuing this last wild Franciscan manzanita, which wasn't extinct in the wild after all. The California Department of Transportation cooperated, using cranes and heavy equipment to move the plant and its ten-ton root ball. It was transplanted to a new home in the Presidio about a mile away, onto a matching patch of serpentine, where it is apparently still doing well.[39]

Most of these Franciscan manzanitas had been planted only recently and were still tiny. The little plants all looked happy to me; their biggest threat was probably from people stepping off the trail and squashing them. A slightly older one labeled "SF 12," from a plant in the San Francisco Botanical Garden, was started from a cutting in 2013 and outplanted here in 2018. It was spreading out and blooming. Helplessly hoping, perhaps, for a mate?

The hope, helpless or not, is that by planting four types of *Arctostaphylos franciscana* near each other here—clones from perhaps four distinct wild individuals—they will eventually begin to cross-pollinate, share their genes, and establish a genetically variable and viable wild population.[40] More than ninety plants of the four types have been established so far.

We walked south along the Presidio Bluffs on the California Coastal Trail, and before long we saw several large patches of another rare manzanita sprawling down the seaward slope. These were clones of the Presidio manzanita, *Arctostaphylos montana ravenii*, also known as Raven's manzanita. They were planted in 1987 and are now large, prostrate mats ten feet or so in diameter. This subspecies of the Mount Tamalpais manzanita, the serpentine endemic I described earlier, was first spotted near here by Peter Raven, a local plant enthusiast, when he was a teenager. He later became a noted botanist, evolutionary biologist, and conservationist, teaching at Stanford University and later directing the Missouri Botanical Garden.[41] Raven's manzanita is listed as threatened under the Endangered Species Act.

Finally, Michael took me to a nearby location to see the "mother plant" from which these patches had been cloned—the one and only surviving, original, wild individual of Raven's manzanita. He swore me to secrecy and nixed photos but at least didn't make me wear a blindfold on the way there. It was a huge hump of a plant with a few patches of dieback, but in general it still seemed to be alive and well.

≈

The California Floristic Province is recognized as a biodiversity hotspot because of its species diversity and the large percentage of species found nowhere else. It is called a "floristic" province, and plants—the flora—are the foundation of all ecosystems, the capturers of the solar energy that powers the whole show. Plant diversity and endemism, through coevolution, underpin all other biodiversity—microbial, fungal, and animal. So in fact this is the California *biotic* province, or bioregion. And serpentine is an important reason for this biotic richness.

Most of the species diversity and endemism in California are encompassed *between* sites rather than *within* them. One reason is that the insular distribution of serpentine outcrops limits dispersal and interbreeding of species populations in ecological and evolutionary time. This is a basic observation underlying island biogeography theory—the same pattern that Charles Darwin and Alfred Russel Wallace observed, which led them to their theory of evolution by natural selection, and which T.D.A. Cockerell also documented on the California Channel Islands.

A second reason seems to be that there is a heightened sensitivity of plant distributions to climatic variation—temperature and rainfall—on serpentine.[42] The climatic sensitivity of serpentine communities isn't really surprising, given that they are already stressful places for plants to live, warmer and drier than other places. Serpentine plant communities are therefore something of an "indicator community," and therefore a good place to monitor and try to understand the ecological effects of the climate warming humans have created by burning fossil fuels.

The reasons underlying the species diversity and endemism of manzanitas, and of California as a whole, have important implications for conserving them: protecting a few sites won't do. Rather, a network of sites spanning and representing the geographic (i.e., topographic, edaphic, and climatic) diversity of California is needed. This conclusion, based on lessons from serpentine and manzanitas, applies across the California bioregion.

Evolution is creative. Life takes advantage of new opportunities by evolving new, genetically adapted populations, subspecies, and eventually species. Manzanitas are the flagship example of the amazing biodiversity of California and the evolutionary forces that created it. "What a wonderful group!" says Dr. Tom Parker, who spent his whole career at San Francisco State University studying them.[43] Manzanitas can be a metaphor, challenging us to think about how our human communities can evolve and become more locally adapted, more finely tuned to the specific places we live, with all of their unique geographies, climates, and ecologies.

5

Butterfly Blues

The blues is sort of a mixed-up thing.
　　　—Billie Holiday, 1957[1]

THE BLUES ARE MEMBERS of the butterfly subfamily Polyommatinae (of the family Lycaenidae), one of the most diverse groups of butterflies in North America, according to lepidopterists. They seem to have found an evolutionary mechanism for adapting to local environments and forming new species and subspecies to a greater extent than most other groups of butterflies, according to recent high-powered genomic research.[2]

The blues are a genre of jazz and the feelings conveyed by that music and its lyrics, feelings of melancholy and sadness, according to musicologists. Enslaved Africans brought that music with them and adapted it to their new circumstances in the New World. It carried and expressed all the dislocation, injustice, and pain of slavery and the slave trade. But the blues were, and are, also a music of resistance and resilience, of "we shall overcome." They're survivor music, make-the-best-of-it music, simultaneous acknowledgment and defiance of hard times.[3]

And the blues—the butterflies, I mean—are singing the blues now. If you evolved in and adapted to the coastal grasslands or the sand dunes of the San Francisco Peninsula for a million years and suddenly someone converted them to housing developments, you'd know the dislocation, injustice, and sorrow of this sudden loss of your habitat and way of life.

Ironically perhaps, and perhaps hopefully, some of the blues are rewilding this place, with our help. The blue butterflies, and others of their butterfly kin, may help teach us lessons in patience and resilience while encouraging our own species to forge on too, adapting, evolving, and rewilding our hearts and spirits toward a future where all species can thrive.

~

The Mission blue, *Icaricia icarioides missionensis*, is a subspecies of a butterfly called Boisduval's blue, locally adapted to the coastal grasslands of the San Francisco Peninsula and the Marin Headlands just across the Golden Gate.

The scientific and common names of this unique butterfly refer to the area where it was first collected in 1934. The Mission District of San Francisco surrounds the original Spanish mission established in the area in 1776, named after Saint Francis of Assisi. The mission was commonly called Misión Dolores; in Spanish, *dolores* means sorrow, or sadness. From the point of view of the endangered Mission blue, the association with Saint Francis—whose reputed love of nature has led some to call him the patron saint of animals—is ironic.

The coastal grassland habitat of the Mission blue would have been much more extensive two and a half centuries ago when a party of men from the Spanish exploring expedition led by Gaspar de Portolá climbed the coastal hills from what is now the San Francisco suburb of Pacifica on November 4, 1769. They were the first Europeans to see San Francisco Bay; earlier Spanish and English maritime explorers had failed to find it, having sailed past its narrow mouth without knowing it was there. The Spaniards did not "discover" the bay, of course: native Ohlone and Miwok people had been living around it for thousands of years. Indian use of fire held woody chaparral and coastal sage scrub vegetation in check and favored the grasslands where the butterfly's lupine host plants occur. The Portolá expedition was soon followed by the establishment of a chain of Spanish missions from San Diego northward, one of which was in San Francisco.

After World War II, residential and industrial development in the Bay Area fragmented and severely reduced their natural habitat, and Mission blue populations plummeted. The subspecies was listed as endangered under the Endangered Species Act (ESA) in 1976. San Bruno Mountain, one of the last best pieces of coastal grassland in the Bay Area, supports the largest population of Mission blues, estimated at about eighteen thousand adult butterflies.[4]

San Bruno Mountain still supports natural vegetation and endangered species only because of the catalytic collective action of a women-led group of local conservationists who formed the Committee to Save San Bruno Mountain in 1971. Committee cochairs Bette Higgins and Mimi Whitney wrote in a 1974 op-ed in the *San Francisco Examiner*:

> Three years ago, when the cry to Save San Bruno Mountain was first heard, it did not come from the formal conservation groups such as the Sierra Club or Friends of the Earth. It came from the working people who are packed into the original "little boxes" that surround the mountain.[5]

The "little boxes" they were referring to were the look-alike suburban homes then sprawling over the hills south of the city, so called in a 1962 song with that title composed by folk singer and political activist Malvina Reynolds, which was first released by Pete Seeger in 1963.[6] It satirizes the environmentally destructive development of the San Francisco suburbs and the mentality of cheap, conformist middle-class materialism impelling it; the houses are "all made out of ticky-tacky," says the song.

The major threat to the mountain was not just the houses, but a proposal made in 1965 to carve off its top so its rock and dirt could be used to fill some of the western shoreline of the bay for more industrial and residential development.[7] In 1975, a story in the *San Mateo Times* described how

> a seemingly rag-tag group of Peninsula residents have banded together in recent years to oppose development of a new community on San Bruno Mountain. Actually, this group of housewives, businessmen, teachers and representatives from virtually every walk of life, have molded into a well-disciplined "grassroots army" whose sole objective is to halt construction of the proposed mountain development.[8]

This group was able to turn the tide away from development, but not without a lengthy, contentious process that pitted many people and perspectives against each other before a compromise was finally reached—a history that needs an entire essay or book to fully explore.

The listing of the Mission blue under the ESA in 1976 supercharged the battle between conservationists and developers, but a half-dozen years of negotiations somehow led to a deal: housing development would be allowed on some part of Mission blue habitat on San Bruno Mountain—resulting in the deaths of some butterflies—in exchange for an agreement, called a "habitat conservation plan," that would permanently protect other butterfly habitat on the mountain or places where, it was argued, the needed habitat could potentially be restored. But this locally negotiated deal was still illegal under the ESA, which prohibited any killing or capture—carefully called "take"—of a listed species for any reason, including destruction of part of its habitat for housing or other development.

Long story made short, the Endangered Species Act was amended in 1982 to allow the Mission blue habitat conservation plan agreement on San Bruno Mountain, and future habitat conservation plans like it. Some ecologists and conservationists thought this saved the ESA from political extinction. This was, after all, in the early years of the Reagan administration, and antienvironmentalist James Watt was secretary of the interior, so the threat to the ESA was palpable. Others, equally credible and passionate—including the Committee to Save San Bruno Mountain and the Xerces Society—thought the San Bruno Mountain plan provided a loophole for development that would weaken and undermine the ESA.[9]

But that's all history now. A part of the critical habitat of the Mission blue on San Bruno Mountain was converted to houses as a result of this compromise, but much of the mountain is now protected as a state and county park, and a critical area of the best remaining natural habitat on the north side of the mountain is an 83-acre ecological reserve managed by the California Department of Fish and Wildlife.[10] A thirty-year review of the effectiveness of the habitat conservation plan was completed in 2015; it concluded that the grassland habitat needed by the Mission blue continues to shrink despite nominal protection of the area from ongoing encroachment by woody native scrub and nonnative invasive species such as fennel, with insufficient funding to control this process.[11] On the national scale, the debate continues even now, and the jury is still out as to whether the habitat conservation plan idea that began with the Mission blue on San Bruno Mountain will work for other endangered species or not.

Given the fragmentation of the Mission blue's habitat, the US Fish and Wildlife Service (USFWS) approved a plan, responding to the ESA listing of the species, to restore it to several areas of its former habitat within the Golden Gate National Recreation Area.[12] A 1982 study found that Mission blues could fly around a quarter of a mile between patches of their coastal grassland habitat. Because of urban development, San Bruno Mountain is an isolated island of Mission blues. On their own, the butterflies are extremely unlikely to reach other islands of suitable habitat that still exist in the area, such as Sweeney Ridge, a mere five miles away as the butterfly flies. It was from this hilltop that the men from the Portolá expedition first saw San Francisco Bay; it is now part of the Golden Gate National Recreation Area, managed by the National Park Service. Mission blues were observed at Sweeney Ridge in the late 1980s, more than a decade after they were listed as endangered under the ESA, but then they disappeared there more than twenty years ago.

∼

A breeze was just starting up as we parked along Quarry Road in Brisbane, California, on the northeastern slope of San Bruno Mountain. I tagged along with a local butterfly conservation scientist, Stuart Weiss, and a two-person team from the Golden Gate National Recreation Area. Mission of the day: to capture and translocate some Mission blue butterflies from this area to Sweeney Ridge. The motive was to reestablish another population of Mission blues there, which would reduce their vulnerability to factors that might cause them to disappear from San Bruno Mountain, and thereby enhance their long-term survival. The translocation project was being conducted with the permission and blessing of the USFWS, which has the responsibility and authority for safeguarding the Mission blue and other species listed under the ESA. This year, 2022, was the first year of translocations from San Bruno to Sweeney Ridge; the USFWS-approved plan was to relocate sixty butterflies to reestablish the population there.

We scoured the steep hillside grassland, focusing on clusters of lupines where Mission blue females might be hanging out and males might be patrolling in hopes of mating. Spotting tiny Mission blues, with a wingspan the size of a quarter, was obviously a skill acquired after considerable experience, and I was a novice. Quick and elusive, flying low in the rising wind, the males gave a flash of their blue upper wings in just the right light; the females looked browner. The translocation team was under a strict protocol from the USFWS. Only six females and two males could be taken in this area today, a small fraction of the estimated local population of adult butterflies. After a few hours of searching, the authorized sample had been captured in nets swooped over the lupines and carefully coached into tiny plastic containers, and we descended to our cars.

Three species of perennial lupines, on which the Mission blue lays its eggs and its larvae feed, are important to its survival: silver lupine (*Lupinus albifrons*), summer lupine (*Lupinus formosus*), and varied lupine (*Lupinus varicolor*). All three occur on San Bruno Mountain. The silver lupine is the most common and the most used as a host plant, but it is probably the diversity of lupines, and the ability of the Mission blue to use all three species, that underlie the ecological resilience that has allowed it to persist. The three lupines favor different microclimates, which are determined mainly by topography. North-, south-, east-, or west-facing slopes, canyon bottoms or ridges, exposure to wind, soil type, and soil moisture create a mosaic of microhabitats that favor different lupine species. On top of that is the variability of climate and weather from year to year. Just trying to imagine the complexity stretches my mind like three-dimensional chess. In some years the silver lupine may wilt early from a fungal disease, but the summer lupine or varied lupine may thrive, giving the Mission blue a backup for egg laying and larval feeding. Other years bring other risks and other options.

For many people, the term "rewilding" evokes reintroducing large carnivores and creating connecting corridors of habitat so that they can again roam through wilderness ecosystems at regional or even continental scales. They picture wolves, grizzlies, mountain lions, jaguars. But that definition is too narrow.

From the point of view of the Mission blue, these remnant patches of grassland and lupines in the San Francisco suburbs *are* their world, their continent, their wilderness. The skyscrapers of the city are visible, communication towers command the hilltops, power lines crisscross the ridges, and suburbs of ticky-tacky houses and roaring freeways hem in these small remnant grasslands, which have improbably—only because of the inspiring activism and work of local conservationists over more than half a century—been protected from all that human infrastructure development. These grasslands may not look wild to our eyes, but they would if we saw them through the eyes of butterflies.

From San Bruno Mountain, with the captives chilling in a cooler to keep them comfortable and calm, we drove south on the Bayshore Freeway, then west toward Skyline College; we parked in an upper parking lot and used a shortcut trail to Sweeney Ridge. When we arrived at the release site in early afternoon, the wind was up. In this area, the National Park Service and volunteers from the Golden Gate National Parks Conservancy have been planting more of the lupines that are the Mission blue's host plants. Big squares of tulle-fabric netting were spread over clumps of reestablished lupines and held down with rocks. The butterflies we captured a few hours ago on San Bruno Mountain were released from the tiny plastic containers under these protective shrouds and offered snacks of sugar-water-soaked cotton balls. Within a short time, some females were laying eggs on the lupines in their new home.

Can even small stories of resilience and rewilding, like this one about the Mission blue, help us rewild our human hearts and spirits and motivate us to work toward a future where all species can thrive together?

～

Butterflies are perhaps the most thoroughly studied group of insects, maybe even of all invertebrates. They are active during the day, unlike most of their nocturnal kin the moths, and their conspicuous and beautiful colors and flower-feeding habits have always attracted human attention. Research on butterflies has made them a model system for understanding many facets of ecology, evolution, genetics, and conservation biology, and recent developments in DNA sequencing technology are leading to further insights from these astonishing creatures, as we'll see later in this essay.

The Bay checkerspot, *Euphydryas editha bayensis*, like the Mission blue a rare endemic butterfly of the Bay Area, is another example of what butterflies can teach us about the human-nature relationship in this place. This butterfly is found only on the remaining, and still threatened, patches of serpentine grassland of the San Francisco Peninsula and South Bay, where its larval host plants and adult nectar plants are found. It was listed as a threatened subspecies under the Endangered Species Act in 1987. As such, because of the habitat conservation and population recovery requirements of the ESA, the Bay checkerspot has been called an "umbrella" species, essentially sheltering and helping to protect its serpentine habitat and all of the other unique, endemic serpentine specialist species.[13]

The Bay checkerspot is a member of the largest family of butterflies, the Nymphalidae. It has only one generation per year, with adults emerging in late spring to feed, mate, and lay eggs before their host plants dry up. Annual plantain, *Plantago erecta*, is the primary larval host plant, although caterpillars also sometimes feed on two species of owl's clover. Because serpentine outcrops are scattered and patchy, forming islands of serpentine grassland, Bay checkerspot populations are naturally patchy and scattered too. In some cases they are small, and prone to local extinction because of random fluctuations in weather and other factors.

This is the species Paul Ehrlich and his students and colleagues studied for decades at Stanford's Jasper Ridge Biological Preserve. Ehrlich (born in 1932) joined the Stanford faculty in 1959. In 1964, he published an influential paper with a fellow Stanford faculty member, plant ecologist Peter Raven (after whom Raven's manzanita, mentioned in the previous essay, is named), in which they described reciprocal evolutionary interactions—"coevolution"—between butterflies and plants.[14] Ehrlich detailed his research on the population dynamics of the Bay checkerspot in a paper in the journal *Evolution* in 1965.[15] His book *The Population Bomb* exploded into creative controversy in 1968. Ehrlich and his students and colleagues continued to study *Euphydryas editha bayensis* at Jasper Ridge until, in 1998, it disappeared.

In April 2022, I wandered the ridge road through the serpentine grassland at Jasper Ridge with Dr. Nona Chiariello, a longtime senior scientist at the preserve (Nona was mentioned in an earlier essay because of her important involvement in the development of the Golden Gate Biosphere Reserve). The morning sun was hot and the grasslands were starting to dry and brown, but at some of Ehrlich's old research sites the hills were awash with golden-orange California poppies, which apparently had liked the heavy rains at the beginning of the winter. There are no more Bay checkerspots at Jasper Ridge, for the time being at least, until by some miracle of dispersal they recolonize this tiny patch of serpentine, or in an act of rewilding by humans they are reintroduced in their former habitat here.

Even early studies of the Bay checkerspot showed it to be quite sedentary, and not good at long-distance dispersal and colonization. That led to something of a paradox: how has a poor disperser, scattered across the landscape on islands of serpentine grassland where it is prone to local extinction, managed to persist? To try to answer that question, Susan Harrison studied the dispersal of the Bay checkerspot at Coyote Ridge, between San Jose and Morgan Hill, the largest serpentine grassland habitat—about five thousand acres—left in the Bay Area. Compared to the sixty acres of serpentine at Jasper Ridge,[16] Coyote Ridge is Bay checkerspot paradise. Harrison's 1989 study confirmed that this butterfly is indeed not a good disperser, and that "the key to the paradox of the Bay checkerspot's regional survival may not be adaptation for dispersal and colonization, but rather the existence within its range (until recently, when the others were destroyed by development) of a few large, persistent populations."[17] Stuart Weiss called the Coyote Ridge population a "reservoir-satellite metapopulation,"[18] the last home on the range of *Euphydryas editha bayensis*.

During my visit in April 2022, I had the opportunity to meet and talk with Paul Ehrlich again. His longtime student, lab assistant, and research colleague Dr. Stuart Weiss had persuaded Paul to come butterfly chasing with us at the Coyote Ridge Open Space Preserve, where Stu had found a few late-season Bay checkerspots still flying a few days earlier. We picked Paul up at his retirement residence, with his trekking poles and sun hat, somewhat frail at ninety but eager for the expedition. The hour-long drive to Coyote Ridge gave us a wonderful chance to talk. In the field, Stu managed to catch a couple of the elusive *Euphydryas* on the last, greenest patches of drying serpentine grassland in the area. I'll never forget how gently, and fondly, Paul held his favorite butterfly between his thumb and forefinger and brought it close to his face so he could see it better.

In the introduction to the book he edited in 2003 with Carol Boggs and Ward Watt, *Butterflies: Ecology and Evolution Taking Flight*, Ehrlich wrote:

> Humanity is now faced with the greatest crisis in its history, a crisis that in some senses is shared by butterflies, and which, as an important test system, they can help to ameliorate. . . . Biologists doing research on butterflies are developing these insects into one of the most important model systems for basic biological research. . . . They are in the enviable position of both working with lovely and intriguing creatures and helping to save the world. What more could any scientist ask?[19]

∼

Only a little more than a century ago, a dynamic sheet of sand dunes covered the southwestern third of what is now the city of San Francisco. William Keith, a landscape painter and friend of fellow Scotsman John Muir, captured a scene from this surreal landscape in his painting *Sand Dunes and Fog, San Francisco*, made sometime in the 1880s.[20] Historic photos from 1910 and even later show dunes and dune vegetation throughout the Richmond and Sunset Districts. Farther inland, older dunes were stabilized by dune scrub vegetation.[21] When photographer Ansel Adams was growing up in the Sea Cliff neighborhood in the early 1900s, Lobos Creek still flowed through dunes south of the Presidio to its mouth at Baker Beach.

And through these dunes fluttered another blue: *Glaucopsyche xerces*, the Xerces blue butterfly, famous because it is said to be the first recorded extinction of a North American butterfly. Its name was used in founding the Xerces Society for Invertebrate Conservation.[22] It was last seen in the Lobos Creek dunes in about 1942.

But no wonder it disappeared. San Francisco's dunes were seen as wasted land and had been steadily covered and converted for decades. In the 1870s the US Army, in charge of the Presidio, farmed vegetables along Lobos Creek and built a balloon hangar there in the 1920s. A sewer system was installed along the creek, and the area was used for dumping and storing junk from the Presidio. Nearby, urban development sprawled across the dune field and out to the coast in the Sunset and Richmond Districts.

Sayonara, Xerces blue.

But then came a turn of fate for Lobos Creek and its dunes, if not yet for its former blue butterflies. In 1994, the San Francisco Presidio was transferred from the Department of Defense to the National Park Service's Golden Gate National Recreation Area, and the Presidio Trust was established by Congress to generate enough revenue from the most-developed core area of the old Presidio to fund its management. That same year, the city of San Francisco provided mitigation money to restore the dunes habitat as part of a deal to replace the old sewer and stormwater system built along Lobos Creek, because the dunes were home to a small and very rare sunflower-family plant called San Francisco lessingia (*Lessingia germanorum*), found only on the San Francisco Peninsula. When this plant was listed as endangered under the Endangered Species Act in 1997, voilà: twenty acres of the old dunes along Lobos Creek began to be restored.[23]

I visited the restored dunes in June 2021 with Michael Chassé, the National Park Service plant ecologist who showed me the rare manzanita restoration efforts on the Presidio Bluffs described in the previous essay. Now a boardwalk trail about a mile long winds through the restored dunes. Michael has been involved in the restoration of dune vegetation here since the beginning; much of the work has been done by volunteers. Junk dumped at the site over the decades first had to be cleaned up, then invasive nonnative plants removed. A carefully chosen "palette" (as Michael called it) of native dune and dune-scrub plants was then planted: mock heather, coyote brush, Chamisso's lupine, dune gilia, and of course the endangered San Francisco lessingia.

And—a key species—the host plant of the former Xerces blue, deerweed. Deerweed, *Acmispon glaber*,[24] in this case a low-growing, spreading variety adapted to sand dune habitats, was in glorious full bloom. The young, pealike flowers at the top of the flower spikes were butter yellow; the earlier, older blooms below had faded to rusty orange and even tawny port red. Large patches of deerweed seemed to be thriving here, but their pale silvery-green, lupine-like leaves were unnibbled by Xerces larvae. Xerces caterpillars apparently fed only on deerweed and were unable to survive on other, related food plants such as lupines.[25]

Over the decades there has been talk among butterfly lovers and butterfly scientists about the possibility of "resurrecting" the Xerces blue, initiated by Robert Michael Pyle's essay "Resurrection Ecology: Bring Back the Xerces Blue!" published in 2000 in *Wild Earth*. Pyle is an award-winning nature writer, PhD lepidopterist, and founder of the Xerces Society.[26] His essay argued for assisting evolution by reintroducing close relatives of extinct species or subspecies into their restored habitats:

> The thoughtful reintroduction of an organism closely related to an extinct type can result in the functional reconstruction of the animal or plant thought to be lost *in toto* ... reestablishment of near relatives in restored habitats may be an act worth considering in some cases. I would like to nominate the Xerces Blue as a candidate for such radical reconstitution.[27]

As Pyle explains in the essay, the inspiration for this idea came from an actual case he learned about while studying in England in the early 1970s. There, the British large blue (*Maculinea arion eutyphron*) went extinct in 1979, despite heroic conservation efforts, for complex ecological reasons discovered too late to save it. However, across the North Sea in Sweden was another subspecies of the large blue, *Maculinea arion arion*. To make a longer story short, butterfly conservationists in England decided to reintroduce the continental subspecies to found new colonies in carefully managed habitats in western Britain. Does this sound like too much tinkering with evolution, too much playing god with nature?

Several facts suggest that this wasn't really a long reach. Only about ten thousand years ago, at the end of the last Ice Age—a rather short time on an evolutionary timescale—Swedish and British populations of the large blue were probably interbreeding and exchanging genes. Although the Swedish and British large blues were probably somewhat different genetically, those differences have not prevented the introduced continental large blues from surviving and thriving in British meadows. But this was not really the "resurrection" of an extinct species, rather the introduction of a closely related subspecies—or even perhaps only a different variety of the same subspecies.

What about the Xerces blue? Was Xerces a good, solid, full-fledged species in its own right, reproductively isolated from any other close relatives? Probably not. It was probably a subspecies of the silvery blue, *Glaucopsyche lygdamus*, according to taxonomic sleuthing done in the last couple of decades. The silvery blue butterfly is found in the western United States and Canada in a variety of habitats. There are currently seventeen nominal subspecies of this species, and the most recent taxonomic treatment I've been able to find begins by saying that it "is very complex with many unresolved and problematic issues."[28] At least six subspecies of silvery blue are found in California, several in sand dune habitats. Some sources now list the Xerces blue, *Glaucopsyche lygdamus xerces*, as a subspecies of the silvery blue.[29] Local populations of silvery blues, even within the same subspecies, tend to specialize on particular host plants, always pea-family plants like lupines and vetches—and deerweed—which may lead to, or be based on, genetic differences.[30]

If a close relative of the Xerces blue were to be reintroduced to the restored dunes at Lobos Creek to nibble its deerweed and fill its now-empty niche, what are some likely subspecific cousin-candidates? There is *Glaucopsyche lygdamus pseudoxerces*, the false Xerces blue, so named because of its close morphological resemblance to the Xerces. Its larvae also feed on deerweed, but it is found on remote Santa Rosa Island in the northern Channel Islands—a *long* way from the Golden Gate. Well, maybe there's an evolutionary scenario about why butterflies so far apart could be so closely related, but it seems like a long stretch. And then there is the sand dune silvery blue (*Glaucopsyche lygdamus sabulosa*), which has been found much closer, in the Marina Dunes along Monterey Bay.[31] Pyle, in his 2000 essay, proposed that the likely candidate for restoration would be Behr's silvery blue (*Glaucopsyche lygdamus incognitus*), which was found on grasslands in San Francisco and is still flying on San Bruno Mountain.

But wait a minute: with modern techniques of genetic analysis, couldn't butterfly taxonomists get a better handle on this question of which is the most closely related relative of Xerces that is still flying somewhere? Maybe . . . and they are trying. A research group at the California Academy of Sciences is comparing DNA samples taken from museum specimens of the Xerces blue with DNA from various extant silvery blue subspecies, hoping genomic analysis will clarify their evolutionary relationships. "This will pro-vide a genomic 'measuring stick' with which to localize Xerces amongst its closest living relatives and to identify one or more suitable candidate silvery blue populations for reintroduction," according to the website of the non-profit organization funding the work, Revive & Restore.[32]

In this case, the research is seen as part of Revive & Restore's funding for "the development of genomic resources that are used to make applied conservation decisions." That's a relatively straightforward scientific goal that is not really very controversial, but the organization is also exploring using genetic engineering technologies to actually "de-extinct" and bring back to life extinct species such as the passenger pigeon and woolly mammoth, plunging them into the middle of philosophical debates about the ethics of such efforts.[33]

Evolution is always unfinished business. If it weren't, there would be no life; all species would have gone extinct. And sure, messing with evolution raises all sorts of philosophical questions. But what doesn't? Everything im-portant raises all sorts of philosophical questions. As T. S. Eliot asked in his famous poem, "Do I dare to eat a peach?"[34]

Two "bottom line" messages here, I guess. One is that evolutionary biol-ogists still don't really know how to draw boundaries around "evolutionari-ly significant units." Species are such, yes; but even subspecies, and all their messy populations, subpopulations, and variants, are also evolutionarily sig-nificant. And the second is that it is a good thing that the Endangered Species Act allows at-risk subspecies and evolutionarily significant units to be legally protected, whether they are full, reproductively isolated species or not. That is the tool within the ESA that can help us conserve the process of evolution itself, not just its current end points. Those may be the branch tips on the tree of life, but the tree is still growing.

~

Let's circle back to the butterfly genomics research alluded to at the be-ginning of this essay. An article titled "Genomics of a Complete Butterfly Continent," released in 2019 as an online preprint, described results from a team of evolutionary geneticists from the University of Texas Southwestern

Medical Center, led by Nick Grishin and Jing Zhang.[35] In a mind-boggling display of the power of modern DNA sequencing technology, they were able to analyze the protein-coding gene sequences for all 845 species of butterflies found in the United States and Canada. That allowed them to build an evolutionary family tree for all North American butterfly groups and estimate the rates of their diversification and speciation. I picture it as looking with a genetic telescope back in evolutionary time to see what the genes and proteins have been doing over tens of millions of years inside the butterflies fluttering over the continent—maybe like a Hubble or Webb space telescope, but looking into the genetic history of butterflies rather than the history of galaxies and stars.

And what they saw was fascinating: they found dramatic variation in the evolutionary rates of different groups of butterflies. The blues, subfamily Polyommatinae, stand out, evolving at least twice as fast as most other butterfly lineages. The mechanism for their rapid evolution seems to be that the blues can readily exchange genetic material with closely related subspecies, or even sister species, after a period of separate evolution and adaptation.[36] This genetic trick, called "introgression" or "introgressive hybridization,"[37] brings together new combinations of genes, some of them perhaps preadapted to the new conditions in which hybridization is occurring.

The image I think of is my fig tree (*Ficus*) houseplant; when I braid the new shoots sprouting up from the base together, they start to grow together where they touch after a couple of years, their separate stems dissolving and eventually fusing into the main trunk. The idea that what were thought to be reproductively isolated "species" can interbreed and merge back together again shook up the hard-core model of species as reproductively isolated forever after speciation. That model pictured evolution as an inevitably branching tree—obviously not a *Ficus*. But recently the whole topic of "reticulate" or "network" evolution—the origin of new evolutionary lineages through the partial merging of two ancestral lineages, rather than through branching from an ancestor—has come into vogue, and plenty of examples are being found. Such examples are best pictured as an intertwining *Ficus* trunk rather than a branching tree.

In the blue butterfly subfamily, this process seems to have led to quite rapid speciation and adaptive radiation in the last couple of million years, a creative flourishing for the blues and a morass for taxonomists.[38] This pattern is similar to the case of the manzanitas described in the previous essay.

Many species of blue butterflies have complex ecological relationships with ants, most of which are mutually beneficial. The caterpillars of many blues have special glands that secrete "honeydew" containing carbohydrates and other nutrients that attract and feed ants, which in turn tend and protect the larvae from predators and parasitoids.[39] The authors of the "butterfly continent" genomic analysis I've been discussing here identified a suite of genes that have been positively selected only in the blues compared to other butterflies, many of which encode proteins that may be related to these interactions with ants, and they propose that the driver of the rapid evolution of the blues may be their relationship with ants.

~

The blues, and the blues.

Blues music is characterized by call and response patterns derived from African music brought by slaves, which evolved in the American South into communal work songs, field hollers, and spirituals. That basic musical form is "a durable and supremely versatile template, the single most common form jazz musicians play and improvise over," according to jazz scholar Kevin Whitehead.[40] Repeated melodic or harmonic phrases, called riffs, often provide the underlying architecture for improvisation.

Blues are played on European instruments like pianos, saxophones, clarinets, trumpets, and trombones, but the blues are characterized by notes from African scales that don't quite match the conventional scales of European music. According to Whitehead,

> the blues also has a distinctive scale that splits the difference
> between Europe's major and minor scales. Where those scales
> diverge is where the blues scale is most ambiguous, hovering
> between flat and natural. These slightly flat "blue notes" give
> blues melodies their distinctive tang and grit. To approximate
> those in-between notes not found on a piano keyboard, blues or
> jazz pianists may sound major and minor thirds simultaneously.

Major keys are generally considered optimistic, and minor keys sorrowful. To play both at once reinforces the blues' simultaneous acknowledgment and defiance of hard times.[41]

The blues, blending musical forms and scales from Africa to Europe, but made in America . . . it all sounds like introgressive hybridization to me. And oh, the creative power of that introgression: the power of that remixing of distantly related forms, that bringing together of preadaptations to new circumstances, that creative power to go to new places and adaptively radiate, fast.

When I think of the explosion of creativity in jazz and the blues, I can't help hearing echoes from scientific reports about the critical role of introgression in the rapid adaptive radiation of blue butterflies.

And even more intriguing echoes. Cultural introgression unleashed the creative power of blues music, and our cultural virtuosity as a species may itself be the product of rapid evolution through the kind of genetic introgression seen in the blue butterflies. "Looking beyond butterflies," write Zhang, Grishin, and colleagues, "we see parallels in the evolution of hominids."[42] The human lineage diversified into multiple genetically isolated populations during the past few million years, some perhaps as different as species, but certainly as different as subspecies—paleoanthropologists are still trying to understand it all. There is now only one human species, *Homo sapiens*. But the so-called modern human genome contains significant DNA sequences from closely related human ancestors. The Neanderthals and the Denisovans are two now-extinct hominin groups with which we have evidence of introgressive hybridization, and there are probably more such ancestors waiting to be discovered. Ancient DNA has been obtained from Neanderthal and Denisovan fossils, and analysis shows that about 2 percent of the genome of non-African modern human populations is from Neanderthals. Some human populations in Austronesia (e.g., New Guinea, Melanesia, Australia) have around 5 percent Denisovan genes.[43]

There is evidence that some of these ancient hominin genes may be beneficial, adaptive, and positively selected. The science of human paleogenomics has advanced rapidly in the last decade because of the same technologies for analyzing genomes that enabled the "butterfly continent" study. Introgression from ancient relatives has been proposed to help modern human groups with adaptation to high altitudes and diverse climates. It also seems to have been involved in resistance to pathogens of various kinds, including viruses—an especially interesting finding in this post–COVID-19 era.[44]

And who knows? Maybe we will someday learn that genomic introgression is itself in some ways responsible for the human ability for culture. For better or worse, we are the only species on Earth that has produced runaway cultural evolution. It remains to be seen whether we can use our cultural talents to save ourselves from ourselves—from the destructive aspects of that same culture.

At least, in the meantime, we have the blues; we'll forge on, defiant and hopeful no matter how bad things are looking, as we always have, so far.

6
Making Friends with Fire

Fire is an old story.
—Gary Snyder, "Control Burn," 1974[1]

AS YOU STOP AT THE INTERSECTION where Sir Francis Drake Boulevard from Inverness T's into California Highway 1 just a mile south of Point Reyes Station, a number of official highway signs confront you. One points left to Petaluma, the other right to San Rafael and San Francisco. Under those, on the same support pole, is a hand-painted sign on a weathered piece of plywood that says "THANK U Firefighters" in white and turquoise letters. A red heart painted in the middle of the *U* adds emphasis and local love. The sign expresses a common feeling around here; there are many other informal signs with similar messages around town, still up two years after the Woodward Fire, a natural, lightning-caused fire that burned at the nearby Point Reyes National Seashore in August 2020.[2] And these more recent signs echo the feelings of many local residents who still remember the 1995 Vision Fire.

I have to confess that I was tempted to park at the intersection and cross out the "fighter" letters of this sign with a magic marker, leaving the message "THANK U Fires." I didn't, of course. If I owned a house in the naturally fire-prone forests on Inverness Ridge on the Point Reyes Peninsula, I would likely have a preference for firefighters over fires too. But these beautiful ecosystems need and thrive with fire. So, what we have here is a conflicted relationship.

This essay is about the fire ecology of the Golden Gate Biosphere Reserve, especially Point Reyes. As much as I don't want to challenge the assigned obligations of local firefighters, who are supposed to protect homes—some very expensive ones—built in fire-adapted ecosystems on the edges of Point Reyes National Seashore, and as much as I want to sympathize with the people who have homes there, we *should* ask the question: How *should* people think about and interact with fire here in this bioregion? We haven't asked that enough, or as seriously as we need to.

Point Reyes National Seashore provides a perfect laboratory for pondering that question. Why? The ecological reason is its two experiences with wildfire in its natural ecosystems in the past quarter century, and also a baseline of research documenting the long-term history of fire here. The political and institutional reason is that it is managed by the National Park Service for multiple uses that include both the conservation of natural ecosystems and social and economic benefits for all of us—from the local to the national level. As you might imagine, harmonizing experiences, perspectives, and values across that vast spectrum (national to local) is a challenge.

≈

Evidence of the 2020 Woodward Fire was all around as soon as I started up the Meadow Trail from Bear Valley in Point Reyes National Seashore on a sunny, warm, barely breezy afternoon in June 2021. The trail climbed up out of the valley through an area burned with only moderate severity. Before I had gone very far, a couple coming down greeted me, and the man couldn't resist saying, "It's good to see that the fire didn't do too much damage!" His use of the word "damage" in relation to wildfire reflects a common misunderstanding of the important role of fire in shaping the Point Reyes ecosystem—and most ecosystems in North America.

The fire had burned through the understory in most places, killing understory shrubs; charred bark showed where flames had licked up the trunks of the big Douglas-firs, sometimes thirty or forty feet, but mostly only on one side. Almost none of the big trees here had been killed, as the flames hadn't touched their needles and crowns. Evergreen huckleberry, bay laurel, tanoak, and sword and bracken ferns were sprouting from their burned bases, rising, phoenixlike, from their own ashes. Wild cucumber ran rampant, climbing the dead, burned stems of huckleberry bushes and thirty or forty feet up fir trunks to the lower branches. In some places the burned ground was laced over with a web of California blackberry, which apparently loved the release of nutrients by the fire.

In a sunny patch of bare soil along the trail, a miniforest of baby Doug-firs an inch or two tall were sprouting—big old mother trees nearby had seeded into the light gaps created by the fire. Approaching Inverness Ridge, the trail crossed a meadow—this trail was called the "Meadow Trail" for a reason, I guess—where crowded stands of young Douglas-firs that had been pushing into the meadow had all been killed. But in a few places, young trees that had sprouted farther out from the forest edge in the grassland had not been killed, but only singed.

One of those partially killed young trees provided a telltale clue to something I'd observed at several places along the trail in deeper forest: what I called "octopus trees." These were big Douglas-firs with basal trunks large enough to be a hundred or two hundred years old; but instead of the tall, straight, self-pruned, single trunk typical of this species, these octopus trees were multitrunked monsters, with a candelabra of big branches reaching skyward as if they were an overgrown, giant bush. The cause was revealed by those few young trees that survived in the meadow. The fire had killed the tallest, leading tip of the young trees, and a bunch of side branches were then released to grow out and up, baby octopus trees in the making.

In 250 years, these little trees will be octopus trees, perhaps embedded in a younger forest of tall, straight trees like I had observed elsewhere along the trail. If, that is, fire continues to be infrequent and deliberately suppressed, and the young forest encroaching on the meadow continues along its successional pathway. One old octopus tree in deeper forest had a diameter of about five feet—my guess is it would be at least two hundred, and maybe three hundred years old or more. Trees like that are the ghosts of the pre-European landscape here, when today's deep forest would have been grassland with encroaching Douglas-firs, as in the modern meadow fragment. Mapping and coring these octopus trees to determine their ages could allow forest ecologists to run ecological succession backward in time and determine the balance of forest and meadow for the past few hundred years.

I kept my eye peeled for fire scars and found only one, on an old Douglas-fir. The recent Woodward Fire had barely burned into the bark around the old scar, enclosed in an alcove of healing curls—several inches of new wood growing over and around it as the tree tried to close the wound, showing that it had been decades, at least, since the last fire here. The edge of the old scar was surrounded by six inches of corky bark, which had completely insulated the sensitive growing tissue of this tree from the recent fire.

Most of the big Douglas-firs in this area, where the fire burned with moderate intensity, survived, maintaining the seed source for the future forest. The understory is rebounding, resilient, and more diverse because of the fire. The species here seem generally well adapted to fire, demonstrating their evolutionary dance with it in various ways: the thick, corky, insulating bark and self-pruning form of the Douglas-fir; the root or stump sprouting of tanoak, bay laurel, and evergreen huckleberry; the quick uptake of nutrients and rapid growth of wild cucumber and California blackberry.

Ecological succession slowly heals over the edges created by an ecological disturbance like fire. Many ecosystems in California and western North America have burned repeatedly for millions of years, and some have been called "fire disclimax" vegetation types—"disclimax" because ecological succession never has time to reach a stable, old-growth state before another fire comes along and resets the process. After the fire or other disturbance, an ecological "reset" begins and a series of ecological communities develop and occupy the habitat until the next disturbance comes along. Because evolution is creative and species are adaptive, different species have evolved to take advantage of one part of this successional timeline or another. Thus, in order to conserve the full range of biodiversity in such ecosystems, we also have to conserve the disturbance regime that allows them to persist. Here, that means restoring the natural frequency of fire. A recent case study of the Woodward Fire by fire ecologists concluded that it may have "net positive ecological effects across the burn area" because it increased the heterogeneity of vegetation types across the landscape and reset succession to create the niches needed by fire-following species.[3]

Just as I reached the bottom of the trail at Bear Valley, I met another couple coming up the trail, just about where I had met the other couple as I was going up. They greeted me, and the woman couldn't resist saying, "Isn't it wonderful how all of these plants are rejuvenating after the fire!" Yes, wonderful! I responded.

⌇

Over the last half-dozen years, with the continent heating up and drying out, especially in the West, there have been a lot of record-breaking wildfires—in size, intensity, and economic impact. Media reporting, as is common with other kinds of natural disasters like hurricanes or floods, has mainly emphasized the human impacts: loss of life and property and displacement of people from their homes in the woods. The fires are often portrayed in apocalyptic terms. Perhaps the poster fire in this regard is the Camp Fire, which burned 250 square miles in the western Sierra Nevada foothills about 150 miles northeast of the Bay Area in November 2018. As the fire erupted into a firestorm, fifty thousand people were evacuated, but eighty-eight people still died. It burned fifteen thousand homes and other structures and was reported to be the deadliest and most destructive fire in California history, and the most expensive natural disaster in the world in 2018.[4] A town called Paradise was completely destroyed, and its story became the basis for a whole book, *Paradise: One Town's Struggle to Survive an American Wildfire,* by Lizzie Johnson, published in 2021. Given all the recent emotional news coverage of wildfires, I wasn't that surprised by the hiker's comment about "damage" from the Woodward Fire on that hike at Point Reyes.

American society has been brainwashed to fear and hate wildfire for a *long* time. The "Smokey Bear" ad campaign of the US Forest Service is probably the most well-known cultural reflection of this attitude: ONLY YOU CAN PREVENT WILDFIRES! During World War II (probably anticipating the postwar housing boom and demand for cheap lumber), the Forest Service started a public outreach campaign to prevent wildfires, and Smokey Bear debuted on posters in 1945. An orphaned bear cub found by firefighters in a fire in the Lincoln National Forest in New Mexico in 1950 was taken to live at the National Zoo in Washington, DC, and the real cub's story was conflated and merged with the public behavior–change campaign that had started five years earlier.[5] Smokey is now a venerable old-timer and even has his own website.[6] A photo of a bear cub in a burned tree taken by firefighters in Oregon's 2021 Bootleg Fire[7] mimicked the New Mexico Smokey-cub story and quickly went viral—or, as we used to say, spread like wildfire.

Even before the USFS Smokey Bear campaign, there was the Walt Disney movie *Bambi*, with its dramatic animated scenes of Bambi and the other forest animals fleeing from a wildfire that had spread from a hunting camp. But long before Bambi and Smokey, the fire-is-bad attitude arrived at Plymouth and the other European colonies, so it predates the founding of the United States by a century and a half.[8]

Wildfire policies have been intertwined with politics for more than a century in the United States. It's a complicated and convoluted story, far too much to deal with here. Fortunately, there are plenty of sources for unraveling the story for anyone interested.[9] Fire suppression policies on national forest lands began in 1905 when management authority over national forest reserves was transferred from the Department of the Interior to the Department of Agriculture and the US Forest Service was established by President Theodore Roosevelt (president from 1901 to 1909), with Gifford Pinchot as its head. Trees were basically seen as a crop, and what responsible farmer would allow fires to burn up a crop of corn or wheat?

Roosevelt's second term as president ended in 1909, but Pinchot continued as head of the USFS under President Taft until a political controversy erupted between Pinchot and Taft's secretary of the interior, whom Pinchot and Roosevelt accused of backtracking on the conservation of public lands. Taft fired Pinchot over the issue in January 1910, but the bitter fight continued. Then, in August 1910, a huge wildfire called the "Big Burn" or the "Great Fire" burned 4,700 square miles in Montana, Idaho, and eastern Washington. The fire captured national attention and, partly through the political maneuvering of Roosevelt and Pinchot, became a catalyst for an increase in influence and funding for the USFS. That, in turn, eventually led to the creation and expansion of national forests in the eastern United States through the purchase of formerly private forest lands.[10]

A few years after the Big Burn, in 1913, a wildfire burned through Muir Woods National Monument and across the south side of Mount Tamalpais. The fire destroyed the Muir Inn, at the terminus of the Mount Tamalpais railroad. After the fire, in 1917, the Tamalpais Forest Fire District was created by the California legislature, the first such district in the state; Marin County was thus enabled to levy taxes to support fire prevention and suppression efforts. A fire lookout was built on top of Mount Tamalpais. In 1923, a 40,000-acre wildfire burned across the mountain, and the famed tavern at the top of the tourist railroad was destroyed. After another fire in 1929, which destroyed the rebuilt Muir Inn in Muir Woods, the boundaries of the fire district were expanded to include an area from Bolinas north to Inverness on Tomales Bay, and the entire Point Reyes Peninsula. It was expanded again in 1940.[11]

The latest twist in the story is that after more than a century of serious fire suppression policies in fire-adapted forests, anthropogenic climate change is drying out those now-unnatural forests in many places and creating historically large and intense fires. But the other side of the equation is that overcrowded America has fled cities into what is now often called the "wildland-urban interface," places that are often fire-suppressed private lands and often adjacent to fire-suppressed public lands. So, when the more intense wildfires that are the expected result of climate change and fire suppression occur, they affect many more people, structures, and infrastructure than they would have in the past.[12] Hence the media attention and public outcry.

But if we could hear the voices of fire-dependent, fire-following species in many temperate zone ecosystems, they would be saying, "It's about time! *Finally*, we are taking back some of the landscape we are adapted to and need! You non-Indigenous Americans have been hogging it for a hundred years!" Who would say that, if we could only hear them? Bishop pine, blue blossom *Ceanothus*, Marin manzanita, and many other fire-loving species.

~

Wait just a minute, though. The last section breezed through a discussion of the recent history of our cultural and political interactions with wildfire—I say "recent" because it all focused on the past century or so. But what was happening before that with fire and people? What is the "natural" history of fire in the Golden Gate bioregion, which the rich biodiversity of the area seems to be at least partly a response to?

We can look back a few more centuries by reading descriptions of Point Reyes by early European explorers and visitors. When Sir Francis Drake spent a month in 1579 repairing his ship in the bay that now bears his name, the hills and ridges to the east would have been mostly open grassland or coastal scrub because of the Miwok's liberal use of fire as a key tool of their ecological management[13] and because of grazing by herds of elk, which benefited from the anthropogenic burning. The same was true when Sebastian Cermeño, a Portuguese navigator and explorer sailing on the Manila galleon route, was shipwrecked in Drakes Bay in 1595. Richard Henry Dana, visiting San Francisco Bay in 1840, described the herds of elk he could see on the open headlands.[14]

For a more detailed view or to go back beyond the eyes of the earliest European historical records, we have to turn to other fire-ecology methods. Most common are dendrochronological studies—"tree-time" studies—that analyze annual growth rings and fire scars to reconstruct the history of fire in a forest. Fire scars form when a fire burns along the ground at the base of a tree and kills part of the living, growing layer, the cambium, that surrounds the trunk, but not enough to kill the tree. The tree survives and begins to grow healing curls of new wood that can eventually overgrow and protect the fire-scarred area. Fire scars on 210-million-year-old fossilized trees in Petrified Forest National Park show that fire in forests is a very old story, and an evolutionary force that has had plenty of time to select fire-adaptive traits like resprouting or serotiny in plants.[15]

By coring these scars and counting the annual rings of new wood in the healing curls, we can determine the date of an old fire. Since many forest trees can live many centuries or even more, dendrochronological studies can create fire timelines that reach back that far. For Point Reyes, a 1999 fire-scar dendrochronology study by Peter Brown and colleagues provided information on historical fire frequency, spatial patterning, and seasonality in Douglas-fir and coast redwood forests back to around 1800. They could not do so for bishop pine forests there because of the generally stand-replacing nature of fires in those forests—which completely kill the trees rather than leaving some of them alive but with a scar—and their generally younger ages.[16]

Brown and his colleagues found that fire was frequent from the mid-1800s until the early 1900s; average fire return intervals in both Douglas-fir and coast redwood stands were around eight or nine years. But after World War II, wildfire was essentially absent in these ecosystems until the Vision Fire in 1995 and the Woodward Fire in 2020.[17]

Standard fire-scar dendrochronology doesn't really reach back very far at Point Reyes—only about two hundred years, which was after the arrival of the Spanish missions and the American gold rushers. How can we learn what was going on with fire and vegetation before European settlement? Sediment deposited in lakes, ponds, and other wetlands traps and sometimes preserves a proxy record of the surrounding ecosystem that can push the timeline back much further. Pollen and other microfossils such as fern and fungal spores in the sediment indicate what was growing nearby, and charcoal and ash layers indicate episodes of fire. Carbon-14 dating can determine when a given sediment layer was formed. By analyzing sediment layers in a twelve-foot core taken from a small marsh near Glen Camp in the southeastern part of the national seashore, Scott Anderson and his team were able to reconstruct a picture of vegetation and fire reaching back 6,200 years, to around the time of the first archaeological evidence of humans in the area.[18] It's amazing!

What did they find? For more than 2,000 years, until around 4,000 years ago (or around 2000 BCE), there was not much charcoal in the marsh sediments. Then, starting around 3,500 years ago, charcoal is consistently found, indicating relatively frequent fires in the area. During that period, according to the pollen record in the core, the vegetation began to resemble that of today's ecosystems, mainly a mix of conifer forest and coastal scrub grassland. Charcoal deposition increased around 2,500 years ago, at a time when the archaeological record shows an increasing population and a proliferation of village sites in the Point Reyes area. Charcoal in the sediment core remained high for around 1,500 years, during the period that has been described as the "cultural climax" of the ancestors of the Coast Miwok, when their material culture became more complex, acorn processing became the dominant subsistence activity, villages became more permanent, social stratification increased, and burial offerings became wealthier. Anderson and colleagues state that "these pollen and charcoal stratigraphies suggest a tight coupling of fire history and vegetation change" in the area during this period.[19] And a tight coupling of both with human activities.

Lightning is not common in this area today, especially late in the dry season when ignitions would be more likely—although the Woodward Fire was started by August lightning. Therefore, the consensus among fire ecologists seems to be that the relatively frequent fires that have shaped the vegetation of Point Reyes over the past several thousand years were caused mostly by humans.[20] The fire history based on sediment cores from Point Reyes shows that anthropogenic burning is a very old Indigenous cultural tradition.

In 1793, the Spanish governor of Alta California issued a fire suppression proclamation banning all use of fire by Native people. The sedimentary fire history from Glen Camp marsh shows a sharp drop in charcoal at around that time, as Coast Miwok were moved off the land and resettled around the mission at San Rafael, which was founded in 1817. Around that time, the fire-scar history of Peter Brown and his colleagues picks up the fire record.

Deliberate and frequent use of fire by Native peoples to manipulate the environment was common and well documented at the time of European contact and would have shifted the spectrum of vegetation from conifer forests toward coastal grasslands, explaining the landscape observed by Drake, Cermeño, and other early European visitors.[21] The forests of the Point Reyes area are not burning today with nearly the frequency they did in the past, which is likely to have "cascading effects on landscape patterns and ecosystem processes."[22] The conversion of grassland to forest will continue without an increase in fires, and the forests will become more dense and prone to intense, stand-destroying crown fires when they do burn, thereby increasing the risk to communities nearby.

The long-term fire history of the Point Reyes area leaves us with a somewhat ambiguous understanding of what is natural, and what condition our current policies of ecological management and restoration should be aiming toward. We certainly want a diverse mosaic of vegetation that reflects millions of years of adaptation to California's dry-summer, wet-winter climate, with its many fire-loving and fire-dependent species. Such a landscape is more likely under a fire regime more like that of the thousands of years of Indigenous fire use. Do we want that? Or do we want to "let nature take its course"—and leave homes and communities embedded in the kind of fire-prone forests that developed naturally after Indigenous burning was stopped and wildfires were suppressed, just waiting for a spark?

⌒

The Vision Fire started on October 3, 1995, and burned for about a week in an area mostly designated as park wilderness, eventually burning almost twelve thousand acres.[23] Some local boys apparently thought they had drowned their campfire, but they hadn't. It's a story that reminds me of Henry David Thoreau; on a camping trip with a friend in April 1844, their campfire got out of control and almost burned down their hometown of Concord, Massachusetts. Many years later, that experience led Thoreau to investigate the fire ecology of his local ecosystem. He recognized the influence of past Native American burning on the landscape and became essentially the first published fire ecologist through his writing on the subject.[24]

The Vision Fire burned an area partly dominated by bishop pine, *Pinus muricata*. Bishop pine became so familiar with fire that it evolved a relationship that could be called "friends with fire," or probably even more intimately, "I love fire!" *Pinus muricata* is a "c'mon baby light my fire" species.[25]

Bishop pine has two closely related cousins, *Pinus radiata*, Monterey pine; and *Pinus attenuata*, knobcone pine. All three of these Californian "closed-cone" pines are fire adapted and have serotinous cones that generally remain closed until heated by a fire. All have disjunct, island-like distributions—perhaps because they are relict populations left from a time when the climate was different and they were more widely distributed. Two of the three, bishop pine and Monterey pine, are found only close to the coast in sites where fog is common, whereas knobcone pine is found in drier, interior montane sites.[26] I discussed the three small populations of bishop pine found on Santa Cruz Island (more than three hundred miles south of Point Reyes) in an earlier essay.

I wanted to learn about the fire ecology of bishop pine forests firsthand, so I took several hikes on trails that cross the area burned in the Vision Fire, and also in an old bishop pine stand that escaped that fire and has probably not burned in a couple of hundred years, at least. The experience, feeling, and gestalt of these areas create a kind of time travel in which it is possible to imagine what the area burned by the Vision Fire will look like in a century or two, and what the sure-to-burn old-growth bishop pine stands on the north slope of Mount Vision will look like after they burn. For me, as an ecologist who has done some fire ecology research, this was heaven. Or, er . . . isn't hell where things are supposed to burn? For many fire-adapted, fire-following, fire-loving species besides bishop pine, this was heaven too.

Saturday, April 16, 2022. A steady rain in the night and still sprinkling in the morning, so I had a chance to do some reading, catch up on emails, have a slow breakfast. The wind came up around 11:00 a.m. and the sky brightened, luring me out for a hike in the area burned by the Vision Fire. I parked at the trailhead along Limantour Road and headed up the Inverness Ridge Trail, the day now sunny, clear, and windy. Near the top of the ridge, where the fire had burned with high intensity, blue blossom ceanothus (*Ceanothus thyrsiflorus*), Marin manzanita (*Arctostaphylos virgata*), orange bush monkeyflower (*Diplacus aurantiacus*), and silver lupine (*Lupinus albifrons*) were thriving—a perfect demonstration of the response of these chaparral species to fire. On the crest of the ridge, the fire had burned to the backyards of several houses in the private "Paradise Ranch Estates" subdivision that borders national seashore land at the top of Drakes View Drive. I guess they had survived the fire or else been rebuilt in the years since.

Then I went down the Drakes View Trail into a dense young forest of bishop pine in an area that had burned intensely. It was what is often called a "dog-hair" stand, thin limbless trunks closely crowded together in a reach-for-the-sky competition for light. It looked a lot like a lodgepole pine forest in the Colorado Rockies (lodgepole is also a fire-loving species) where I've done fire ecology research. The understory looked like a giant's game of pick-up sticks, or a wind-thrown I Ching. Almost half the original trees had died and fallen in many places, sometimes arrayed in the same direction by the wind but sometimes at all angles, just a jumble. The branches and trunks of live and fallen trees were thick with fog-drinking filamentous lichens. The dense young forest blocked any view of Drakes Bay from the Drakes View Trail, or from the Bucklin Trail once you dropped out of the chaparral at the top of Point Reyes Hill into the forest.

A few days later, by way of comparison and a sort of time travel of 150 years or so, I went up into an area of bishop pine forest on the steep north slope of Mount Vision that hadn't been burned in the Vision Fire. The trees here were widely scattered, maybe two or three feet in diameter, and maybe a hundred feet tall—about the same height as the trees in the dog-hair forest in the burned area. But there were far fewer trees, exponentially fewer per unit area compared to the young stands. The trunks were straight, with no branches—which were shed in the dog-hair era as the trees shot for the sky—until the branches flattened out to form a twisted canopy. The trees had thick, furrowed bark somewhat like that of ponderosa pine, which looked like it would insulate them from a light ground fire. These were the old survivors from the last postfire dog-hair forest. As their densely packed fellows died out, the surviving trees sprawled out at the top like octopuses reaching arms in all directions. I took a photo of one tree with its branches almost tied in knots—branches reach down, arc across other branches, then hook back up, over, under, around, and through.

No other pine that I have ever seen has this growth pattern of unique, suggestive curves, and no other forest I've seen has this gestalt—so green and cool and hung with fog-catching lichen, just waiting for the fiery orgasm that will seed the next generation from the tight, serotinous cones clinging on the old trees.

~

We are overdue for a pendulum swing toward restoring ecological fire and natural—at least pre-Columbian—fire regimes in terms of fire return interval and intensity. That will require some adjustment of the current obsessive focus on forest fuel reduction in areas with houses, the so-called wildland-urban interface, and a rethinking of the wisdom of building houses in fire-suppressed forests in the first place. Such a rethinking, and policies to implement it, will reduce both the risk of wildfire to people, and the risk of suppressing wildfire to biodiversity. I think they call that "win-win"?

Point Reyes National Seashore has done an exceptional job of providing information to the public about fire ecology and its fire-management policies.[27] It is trying to walk a tightrope—or maybe a better metaphor would be jumping through a flaming hoop like old-time circus performers—to both support public education about the ecological benefits of fire and promote strategies for reducing the risk to public safety for those living in California's naturally fire-prone ecosystems. Despite this balancing act, the bottom-line policy (politics trumps ecology, as always, it seems) is fire suppression: "All unplanned wildland fires at Point Reyes National Seashore receive aggressive initial attack action by the nearest available suppression forces. Initial attack is an aggressive suppression action consistent with firefighter and public safety and values to be protected."[28]

Beyond Point Reyes, other partners in the Golden Gate Biosphere Network[29] are working to better understand how to make friends with fire. The "Good Fire Alliance" and "Fire Forward" program, led by Golden Gate Biosphere Network partner Audubon Canyon Ranch, is working with private landowners and communities in Marin, Napa, and Sonoma Counties to restore beneficial fire.[30] Other initiatives, such as the Indigenous Peoples Burning Network, a project administered by The Nature Conservancy,[31] and the Climate Change projects of the Karuk Tribe,[32] are also sources of information and inspiration about restoring ecological fire.

Another hotspot of research and experimentation in fire restoration and resilience is the Pepperwood Preserve, also a member of the Golden Gate Biosphere Network. Established in 2005, Pepperwood is a 3,200-acre private nature preserve tucked into the hills of wine country between Santa Rosa and the Napa Valley.[33]

The preserve is located in beautiful, rolling oak woodland and grassland, with Douglas-fir on the cooler slopes, and views of Mount Saint Helena and down into the valleys east and west from its ridges. The 2017 Tubbs Fire burned 90 percent of the preserve.[34] Two years later the Kincade Fire burned 60 percent of the preserve, almost all of that over the footprint of the Tubbs Fire. More than one hundred vegetation monitoring plots at Pepperwood are tracking ecological recovery and succession after the fires and will allow manipulations to test management interventions, including controlled burning. David Ackerly, a professor at UC Berkeley, has been monitoring vegetation on fifty-four of the plots at the preserve since 2013, before the fires; his plots are for monitoring only and provide a prefire baseline.[35]

I visited one of the Pepperwood monitoring plots on a cool late April morning with the preserve's ecologist, Michelle Halbur. Michelle and her assistant were noting every plant in the large circular plot. A high percentage were poison oak, and I tiptoed around warily as I watched them work. In 2016, before the Tubbs Fire, they had found thirty-eight plant species in their monitoring plots, Michelle said; now, since the fires, they are up to seventy-seven different species. That's a stunning statistic that validates the role of fire in increasing species richness and maintaining biodiversity. Along with the increase in plant species, however, the fires caused a shift in species composition; native understory species, especially of the pea family, increased, but seedlings of oaks and Douglas-fir were burned and their numbers reduced dramatically.

Lisa Micheli, the executive director of Pepperwood, said that for them the fire experiences were "a wake-up call"—in the social sense—in orienting the attention of the local community to wildfire issues. But it also applies to biodiversity. Fire "woke up" a lot of fire-loving plants whose seeds must have been sleeping in the soil, just waiting for fire—like the phoenix rising from the ashes, or Sleeping Beauty awakened by the kiss from the Fire Prince.

∿

To keep the meadow on the Point Reyes National Seashore "Meadow Trail," we have to make friends with fire. To keep bishop pines, and to conserve blue blossom *Ceanothus* and manzanitas, we have to make friends with fire. To conserve the biodiversity of Douglas-fir and bay laurel forest, we have to allow the natural, dynamic disturbance of periodic fires and conserve the full spectrum of ecological succession.

So, what can you do to become friends with fire? Learn about the fire ecology of your bioregion. If your house is in a habitat that burned naturally, learn about the historic fire frequency and how to live with it: defend your space, fireproof your house, and pack your go-bag. Bury those power lines, sure; and electric customers, prepare to pay for that. Insurance against wildfire? Don't count on it unless you have done a certified job of fireproofing your property. Invest in both public and private ecological forestry that may hasten the return of less fire-prone forests. Get used to the prescribed and controlled use of fire as a tool for ecological restoration. Encourage land managers, public and private, to reconcile their policies with the fact that fire is an old story, a very old story in our ecosystems, and one that has made them as biodiverse and beautiful as they are. Fire is part of nature, nature's friend. We need to change our views about fire and learn to live with it as at least a neighbor and, really, as a friend.

Thank you, fires! Thank you, firefighters, too, of course, but in a fire-adapt-ed future, you won't have to risk your lives for antiecological expectations to protect people from wildfire. It's not a war we can win, or a goal we want, all things considered.

7

Séance at Sky Camp

Before I built a wall I'd ask to know
What I was walling in or walling out,
And to whom I was like to give offense.
Something there is that doesn't love a wall,
That wants it down.
　　　　　—Robert Frost, "Mending Wall," 1914[1]

AND THE SAME SOMETHING doesn't love a fence. Before I built a fence, I'd ask to know to whom the fence may give offense. Did anyone ask the elk? Build a fence around a herd of elk, and you can count on them wanting it down, wanting out, and getting over or around.

As I was driving to the Pierce Ranch trailhead on Tomales Point at Point Reyes National Seashore, I stopped at the boundary of the Tule Elk Reserve to take pictures of the fence that is supposed to keep the elk and cows apart. It's ten feet high and looked pretty elk-proof to me. Then I chatted with a ranger at Pierce Ranch and asked him about the elk. There are about three hundred here in the reserve, he said, and a bunch more in the Limantour area, south of Drakes Bay. I asked him about the fence. "We're trying to keep this quiet, but six elk are outside the fence right now. We don't know how they got out. Maybe walked around the end through the water, or something."

I had read about the squabbles over elk on the loose on historic dairy and cattle ranches of Point Reyes National Seashore, where they aren't supposed to be. Where they aren't supposed to be? I mean . . . according to whom? Some people think the elk should be able to roam everywhere, and others want them kept in their place. We aren't talking about the elks' opinion, obviously.

The controversy swirling around the tule elk at Point Reyes is a whetstone on which we can hone our thinking about how to protect and restore the biological diversity that humans have hammered. Who shall "have dominion" over nature, over the Earth? The tule elk controversy is the tip of the antler, to twist a phrase. Whose coastal headlands and meadows are these, anyway? Whose vision of the greatest good for the greatest number should we choose? Good fences don't always make good neighbors. Assuming that humans have the right to make the decision alone is what some environmental philosophers are now calling a "human-supremacist" worldview.

∽

Elk once ranged across most of North America, but commercial meat hunting, conversion of their habitat to agriculture, and competition for forage from livestock grazing led to their extirpation in many places. Four subspecies of elk evolved on the continent, and one of those, tule elk (*Cervus canadensis nannodes*), is found only in California. Its common name comes from the tule, a giant sedge found in the wetlands where these elk were once common; it could just as well be called the California elk. All North American elk, whose scientific name is *Cervus canadensis*,[2] are evolutionary cousins of the European red deer, *Cervus elaphus*, and of several more species of *Cervus* found in Japan and China.[3] Tule elk once inhabited the oak woodlands, grasslands, and wetlands of the Central Valley and the Coast Ranges from about Santa Barbara north to Bodega Bay. It is estimated that just before the 1849 Gold Rush there were half a million tule elk.[4]

When Francis Drake overhauled his ship the *Golden Hind* (the word "hind" in old English referred to a female European red deer, *Cervus elaphus*) on a beach in the bay now named for him in the summer of 1579, the landscape of Point Reyes would have looked quite different. The ship repairs lasted only thirty-six days before Drake was off across the Pacific for the rest of his three-year, around-the-world voyage. It was the first known European encounter with the native Coast Miwok inhabitants of this part of the California coast, and it was described in detail by the ship's chaplain, Francis Fletcher.[5] The hills and ridges east of Drakes Bay—Inverness Ridge and Mount Vision—are now mostly forested, but they were mostly grass-lands when Drake saw them because of Indigenous burning and grazing by elk. Chaplain Fletcher noted, "The inland we found to be far different from the shoare, a goodly country and fruitful soil, stored with many blessings fit for the use of man: infinite was the company of very large and fat deer, which there we saw by thousands as we supposed in a herd."[6] Fletcher was familiar with the tule elk's cousins in England, there called "red deer," and so called them "deer." There were *thousands*, he said.

The second recorded European visit to the area was by Portuguese navi-gator and explorer Sebastian Cermeño in 1595, sailing for Spain, whose ship the *San Augustin* was wrecked in Drakes Bay in a November storm, return-ing from Manila laden with luxury goods. The crew spent about five weeks among the Miwok as they built a small boat in which they continued on to Mexico.[7] Near a Miwok village on the beach where their ship wrecked, they recorded that they saw many deer, "the largest ever found, as could be seen by the antlers, of which the Captain carried away a sample," and that the In-dians hunted them.[8]

And when Richard Henry Dana Jr. visited San Francisco Bay in 1835, he wrote about vast elk herds near the Golden Gate: "We came to anchor near the mouth of the bay, under a high and beautifully sloping hill, upon which herds of hundreds and hundreds of red deer, and the stag, with his high branching antlers, were bounding about."[9] He was probably describing the Marin Headlands to the north, but there were probably large herds of tule elk on both sides of the Golden Gate in that day. Russian explorer Otto von Kotzebue, visiting San Francisco Bay for a month in 1816, described seeing two types of "wolves," which are presumed to have been gray wolves and coy-otes.[10] The gray wolves must have hunted the elk.

After the 1849 Gold Rush, hunting pressure, livestock grazing, and land conversion for agriculture caused the rapid demise of tule elk. By 1870, none had been seen for years, and they were thought to be extinct. Surprisingly, in

1874, a few were found in a wetland that was being drained for agriculture on a ranch in the southern San Joaquin Valley. Some reports say only a single pair was found, but modern genomic studies show there must have been at least three individuals, to account for the genetic diversity—albeit very low—of the surviving tule elk population. The ranch owner somehow felt an obligation to protect them, and a small herd grew from these few individuals. By 1905 there were 140, and the ranch owner, fed up with their grazing impact and fence-busting habits, had them moved to other locations.[11] In 1976, as part of further state and federal efforts to protect the tule elk, Congress directed federal land managers from the Departments of the Interior, Agriculture, and Defense to look for new homes for them. The law justifies this by stating that "the protection and maintenance of California's Tule elk in a free and wild state is of educational, scientific, and esthetic value to the people of the United States."[12] In 1978, as part of the implementation of that law, the Tule Elk Reserve was created on the northern part of Tomales Point in Point Reyes National Seashore, and ten elk were released behind that supposedly elk-proof fence. Within twenty years there were more than five hundred elk in the reserve.[13] Yes, elk are prolific. The old phrase for rapid reproduction is to "breed like rabbits"; it could just as well be to "breed like elk."

Thus, in 1993, as the problem of exponential growth of the confined elk population on Tomales Point was becoming apparent, the National Park Service convened a scientific advisory panel to make recommendations about controlling and managing the herd. The panel noted that "the need for control of overpopulation of deer and elk in parks is becoming commonplace in the United States" and that the tule elk population on Tomales Point "has built up to a population size at which the need for control must be addressed."[14] The elk scientists enumerated the alternatives for controlling the elk population at Point Reyes. Alternative 1 was to just let nature take its course, allowing natural regulation of population size at the ecological carrying capacity of the habitat. Alternative 2 was to put the elk on the pill, elk contraception. And number 3 was culling—a sanitized technical term for shooting elk to reduce the population. Alternative 1 would mean that in some years there would be starving, emaciated, and dying elk, and serious overgrazing of the habitat, given that there are no longer natural elk predators around. Alternative 2, elk contraception, was deemed technically infeasible after brief consideration. Without saying so explicitly, the scientists basically concluded that culling would be necessary to keep the elk population in check.

An option they didn't explore, but which of course would have been the most natural of all, was to reintroduce the nonhuman natural predators that once controlled the elk population here, wolves and grizzlies. In Yellowstone National Park, the solution to elk overpopulation was to reintroduce wolves to the ecosystem, which took place from 1995 to 1997. By contrast, near Grand Teton National Park, elk are fed hay in winter on the National Elk Refuge in Jackson Hole to keep them from starving. And in Rocky Mountain National Park, the chosen course of action has been to cull them and also let them range outside the park into Estes Park, where they graze on the golf course.

The final recommendation of the scientific advisory panel in 1993 was that

> the long-range goal of elk management at PRNS should be the
> re-establishment of free-ranging elk throughout the seashore and
> associated public lands. This would involve . . . removal of the fence
> across Tomales Point. NPS and CDFG [California Department
> of Fish and Game] should develop a long-range management plan
> with the goal of achieving a large, healthy, free-ranging elk popula-
> tion subjected to a minimum of management intervention.[15]

Five years later, in 1998, twenty-eight elk from Tomales Point were captured and translocated to the Limantour area of the national seashore, south of Drakes Estero, which had been designated as "wilderness."[16] The idea was to establish a free-ranging herd per the panel's recommendation. It didn't take long for some of the translocated elk of the "Limantour herd" to swim across Drakes Estero and establish a new herd near Drakes Beach, and then expand west into areas designated for both dairy and cattle ranching. A recent map of the range of elk within the national seashore shows the avant-garde of the unfenced Drakes Bay and Limantour herds pushing north and east into the historic dairy farms and ranches.[17]

Fast-forward to the present. The elk herd confined in the Tomales Point refuge is thought to be roughly at carrying capacity—in ecological terms that means at the population size that the available habitat can support, with the balance of births and deaths regulated largely by the availability of forage and water. Several recent years have been drier than average—with less forage and water—and elk have been dying at rates noticeable by visitors, just as the scientific committee predicted in their 1993 report. Media stories with titles like "Apocalypse Cow,"[18] "Unique Elk in California May Be Killed under Controversial Plan,"[19] and "Captive Tule Elk Are Dying in Point Reyes"[20] have dramatized the situation and hyped the controversy.

Finally, in the fall of 2021, after enough complaints by local conservation activists and sensational media stories, the National Park Service installed watering devices—tanks and drinking troughs like those used for cows on some of the historic ranches—to help the elk make it through the supposedly unusual drought, which probably isn't unprecedented but may be becoming the new normal in a world of climate change.[21] In installing the watering troughs, national seashore managers had to ignore—or at least reinterpret—the "wilderness" designation of the area, and they are now wrestling with how to come to terms with that. Point Reyes National Seashore superintendent Craig Kenkel put it this way:

> Because of extreme drought conditions, last year we made the
> decision to provide water to the tule elk at Tomales Point. We
> imposed upon the wilderness condition by bringing in temporary
> infrastructure—tanks, troughs, and pipes. This is an example
> where land designations become challenging.[22]

Of course, if the elk at Tomales Point weren't fenced in (or is it out?), they would move south and disperse in search of food and water, solving the water problem in the short term, but at the cost of competition with cattle on the ranches they expanded onto.

The National Park Service is currently updating its management plan for Tomales Point and the Point Reyes National Seashore elk, following a process spelled out by NEPA, the National Environmental Policy Act. An initial public comment period has already occurred, and the park is collaborating with the Federated Indians of Graton Rancheria, the Coast Miwok tribe that traces its ancestry to Point Reyes, "to incorporate tribal views and traditional ecological knowledge throughout this process."[23] A final plan is expected by August 2024. In the meantime, elk will be elk—breeding, moving, exploring, jumping fences. And humans will be humans—debating, arguing, stereotyping the other side, pitting "historic rancher" against "elk-loving conservationist."

My sympathies are with the NPS scientists and managers who have to listen to the howling debate but are responsible for deciding what to do. They have a tough job, mediating between factions of the public with dramatically different views about the proper relationship between people and nature. Yes, that's what I mean, not just different views of the relationship between cows and elk, but between humans and nature. I hope it's not an impossible job. Somebody has to do it; we need them, badly. But then again, my sympathies also lie with the eco-satyagraha conservationists who took a lesson from Gandhi and smuggled "illegal" water troughs onto the Tule Elk Reserve during the drought, in a dramatic gesture to speak truth to power on behalf of the elk, essentially shaming the NPS into backing down and finally doing the job itself.

∾

But let's go back again to the bigger story here. This is not just about elk and cows. It's not just about Point Reyes. This controversy, as I said earlier, is the whetstone to sharpen our understanding of the human-nature relationship. This story is about the whole biosphere.

To make that argument, some historical background will help. I've been visiting Point Reyes National Seashore for a half century, since just before its official establishment in 1972. I loved hiking with my college friends on the Bear Valley Trail or up Mount Wittenberg, and camping at Sky Camp, looking across the Limantour and Drakes Bay coast to the grasslands and dairy farms farther north. There were no tule elk at Point Reyes in those days.

I have always thought of Point Reyes as a place where a balance—some kind of harmony, or at least truce—between nature and humans could be observed, scrutinized, tinkered with, and hopefully improved. Point Reyes is the geographic heart of the Golden Gate Biosphere Reserve and "ground zero" for the biosphere reserve's mission. If we can crack the code of Point

Reyes National Seashore and figure out how to make the human-nature relationship work at that scale, wouldn't that be a template for how to make it work in the larger regional landscape and seascape? And ultimately at the scale of Earth's biosphere? Maybe. Let's dig in and have a closer look. Let's put Point Reyes into the context of a longer history, a longer struggle.

The first movement to create a broader category of protected areas than national monuments, national parks, and national forests came in 1936, when Congress passed the Park, Parkway, and Recreational Area Study Act. It gave the National Park Service a framework to designate and protect sites and areas that included a variety of recreational uses. It soon led to congressional authorization of Cape Hatteras National Seashore in 1937, where beach going, fishing, and hunting were popular. Controversy over hunting and land ownership continued until 1953, however, when philanthropist Paul Mellon donated millions for land purchase, and this first national seashore was fully established. A survey by the National Park Service in 1955 recommended sixteen areas on the Atlantic and Gulf Coasts that could qualify as national seashores, but only when John F. Kennedy took office in 1961 was there much movement. Kennedy was keen to protect Cape Cod, and Cape Cod National Seashore was authorized in 1961. In California, some conservation-oriented individuals and organizations had been waiting for this opportunity and persuaded Kennedy's secretary of the interior, Stewart Udall, that they should have a national seashore of their own on the West Coast.

Efforts to establish Point Reyes National Seashore had begun almost as early as those at Cape Hatteras. In 1935, the National Park Service proposed that land at Point Reyes be acquired for a national seashore because of "the peninsula's exceptional qualities . . . and accessibility to the concentrated population of Central California," but Congress refused to fund the idea. The momentum built again in the 1950s, when post–World War II development pressures threatened the peninsula with logging and housing development.[24] California representative Clem Miller and Senator Clair Engel succeeded in passing the act authorizing Point Reyes National Seashore in 1962, and President Kennedy signed it into law. But wrangling over what uses would be permitted and how to acquire private lands to include in the park continued, often just one step ahead of developers. The Sierra Club's 1962 large-format book, *An Island in Time: The Point Reyes Peninsula*, with photographs by Philip Hyde and text by Harold Gilliam, created an artistic environmental hype that drew national attention. Key individuals who supported and promoted the national seashore at Point Reyes before and after 1962 are a who's who of California conservation heroes: Clem Miller, Clair Engel, Peter Behr, Phillip Burton, Caroline Livermore, Margaret McClure, David Brower, Ansel Adams, Huey Johnson, Edgar Wayburn, Martin Griffin, Anne Kent, and many others.[25] Finally, in 1972 the national seashore was officially established, even while contentious negotiations about how its lands should be managed continued.

One outcome was a win for conservationists. In 1976, Congress exercised its authority under the Wilderness Act of 1964 to make more than thirty-three thousand acres (almost two-thirds) of Point Reyes National Seashore (PRNS) a wilderness area, which was named the Phillip Burton Wilderness after the California congressman who had been a strong proponent of the Wilderness Act. The lands designated "wilderness" had been former ranchlands with roads, fences, and structures. Coastal waters on the southeastern shore of the peninsula, up to and including Limantour and Drakes Esteros, were also included in the wilderness designation.[26] That wilderness designation created a unique challenge—and opportunity—for PRNS. California writer John Hart, in his 2012 book, *An Island in Time: 50 Years of Point Reyes National Seashore*—the title echoing the 1962 Sierra Club book—wrote: "In the national park system, Point Reyes has been a kind of pilot boat, always testing new waters. It was a place where *wilderness* was to be restored on lands that had been intensively used and modified."[27] In an interview in April 2022, PRNS superintendent Kenkel acknowledged the challenge his agency faces, saying,

> Even though it's designated wilderness, it's an altered landscape, not a pristine ecosystem. Human impact has altered ecosystems globally. We're actively managing Point Reyes' ecosystem, trying to repair it and to reach the desired condition of a balanced ecosystem. There's always tension when we do that.[28]

~

If we move from conservation history to conservation philosophy, what about this idea I had that Point Reyes National Seashore has been and should be a laboratory for harmonizing the human-nature relationship? Both John Muir and Aldo Leopold were pioneers in exploring and advancing our thinking about humans and nature: What would they make of Point Reyes today?

Muir tried to inspire, in the historical context of his time, the conservation of sublime natural landscapes; his argument hinged in part on the emotional, psychological, aesthetic, and spiritual values of wild places and nonhuman species. Although Muir is often labeled a "preservationist," his own writings suggest that this is at least an oversimplification, maybe even a misunderstanding. First, it implies that Muir thought that ecosystems were somehow static and could be "preserved" in an unchanging "pristine" state, if only humans were not messing with them. But Muir was well aware of the dynamics of ecosystems and of how humans, including Native Americans, had shaped them across North America and in his beloved California. He knew well that there was no such thing as a "pristine" ecosystem. Second, it ignores Muir's clearly stated recognition of and support for the direct material benefits to humans from ecosystems, not just their nonmaterial values. In an article that argued for the creation of a system of national forest reserves, titled "A Plan to Save the Forests" and published in *Century Magazine* in 1895, Muir wrote: "It is impossible . . . to stop at preservation. The forests must be, and will be, not only preserved, but used. Forests, like perennial fountains, may be made to yield a sure harvest of timber, while at the same time all their far-reaching beneficent uses may be maintained unimpaired."[29] His pragmatic view was a balance between sustainable use and long-term protection of the multiple values of nature and was aligned with the progressive political thinking of his era. Then, and today, such a view is best called "conservation," not "preservation."

Unfortunately, stereotypes of Muir as a narrow, misanthropic preservationist are common. They probably began toward the end of his life, when he was engaged in the bitter debate over Hetch Hetchy Reservoir, and politicians who supported the dam at both the state and national level were seeking ways to undermine his stellar public reputation.

And what about Leopold? Much of his writing lamented the abuse of ecosystems by humans that had occurred since Muir's time. He wrote from firsthand experiences, gained during his career in the US Forest Service, with human damage to ecosystems—from the overgrazing of public forest lands in Arizona, to the elimination of top predators that upset ecological balances, to agricultural practices that created the Dust Bowl, to destructive farming practices at Coon Valley in northwestern Wisconsin. At the end of his life, in his ecocentric manifesto, *A Sand County Almanac*, Leopold was arguing for what I think was an essentially Muirian view of the sacredness of intact ecosystems.[30]

A close, historically contextualized, fair reading of both Muir and Leopold suggests to me that these two men were on the same trail, the same vision quest. I can trace it to Muir's reflections on growing up on a homestead farm at Fountain Lake, Wisconsin, described in *The Story of My Boyhood and Youth*, not far from Leopold's "shack" on the Wisconsin River that was the focal point for *A Sand County Almanac*. Both Leopold and Muir were striving to assemble an ecocentric, rather than an anthropocentric, worldview. Both Leopold and Muir were seeking a way to create a harmonious "biotic community" of humans and nonhumans. I don't believe their vision would be of a dichotomized landscape where fences that attempt to separate wild elk and domestic cattle create endless arguments within the human community.

~

Our ancestors don't abandon us when they pass on to the next phase of life. They invite us with their words and wisdom to consult them and learn from them. To some cultures, like the Shona of Zimbabwe with whom I've worked, this idea is commonplace. Their traditional mbira music, played continuously in all-night ceremonies with plenty of dancing and maize beer, is said to be irresistible to the ancestral spirits. When the spirits arrive, they are consulted for advice about issues of the day. For us it may take a bit of imagination. But still, let's try it.

I remember camping here at Sky Camp with college friends. From the camp we had a clear view across open grassland toward Limantour Beach and Estero, with Drakes Bay and the hook of Point Reyes farther off. In my memory, the top of Mount Wittenberg, now buried in a Douglas-fir forest, was a meadow with only a few little trees creeping in.

Let's camp at Sky Camp again. We'll invite John Muir and Aldo Leopold to join us and watch the sunset, nibbling some nuts or cheese and crackers, and imbibing a wee nip of something. The fog slides slowly inland, obscuring the view of Chimney Rock, Drakes Bay, Drakes Beach, and Limantour Spit. Low sun paints the irregular top of the fog layer pink; the pink swirls and climbs toward us until at last we are enveloped in a glow of color, and then only a chilling humid gray. And the conversation begins.[31]

We cooked a simple dinner of ramen noodles on a backpacking stove. John was so amazed by this apparatus that his apparition seemed to fade for a moment, remembering, I suppose, the Sierran campfires on which he had boiled water for his supper of tea and bread so many times, and struggling to imagine this new technology. But he was soon back, and after dinner the conversation continued around a campfire, familiar and comfortable to us all. At times it seemed we could hear voices and see shapes moving at the edge of the circle of firelight, and we imagined ancestors of the Miwok listening to our conversation, but they never approached closer and we didn't know how to invite them in.

I'd brought a small bottle of bourbon—Buffalo Trace—just in case the conversation needed lubrication. I'd heard that Aldo occasionally enjoyed a drink, sometimes bourbon I'd been told, but I'd never heard any mention of John's drinking habits. I doubted he imbibed much given his teetotaling upbringing, but he went to his knapsack and brought out a bottle of wine that he and his father-in-law, Dr. Strenzel, had made from grapes grown at their Martinez ranch. Later, Aldo pulled out a small silver flask of a homemade cordial he called "cherry bounce," apparently a family favorite. John took to it right away, asking Aldo what kind of cherries he should grow in his orchard to make it, what spirits he used, and how much sugar to add.[32]

One of the first topics to come up around the fire was John's friendship with President Theodore Roosevelt, who had dedicated a nearby national monument, Muir Woods, in his name in 1908. Then Aldo brought up the name of Gifford Pinchot, whom Roosevelt had chosen as the first chief of the US Forest Service after it was moved from the Department of the Interior to the Department of Agriculture in 1905. John then recalled how he had visited the Pinchot family mansion in New York City on a trip east in 1893 and met young Gifford there, just back from forestry school in France, and also how he had camped and worked with Gifford on the National Forest Commission survey of western forests in the summer of 1896. Aldo noted that he had graduated from the Yale Forest School, founded and funded by James Pinchot, Gifford's father, and had attended the school's forestry camp one summer at Grey Towers, in Pennsylvania. He and Gifford met and communicated occasionally after that for the rest of their lives. Although Leopold and Muir never met when alive, there were obviously many connection points in their partially overlapping lives.

They reminisced about their days—roughly a century apart—at the University of Wisconsin–Madison. John was happy to learn that Aldo and some colleagues led a campaign to conserve his boyhood farm at Fountain Lake, Wisconsin, as a historical site.[33]

"Oh, I loved those Wisconsin oak openings!" exclaimed John. "The birds and flowers were so wonderful!"

Leopold, whose little family camp along the Wisconsin River, called the Shack, was also in oak-openings country, chimed in with "Yes, so did I!"

"And you know," John said, "it was the Indian burning that kept them so open and beautiful. They started to close in while we lived at Fountain Lake, with the farming, grazing, and fire suppression. I first learned how the Natives' burning shaped our North American landscape from reading Thoreau. And California would have been the same; it has its own oak savannas and fire-gardened forests. This mountain we're camping on, right here, would have been a grassy meadow full of elk, back in the Indian days!"

When I tried to raise a current issue and asked about cattle and dairy ranching at Point Reyes, both men brought up their experience with the effects of domestic livestock on public lands. John mentioned his first summer in the Sierra Nevada, in 1869, when he herded sheep on contract. He later called sheep "hooved locusts" for the damage they did to the mountain ecosystems he came to love. Aldo described his struggles to prevent ecological damage from sheep and cattle on rangelands managed by the Forest Service in Arizona and New Mexico early in his Forest Service career—although he also noted how grazing could be ecologically restorative in some situations.

Then, of course, the cows-versus-elk controversy here came up, and I described the current situation. I first mentioned how close these tule elk had come to extinction. Both shook their heads in sadness, but not surprise, I noted. With the mention of near extinction, Aldo launched into a mini-sermon about the importance of conserving, studying, and learning from wild ecosystems and their whole suite of constituent species, in part for very practical, utilitarian reasons. He used the example of the research of a prairie ecologist at the University of Nebraska who studied the ecological function-ing of a tiny protected patch of native grassland during the Dust Bowl. Pro-fessor Weaver found, he said, that the native plants and undisturbed prairie ecosystem maintain soil structure and retain moisture even during droughts, and he concluded that it was ignorant and indiscriminate plowing and graz-ing that had caused the Dust Bowl. "If prairie flowers are that important," Aldo said, "who can say for sure that someday we won't need cranes and condors, otters and grizzlies, and elk and wolves, even if we think of them as expendable now? The first rule of intelligent tinkering with ecosystems is to save all the pieces."

Aldo then confessed that before he came to this broader view of the importance of all species, he had copied a passage from John's 1901 book, *Our National Parks*, into his personal notebook when he was a student at the Yale Forest School. "I should have thought harder about it sooner. It was the one about rattlesnakes. You remember, John? I have it memorized still. You wrote, 'Again and again, in season and out of season, the question comes up, "What are rattlesnakes good for?" As if anything that does not obviously make for the benefit of man had any right to exist; as if our ways were God's ways.'"

I think maybe Aldo was feeling a little guilty. An avid hunter all his life, he then described his experience with overpopulation by deer on Arizona's Kaibab Plateau after predators had been eliminated. In his younger days he'd been keen to kill wolves himself, he said, and described a situation in which he shot a mother wolf and then reached her just in time to see the "green fire" in her dying eyes.

"That changed me, John," Aldo said. "You know, when I was young and full of trigger-itch, I thought fewer wolves meant more deer, but I came to know better."

"I realized then," he said, "that there was something new to me in those eyes, something known only to her and the mountain. I watched, later in my career, how the deer denuded the vegetation on mountain after wolfless mountain, and I realized how much we need both the predators and the prey. We need the whole, intact biotic community. We need to save all the pieces of the ecosystems we are tinkering with. They know better than we do what's good, what's right. We need to think like a mountain."

Here at Sky Camp, not far from the summit of Mount Wittenberg, the highest point on Inverness Ridge, we wondered silently together: What would *this* mountain think about the elk and cows, about thirty-dollar-a-pound artisanal cheese and fire-dependent bishop pines? No, we agreed: ecosystems—the biotic community—can't be managed by dichotomies like "wilderness" versus "working landscapes." An ecosystem divided against itself, half slave and half free, cannot stand. We felt a shared vision of where we had been and where we needed to go. The fog enveloped us, but our thoughts flew back in time and forward into the future.

From below and not that far away, in the direction of Limantour, came the bugle of a bull elk. And then another, from farther south. We were silent, spellbound.

It was rutting season, and the big bulls were bugling and challenging, gathering up their harems and breeding. Come spring, there would be another boom of babies, a cascade of calves, in these herds.

Finally breaking the silence, teasing Aldo, John asked, "You've talked about crane music . . . but what may elk music be good for? To heal our souls?"

"Yes, of course," Aldo responded after a reflective pause. "But it's an incomplete symphony. It needs a wolf section to bring in the right harmony."[34]

"Oh, Aldo! Can you imagine how these cattle and dairy people would howl if you told them you wanted wolves too, not just elk!?"

"I know, John, I know. We have to be patient, I guess."

The bugling continued. The fire died down. The fog thickened. The spirits finally slipped away into the night.

We crept into our tents and snuggled into our sleeping bags.

Sky Camp was still swaddled in fog when we woke and started the stove to make coffee. Last night's conversation around the campfire felt . . .

dreamlike, real, powerful. Had we really encountered those spirits of the past? we asked ourselves. The consensus was yes, that they were present and wise, and we resolved to work to link the wisdom of Muir and Leopold and strive toward a true community of all species, including humans, here, in this place.

~

As I was returning along the trail back to Pierce Ranch in late afternoon after a long hike out to Tomales Point, a gang of about two dozen elk were lounging on the ridgetop in the late sun, chewing their cuds, and I suppose enjoying the spectacular view: Tomales Bay to the east, filling the depression where the San Andreas Fault cuts off the Point Reyes Peninsula from North America, and to the west the steep cliffs falling into the shining silver ocean. I approached slowly, expecting them to jump up and bolt away. But they didn't. In fact, they seemed to mostly ignore me. The few who looked at me with half-wary eyes had a look that said I was the intruder in their space, not vice versa. The elk, I imagine, assume they are supposed to be wherever there are tender plants, water to drink, and meadows to bugle and mate in. Anyone else is just an intruder in their territory, whether a benign one like me or a potential enemy.

After all, according to the Old Elk Testament, "God created elk in his own image, in the image of God he created them; bull and cow he created them. And God blessed them, and God said unto them, be fruitful, and multiply, and fill the earth, and graze it, and spread across it to fill all of its habitats. With the help of your God, you will outrun all the wolves and break through all the fences your enemies may place in your way!"

A-men!

Er ... A-elk!

8

The Salmon Sermon

Water does not flow up; it always flows down.
—Shunryu Suzuki Roshi[1]

THE WOODEN FLOOR OF THE ZENDO gleams with quiet natural light reflected from its polished surface. It was originally a dairy barn, built directly over Green Gulch Creek so that manure could be mucked straight into the creek and washed away to the ocean at Muir Beach—at least during the season when the little creek was flowing. The floor is made of thick redwood planks, designed to hold the weight of the cows. In the half century since the San Francisco Zen Center acquired Green Gulch Farm and repurposed the barn as a temple and hall for sitting meditation practice—zazen—the oil and sweat from thousands of bare feet have permeated the old wood and given the floor a beautiful sheen. The zendo is a largish space with enough room for perhaps a hundred meditators. A statue of Manjushri, bodhisattva of wisdom, stands at one end of the hall.

I visited the farm and Zen Center on a sunny mid-April morning in 2022. Sara Tashker, the farm manager and a longtime resident, led me on a tour and oriented me to the place and its history. After looking around the zendo, we wandered down the road along the creek and beside the farm fields. We peeked into a greenhouse to check flats of tender baby lettuces waiting to be outplanted and then walked down to look at the ecological restoration work that has been happening here for more than fifteen years. "What inspired that?" I asked Sara. "How did that get started?"

The winter of 2004–2005 was a wet one, Sara told me. That winter, after the rains had recharged the Redwood Creek watershed and broken through the sandbar at Muir Beach that usually cuts it off from the ocean during the dry months of the year, someone spotted a big red fish thrashing around in Green Gulch Creek, the lowest tributary of Redwood Creek, not far below the zendo. It was a male coho salmon in full spawning colors. Everyone was amazed. At least one pair must have spawned successfully at Green Gulch that winter because in April, the Golden Gate National Recreation Area's aquatic ecologist found baby coho in the creek.[2]

The discovery of the salmon reoriented the Green Gulch community. In discussions over the next few years, they resolved to "free the creek" and make it the "center" of Green Gulch. The creek had shaped the valley and deposited the soil they were farming, and now endangered salmon were trying to come back. "Our life as a community didn't reflect the centrality of the creek to this place," Sara said. "That led us to a watershed view." The vision statement that emerged from the discussions said:

> As the vow to benefit all beings grows more rooted in this valley, the Green Gulch Farm community enters into a more intimate relationship with this beautiful and bountiful place. The profound listening that comes out of this relationship helps us to hear more clearly the voice of the land and of the watershed itself and to realize our deep interconnection with the natural world. Recognizing that the world is at a critical moment in time, facing the challenge of preventing the irreversible loss of planetary capacity to support life, it is with humility and an understanding of our role and responsibility to act interdependently with the wider community—the soil, water, plants, animals *and* people—that we propose a long-term vision for Green Gulch Farm.[3]

I tried to imagine that view: a view of everything connected, upstream and downstream, from clouds to ocean, from Mount Tamalpais above to Muir Beach below and out into the ocean beyond, where the salmon wait for the rains so they can swim upstream and where people, embedded in the ecosystem, wait to greet them.

∼

The coho salmon (scientific name *Oncorhynchus kisutch*) found at Green Gulch belong to a genetically distinct and evolutionarily significant subgroup of the species. Coho in this area of the Central California Coast were first listed as threatened under the Endangered Species Act in 1996 and uplisted to endangered in 2005. A final recovery plan was published in 2012 and is still being implemented.[4]

Coho begin their life cycle in freshwater rivers and streams and then spend three years feeding and growing, much of that time in the ocean, before returning to spawn in the streams where they hatched. Biologists call such a reproductive life cycle "anadromous." In spawning, females build nest-like depressions called "redds" in the gravel of a stream, and as they release eggs into them, male salmon swish over, releasing sperm to fertilize the eggs. Salmon are mostly faithful in returning to the same stream where they hatched, apparently navigating "home" from the ocean using chemical cues that give their natal water a unique flavor. To a coho, Green Gulch Creek must have its own special taste.

In a given year, the returning salmon are the offspring of parents that spawned three years earlier—and with luck will be the parents of the generation that will return to spawn in another three years. This three-year anadromous life history apparently evolved as an evolutionary strategy to allow salmon to survive in a dynamic environment—the North Pacific Ocean—and it has been successful for the many millions of years they have existed there. Still, there are many climatic "what-ifs" that affect the salmon. When the sandbar at Muir Beach is breached after winter rains have swollen Redwood Creek, some returning spawners may sprint to the tributaries upstream. Other fish may loiter lower in the watershed to spawn, maybe even in Green Gulch Creek, which enters Redwood Creek near its mouth. Then the odds kick in. If the rains are not strong, the baby fish in the upper watershed may get stranded as their pools dry and become disconnected from the flow later in the season. But if the rains are serious, high flows in the lower creek may wash the eggs and baby fish from redds there, and those in the upper watershed might have a better chance of survival. Given all the environmental variables, the more stream miles with suitable flows and good gravel for redd making that the fish have access to, the better. "Coho Salmon have evolved to play the odds," wrote Eric Ettlinger, an aquatic ecologist with the Marin Municipal Water District, in an email in April 2022, describing coho monitoring results from the past winter.

Spawning coho in Redwood Creek and its two largest tributaries, Kent and Fern Creeks, have been monitored every winter since 1997–1998 by the National Park Service.[5] This population monitoring is based on counting redds, as well as trapping and counting juveniles making their way to the ocean as smolts roughly a year after they hatch. Redd counts show dramatic fluctuations in fish numbers. In wet years there can be nearly one hundred redds in the Redwood Creek watershed, while in some years there are fewer than ten. The recovery plan for Central Coast coho set a target of 136 redds in the Redwood Creek watershed; the actual number is still far below that.[6] Each of the three-year cohorts has had a relatively good year sometime in the past twenty-five years, but it can be many years between good years for a given cohort. Ocean temperatures and feeding conditions are part of the equation too, of course, which may explain why a lot of spawning one year may not predict a larger population returning to spawn three years later.

Each of the annual cohorts is likely to be somewhat different genetically, and each cohort is undoubtedly genetically diverse itself, made up of fish with different behavioral strategies for spawning and feeding. Research enabled by salt marsh restoration in the Salmon River estuary in Oregon—within the UNESCO Cascade Head Biosphere Reserve—found four different life history and feeding strategies in juvenile coho salmon there.[7] One type fed and grew for a year in freshwater streams before migrating to the estuary for a brief period to adjust to salt water, then went to sea. This life history type was what many fisheries managers thought was typical for coho, and they had based their estimates of adult returns on surveys of stream habitat capacity, ignoring the importance of estuaries. But the research showed that there were three other types of juvenile coho that used estuarine habitats extensively in the first year of life, and that when adults returning to spawn were sampled, those estuary-feeding types made up between 20 and 35 percent of the population, a very important contribution.

Something similar is likely to be true in Redwood Creek and the other streams and estuaries around Mount Tamalpais. Although coho populations here are too small right now for studies like those at Oregon's Salmon River, it's a good bet that the restoration of the lower Redwood Creek watershed, including along lower Green Gulch Creek and at Big Lagoon at Muir Beach, increased the feeding habitat for juvenile coho of the life history types that like to hang around in fresh or estuarine water before heading out to sea. The same must be the case where Lagunitas and Olema Creeks flow into Tomales Bay at Point Reyes Station; restoration of the Giacomini Wetland there must be good for coho also.

Diversity within a population leads to resilience for the whole population, something ecologists have recently called a "portfolio strategy," borrowing an idea from their stockbrokers and 401(k) managers. The idea is, if your portfolio has only one or two investments, and one (or two) of those crash, you are in bad shape, maybe wiped out. More investments, of diverse kinds, reduce the risk of any one thing not doing well. In an article on applying the portfolio concept to ecology and evolution published in *Frontiers in Ecology and the Environment* in 2015, the authors say: "Biological systems have similarities to efficient financial portfolios . . . portfolio effects derive from statistical averaging across the dynamics of system components, which often correlate weakly or negatively with each other through time and space."[8] The portfolio of life history "investments" made by salmon spreads risks in time and space and increases their evolutionary resilience in the unpredictable corner of the biosphere they inhabit.[9]

∾

To understand what I was seeing on my visit to Green Gulch, it helped to have some historical context. People shape landscapes through their choices and actions, which are influenced and guided by their perspectives and worldviews. In some cases, individuals or groups have taken actions that slowed or prevented the destruction of natural ecosystems in a place. They are, to me, the "heroes" of conservation in that place, and if we know how to look, we can read the landscape and see the legacy of their actions and visions decades and even centuries later. The Tamalpais landscape, including

Redwood Creek and Green Gulch, are what they are today because of many such individuals and groups.

The trajectory of Green Gulch begins with its Indigenous inhabitants, Miwok hunter-gatherers who lived in the area for thousands of years. They used fire liberally in their ecological management, and coastal grasslands would have been much more extensive then. The Spanish mission system severely reduced their population, commandeered their lands, and all but destroyed their ecologically adapted culture. After the mission system collapsed, the Mexican government granted a large part of the southern Marin Peninsula, including Green Gulch, to William Richardson in 1836. Richardson named it "Rancho Sausalito"; it remained mostly unsettled and was used as open cattle range.

In 1856 Richardson sold most of the land to Samuel Throckmorton, a San Francisco businessman and real estate developer, who began to subdivide and lease it, mostly to Portuguese and Swiss dairy farmers. Throckmorton kept much of the Redwood Creek valley and its watershed, reaching north to the upper slopes of Mount Tamalpais, as his private hunting preserve. Most of the redwoods in Marin were being logged at that time, after the 1849 Gold Rush and building boom in San Francisco, but Throckmorton protected them along Redwood Creek.[10] When he died in 1883, Rancho Sausalito passed to his daughter, but in 1889 debts forced her to sell it to a group of investors who formed the Tamalpais Land and Water Company.[11]

Eastern Marin County was growing and developing rapidly, from Sausalito north through Mill Valley to San Rafael and beyond. Until the turn of the twentieth century, Redwood Canyon continued to be protected as a hunting preserve, as it had been by Throckmorton, but the Mount Tamalpais area was attracting an increasing number of hikers and tourists from burgeoning San Francisco. In 1905, William Kent, a prominent businessman, progressive politician, and admirer of John Muir and his nature philosophy, and his wife, Elizabeth Thatcher Kent, a visionary women's suffrage activist, purchased the land that included Redwood Canyon, both to conserve its old-growth redwoods and to develop it as a tourist destination.

In 1907 a private local water company began condemnation proceedings to acquire Redwood Canyon; its plan was to cut and sell the old trees and build a reservoir there. The Kents cleverly used their national connections to block this proposal. They donated almost three hundred acres along Redwood Creek to the federal Department of the Interior, to be designated as a national monument under the recently enacted Antiquities Act. They requested that it be named Muir Woods National Monument in honor of John Muir, and it was established by President Theodore Roosevelt in January 1908.[12]

During World War II, observation bunkers were built on the coastal cliffs above Muir Beach to watch for Japanese ships. Green Gulch Ranch had passed through a series of renters or owners for more than a century, and after the war it was purchased by George Wheelwright and his wife, Hope. Wheelwright was a physicist and inventor who had made a bundle of money from his role in the invention of the Polaroid camera. He turned his engineer's mind toward making Green Gulch into a model modern cattle ranch. He imported prize Hereford cattle from England; cleared the slopes of native vegetation and planted the most-recommended pasture grasses from New Zealand; and with help from his connections at the Army Corps of Engineers, bulldozed the valley floor, channelizing the creek between berms so that it looked like an irrigation ditch. He filled in the wetlands along the lower creek and built a levee to prevent seawater from flowing up from the Muir Beach lagoon into the lower section of his property.[13] Wheelwright clearly had a hard, technology-in-control vision of the human-nature relationship at Green Gulch, but that is not really surprising—his worldview was created by, and reflected, the mainstream worldview of his time.

After the death of his wife, Wheelwright wanted to see Green Gulch cared for and protected, and in 1972 he deeded it to the San Francisco Zen Center—to "a bunch of beatnik hippie Zennies," as Sara Tashker put it—for a fraction of its market value. He stipulated that it was to be maintained as a working farm, with public access to trails on the public land around it. Those criteria allowed it to become an inholding within the Golden Gate National Recreation Area. The deal for Green Gulch was brokered in part with the help of Huey Johnson, then with The Nature Conservancy, a hero of so much of the resistance to residential and infrastructural development in Marin at the time.[14]

Green Gulch then became a laboratory for experiments with a more ecological and spiritual human-land relationship. Horticulturist Alan Chadwick brought and taught "biodynamic" farming techniques.[15] Architect Sim Van der Ryn, a pioneer in ecological design, planned several buildings (including a composting toilet) on the property.[16] Through relationships with several Native American collaborators, Indigenous perspectives and traditional ecological knowledge influenced the work at Green Gulch from its beginning, first through Harry K. Roberts,[17] who had trained under Robert Spott, a Yurok medicine man and chief (and one of A. L. Kroeber's Native collaborators and informants), and more recently through collaboration with Melissa K. Nelson.[18] The farm now includes a patch of coyote willow that is tended and pruned to produce young, straight willow shoots for traditional basketry, for example. And just up Redwood Creek, perched on the slope near Muir Woods, was Druid Heights, another outpost of experimentation with various aspects of human nature and nature. Alan Watts, author of *The Way of Zen*, lived at Druid Heights for a time, as did poet and environmentalist Gary Snyder, and they were frequent visitors to the farm and Zen Center.

Finally, let's take another quick side trail up a tributary in the historical and philosophical "watershed" of Green Gulch. Shunryu Suzuki (1904–1971) was key to bringing Zen to the Golden Gate region. Suzuki Roshi trained at Eihei-ji in northern Japan, the main temple of the Soto school of Zen practice. He had learned English in school and wondered whether Westerners could ever grasp Zen. When he was invited to serve as the interim priest at the only Soto Zen temple in San Francisco in 1959, he accepted the offer. Suzuki Roshi found that there was in fact a deep American interest in Zen, and he was soon giving lectures around the Bay Area, including at the American Academy of Asian Studies, where Alan Watts had once taught. He started a serious zazen sitting group, which evolved over half a dozen years into the San Francisco Zen Center. In 1966, the Zen Center purchased the old Tassajara Hot Springs in the Santa Lucia Mountains above Big Sur and established the Tassajara Zen Mountain Center. Green Gulch Farm Zen Center was opened as an affiliated training center in 1972 at Suzuki's urging.[19]

≈

The actions and visions of individuals—those mentioned in the brief history above and many others—are recorded in the landscape at Green Gulch, some subtly, some more boldly. People make a difference, and their world-views guide their actions and affect the environment and ecology of a place.

Sara showed me what we can see now as the legacy of the Green Gulch community's "free the creek" vision from 2008. Bulldozers had been back at Green Gulch again, undoing what their brethren had done in Wheelwright's day by removing the lower levee road and restoring a natural meander to the creek. Spring Creek, a small tributary of Green Gulch Creek, was reconnected to the main channel in hopes of sending sediments and coarse gravel that spawning salmon need to the restored meander reach.[20] The National Park Service supported this work, which was completed in 2015, through a conservation easement with the farm and Zen Center; many other federal, state, local, and private partners also contributed.

The restoration of lower Green Gulch Creek piggybacked on earlier efforts to restore the Central Coast coho salmon population. In 2009, a multiyear project[21] began to restore the connection between lower Redwood Creek and Muir Beach, where in historical descriptions a large, mostly freshwater estuary called "Big Lagoon" existed behind the sandbar that was seasonally breached by winter rains. Funding for this work came from fees collected at Muir Woods National Monument. Green Gulch Creek joins Redwood Creek at Big Lagoon, so they are now hydrologically connected. Aquatic habitat restoration continues up Redwood Creek through Muir Woods.[22]

~

During the winter of 2021–2022, an "atmospheric river event" and storms in October recharged the watersheds of Mount Tamalpais. Redwood Creek broke through the sandbar at Muir Beach and scoured the creekbed gravels, and salmon swam upstream to spawn, reaching Fern and Bootjack Creeks. Over twenty coho redds had been observed by December, and Chinook salmon (*Oncorhynchus tshawytscha*) were seen in the creek for the first time in at least twenty years.[23] In Green Gulch Creek, baby coho that had hatched that year were seen in late April in the restored meander reach.[24] Monitoring in the spring of 2023 found a record number of roughly year-old juveniles from the 2021–2022 spawning season returning to the ocean as smolts.[25] In three years, depending on ocean conditions, record numbers of adult coho from this cohort may be coming back.

The winter of 2022–2023 was something else: a record number of atmospheric river events blasted the Mount Tamalpais watersheds with rain, and even salmon apparently couldn't cope with the flooding creeks. Only a couple of coho redds were observed; a few carcasses but no live fish were seen. This cohort seems to be on the brink, with climatic variability almost exhausting its portfolio of adaptive investments. Will they be back in 2026?

∾

In a beautiful "dharma talk"—an exposition of Buddhist views on some subject—presented to the San Francisco Zen Center on Earth Day 2021, Sara Tashker described what George Wheelwright did at Green Gulch after he purchased the property as "the engineering of Green Gulch Creek," and she posed a question fundamental to these essays and to the mission of the UNESCO Golden Gate Biosphere Reserve within which Green Gulch lies. She asked:

> What thoughts and ideas might lead to a straightened, gravel-starved creek, with check-dams blocking fish passage and drastically reducing riparian habitat for myriad species? Humans know best; humans can control water, plants, animals, life; the purpose of this land is to support me, my life, my livelihood, human activity; human activity is more important than the activity of other forms of life; the success of my human activity can be separated from the success of other forms of life in this ecosystem; I can control the consequences of my actions; the abundance of the natural world will always be available to me, no matter what I do; and finally, what I see and think is true and complete.[26]

I don't know of a more clear or comprehensive breakdown of the elements of the anthropocentric Western worldview that is the root cause of our ecological crisis than this. This human-supremacist worldview now dominates, and is used to justify, the current unsustainable global economic and geopolitical system.

But there's a problem. The human-centered hubris—or is it merely myopia—that motivated Wheelwright's enslavement of Green Gulch Creek doesn't conform to ecological reality. It is like trying to make water flow uphill. Sara called it what it is in my conversation with her: "a mistaken view of reality." Reality is that we humans are only one of millions of species in the biosphere, on which we are completely dependent, and we are a relative newcomer at that. In Sara's words, we are "completely made up of and in turn are part of making the relentlessly dynamic, complex, interdependent activity of life." Therefore, she said, the aspiration of the Green Gulch community is to "support the unobstructed flow of the creek and of reality."

And with that will come the coho, nosing up under the zendo in another wet year. Another big red fish, a bodhisattva-like messenger bringing instant insight into the reality of interconnectedness, interdependence, interbeing. The first "transmission" of Zen, it is said, was when Shakyamuni, the historical founder of Buddhism, twirled a flower in his fingers and said nothing, but his disciple Mahakasyapa "got" the wordless message of the "flower sermon" and was immediately enlightened. Like the twirling of the flower, a sudden salmon, a sudden awakening. A salmon sermon.

Water always flows down, but salmon swim up!

9

They Say the Sea Is Cold

They say the sea is cold, but the sea contains
the hottest blood of all, and the wildest, the most urgent.
    —D. H. Lawrence, 1932[1]

IN THE 1986 MOVIE *Star Trek IV: The Voyage Home,* Captain Kirk and his old crew from the *USS Enterprise* come to San Francisco sometime in the "late 20th century" to respond to a distress call from Earth's whales that has caused an unknown alien probe, itself like a giant lonely interstellar whale, to wreak havoc on Planet Earth. They land in Golden Gate Park, put out a shield to make the ship invisible, and fan out in pairs to investigate the situation and try to resolve the crisis. Kirk and Spock head for the Cetacean Institute in Sausalito, where a pair of captive humpback whales named George and Gracie seem to be the source of the distress calls. On an initial tour of the institute, Kirk is instantly smitten with Dr. Gillian Taylor, the attractive blond assistant director and whale researcher. In a classic line, Kirk botches his pretended twentieth-century knowledge when he tries to explain Spock's unusual dress and behavior to Gillian by saying, "I think he did too much LDS back in the sixties."

Through various dramatic machinations, Kirk's crew manage to smuggle the two whales into a huge aquarium constructed aboard their starship and leapfrog them into the safety of a future century through time travel, while the rest of their kin are hunted to extinction on Earth. "You know, it's ironic; when man was killing these creatures, he was destroying his own future," Kirk says at one point. When they are returned to the twenty-third-century ocean and sing their whale songs to the lonely alien whaleship, it releases its death grip on the planet and departs, apparently satisfied that the ancient intelligence of whales is once again safe and secure. "You and your crew have saved this planet from its own shortsightedness, and we are forever in your debt," says the leader of the Earth federation, thanking Kirk and his crew.

In one scene, watching George and Gracie swim together in their starship tank, James quotes the opening lines from D. H. Lawrence's poem "Whales Weep Not," which is basically a paean to whale sex. Gillian immediately identifies the title and author, acknowledging her familiarity with the poem. It's a skillful literary nod to the romantic vibes passing between them. At the end of the movie, Dr. Taylor opts to stay on a twenty-third-century Earth to continue her research on the whales that Kirk's efforts saved from extinction. As for their future together? At first, Kirk seems surprised that she's not going to follow him into the galaxy. "How will I find you?" he asks her. "Like they said in your century, I don't even have your telephone number!"

"Don't worry," Gillian replies, "I'll find you."

Actually, it's not literally true that "the sea contains the hottest blood of all." But never mind. Lawrence was not referring to physical body temperature anyway, but emotional temperature. As for whales, he wrote:

> and through the salt they reel with drunk delight
> and in the tropics tremble they with love
> and roll with massive, strong desire, like gods.

Marine mammals are warm blooded like all mammals and maintain a body temperature about the same as ours or slightly higher—99 to 100 degrees Fahrenheit (the average in humans is supposed to be 98.6°F). Hummingbirds, it turns out, may hold the record for the hottest blood of all, with body temperatures of 103°F. Some marine mammals can tolerate water temperatures a little below freezing—seawater doesn't freeze at 32°F because of its salt content. A layer of blubber provides insulation, and large size reduces the ratio of heat-losing surface to heat-generating volume in many species.

Lawrence says:

> All the whales in the wider deeps, hot are they, as they urge,
> on and on, and dive beneath the icebergs.

Their blubber was their downfall. The oil rendered from it was, throughout much of the nineteenth century, the best available fuel for oil lamps and for machine lubrication, until replaced by kerosene and petroleum-based lubricants toward the turn of the century. By that time, the baleen whales were mostly gone anyway.

~

Why San Francisco for the setting of *Star Trek IV: The Voyage Home*? Maybe because it would look so dramatic for the starship *Enterprise* to fly under the Golden Gate Bridge in the fog and then crash-land in the bay. And a "Cetacean Institute" in Sausalito with a cute blond female scientist sounds perfectly Californian. But maybe it makes sense for another reason.

From the time Mexico acquired Alta California in the early 1820s until the Gold Rush in 1849, most of the ships stopping in San Francisco Bay were either American whalers or hide and tallow traders. Whalers came to favor Sausalito Cove, a sheltered anchorage on the Marin Peninsula where wood, water, and beef were readily available and where it was more difficult for Mexican tax collectors and soldiers from the Presidio to interfere with their untaxed illegal trade. Its popularity grew until it became known as El Puerto de los Balleneros, or Whalers' Harbor. If you were a Yankee whaling captain from Nantucket or New Bedford and had to spend two or three years hunting enough Pacific whales to fill enough barrels with oil to sail back home around the Horn and make a profit, the two favorite choices for hanging out and resupplying were Sausalito and Lahaina, on the Hawaiian island of Maui. Lahaina was a laid-back place for that, but after the Gold Rush the booming San Francisco area was more of a lure from a business perspective, and San Francisco businessmen saw to it that pilotage fees were reduced to increase the incentives for whalers to stop there. Whaling was a big business; in 1856, about 2,400 ships were hunting in the world's oceans, and each carried approximately one thousand barrels of oil. San Francisco's role as a base for Pacific whale hunting grew until, from 1885 to 1905, it became the world's largest whaling port.[2]

The most notable of the San Francisco whaling captains was Charles Melville Scammon. Born in Maine in 1825, Scammon agreed to take a shipload of gold rushers to San Francisco in 1850, and he stayed in California, taking advantage of the market for ship captains in the area. In 1852 he captained an elephant seal hunting voyage that returned with 350 barrels of oil. Starting in the winter of 1855, he commanded whaling voyages to the gray whale breeding lagoons on the west coast of Baja California: first Magdalena Bay, then Laguna Ojo de Liebre, which came to be called "Scammon's Lagoon," and finally to Laguna San Ignacio, the last breeding stronghold of these whales. Scammon's party was the first to find a way over the treacherous sandbars protecting its mouth in 1860. Within a few years, gray whales were almost wiped out by intense hunting, and Scammon made his last whaling voyage to Baja in the winter of 1862, catching only a few whales. His sealing and whaling career over after only a decade, he joined the US Revenue-Marine, an armed naval customs enforcement service that was the predecessor to the Coast Guard, and took command of its only ship based on the Pacific Coast, a steam cutter.[3] Scammon worked for the Revenue-Marine for thirty years, but starting in 1869, he wrote seventeen articles for the San Francisco–based *Overland Monthly*, a popular travel and natural history magazine in which John Muir was also published. In 1874 Scammon wrote *The Marine Mammals of the North-Western Coast of North America*, a book based on his close observations while hunting whales, elephant seals, and other marine mammals.[4] He was elected to the California Academy of Sciences because of his scientific work. Scammon had a complex and somewhat conflicted view of American enterprise and its impact on American nature, but somehow the whaler was transformed into a marine mammal scientist.[5]

∼

The sky and water were lead gray as we left the docks in Monterey to look for whales. The morning whale-watching boat was full, partly with a large group of high school students and their teachers. It was relatively calm offshore at first. Some California sea lions rested on a rocking buoy just outside the harbor, and a group of sea otters lounged in the kelp as we passed the Pacific Grove shoreline where I had walked yesterday. Not far out we passed through a large group of several hundred Risso's dolphins feeding closer to shore than usual, the naturalist on board said. The sharp dorsal fins of these large dolphins reminded me of killer whales. One of them was pure white, a Risso's version of Moby Dick, the famous white sperm whale; nicknamed Casper after the friendly ghost of the cartoons, this individual is often seen in the area.

The captain didn't dally crossing the bay, apparently acting on a tip from other whale-watching tours that something interesting was happening just off Moss Landing, where the Salinas River flows into the bay at the head of the Monterey Submarine Canyon. We saw a few humpback whales as we ran, sometimes slowing briefly to observe their tall, straight, puffing blows and the row of small humps along their spine as they rolled above the surface. The twin smokestacks of the Moss Landing power plant loomed from the shore as we approached, and indeed there was some interesting action just off the mouth of Elkhorn Slough: a family of killer whales hunting sea lions for breakfast.

It was a family group seen in Monterey Bay unpredictably but regularly, whose family tree has been worked out by scientists from the Monterey-based California Killer Whale Project.[6] The group is led by an old matriarch nicknamed Star, about forty years old, who has six known children and four grandchildren. Male killer whales stick with their moms, and one of the males in the group was distinctive because his tall dorsal fin was bent over at the top. Our guides said he occasionally came up under boats and bumped them, and that behavior might explain his bent fin. Nicknamed Bumper, he was born in 2003.

The sea lions knew they were being hunted and swam together in tight groups of a dozen or more to escape the orcas, sometimes leaping out of the water in synchrony like porpoises do. The whales circled and dove and sometimes slapped the water with a fluke, a technique that can stun prey, but we never saw a kill in the time we watched. After half an hour or so, not wanting to get in the middle of the hunt for too long and possibly interrupt it, our boat captain headed back across the bay. The wind had picked up and it got pretty rough, but somehow I found my sea legs and never felt queasy. A swirl of gulls ahead marked a group of humpback whales in a feeding frenzy, where half a dozen or more whales were helping each other herd the baitfish they were gulping down. Some of their blows were accompanied by a trumpeting sound, apparently an expression of exuberant delight as they lunged, huge mouths wide, through the schools of silvery fish.

∾

International initiatives to conserve whales began in the 1930s, after many species were on the brink of extinction. Populations of some species, such as the Atlantic gray whale, were actually extinct. The initial whale conservation efforts led to the International Convention for the Regulation of Whaling in 1946; it established the International Whaling Commission, which sets policies and regulations for the conservation and management of whales. In 1972 the US Congress passed the Marine Mammal Protection Act (MMPA), using an ecosystem-based approach to create "a national policy to prevent marine mammal species and population stocks from diminishing, as a result of human activities, beyond the point at which they cease to be significant functioning elements of the ecosystems of which they are a part." The MMPA established the Marine Mammal Commission to implement its provisions in coordination with other international and federal government partners.[7]

Fourteen species of whales are listed as endangered under the Endangered Species Act (passed in 1973), which adds an additional dimension of protection. Authority for their conservation is delegated to NOAA Fisheries, as the oceanic counterpart to the US Fish and Wildlife Service.[8] Now that they have been protected from hunting for around seventy-five years, populations of some species in some areas, including the eastern North Pacific, are rebounding.[9]

As whale populations expand, they are reexploring ocean territory and in many cases reestablishing migration routes and feeding traditions that must have existed before overhunting crashed their numbers. Grays, blues, humpbacks, and killer whales provide examples. As they reinhabit their historic ranges, they are giving whale scientists a chance to get to know these animals for the first time—they could not be studied when they were almost gone—so of course we are learning new things, surprising new things, about these creatures.[10] It's an exciting time for whale research, and cetacean scientists are now being aided by citizen-scientists who take photos of whales and submit them to various whale ID databases; individual whales can be identified by their unique fin and fluke shapes, scars, coloration, and other markings, and their locations tracked.[11]

One example comes from eastern Pacific gray whales, which migrate up and down the North American West Coast every year from their breeding lagoons in Baja California to feeding areas in the Bering Sea. Eastern Pacific gray whales may be back to somewhere around their preexploitation population size—estimated by Scammon to have been around thirty thousand.[12] A small population of behaviorally distinct gray whales that stay along the Pacific Coast during the summer–fall feeding season has now been designated the "Pacific Coast Feeding Group" by the International Whaling Commission. This group is estimated to number around a few hundred whales.[13] These Pacific Coast summer-resident gray whales have been reinventing and restoring old behavioral patterns that could once have been common. It seems perfectly plausible that some gray whale mothers would dally with their calves along the coast if they could find enough food there, and not swim the full five thousand or six thousand miles to the Arctic. They might then continue that tradition, which has been called "maternal feeding ground fidelity," and teach it to their calves, who would themselves pass it on when they became mothers. The Pacific Coast Feeding Group may simply represent the restoration of diverse, adaptive behavioral patterns that were lost or less obvious when this species was nearly extinct.

Another example comes from killer whales (*Orcinus orca*); some people prefer to call them "orcas," from their scientific species name, perhaps because of a perceived negative connotation of their common name. Killer whales are a species of toothed whale found in all the oceans of the world, probably making them the most widely distributed of all mammals. They are a top predator in marine ecosystems, and because they hunt in groups, their social ecology resembles that of wolves. They could be thought of as the wolves of the sea. Like wolves, they are natural killers. And like wolves in terrestrial ecosystems, killer whales have a strong influence on the structure of marine food webs in ways that scientists are just beginning to understand.

Three main "ecotypes" of killer whales are recognized in the northern

Pacific, distinguished by their ranges and feeding behavior. "Resident" orcas stay more or less within the same geographic area year-round, feed mostly on salmon, and live in family groups of ten to forty individuals, called "pods," led by the oldest females of the group. A "northern resident" population ranges from Alaska to Vancouver Island, and a "southern resident" population is found in more inland waters of the Salish Sea and Puget Sound.[14] Some members of the southern resident population have been seen as far south as Monterey Bay in California, however, and critical habitat for this stock, which is listed as endangered under the Endangered Species Act, was recently expanded to include the Washington, Oregon, and California coasts.[15] Another orca ecotype is known as "transients" because they range more widely and unpredictably. Transient killer whales eat other marine mammals—whales, dolphins, seals, sea lions, and sea otters. Transient groups are generally small, with fewer than ten individuals, consisting of the matriarch, her sons, and a generation or two of her daughters. Transients are the most common type of killer whale seen along the California coast, and Star and her family, which we saw hunting at Moss Landing, are transients. Finally, an elusive and difficult-to-study ecotype is called "offshore" killer whales. These range widely (from Southern California to Alaska), often travel in large groups of fifty to one hundred individuals, and are known to feed on sharks.[16] These three orca ecotypes reflect different behavioral traditions in diet and migration, but individuals of a given ecotype also exhibit subtle anatomical differences and so probably represent at least partially separate and genetically differentiated breeding populations. NOAA Fisheries, which monitors and protects killer whales as part of its responsibilities under the Endangered Species Act, currently recognizes eleven "stocks" of this species, based on a combination of ecotype and range.[17] Research continues to probe and refine our understanding of what's going on with these populations and ecotypes. The California Killer Whale Project has observed orcas off the California coast that do not appear to belong to these three ecotypes; other ecotypes may also exist, and killer whale scientists can look forward to decades of interesting research to sort out the whole story.[18]

It's about twenty-five miles across the mouth of Monterey Bay. Gray whales, especially mothers heading north in March or April with calves born in Baja lagoons the winter before, normally hug the shore for safety from killer whales but sometimes venture across the more open water here. Transient orcas have figured that out and are most frequently seen in Monterey Bay in March and April when they target these migrating mothers and their calves. The whale with scarred flukes that I once saw at Rocky Point, Oregon, and nicknamed Paint Drip in "Whale Haven," an essay in my book about the Cascade Head Biosphere Reserve, recorded a close encounter with orcas, perhaps as it was crossing Monterey Bay as a mother or calf.[19]

~

The lunge-feeding, trumpeting humpbacks that delighted me on my whale-watching trip in Monterey Bay provide another example of rebounding whale populations that are giving us a new view of their ecology and behavior. Humpback whales (*Megaptera novaeangliae*) are found worldwide. Commercial whaling reduced their populations by 95 percent or more in many areas, but with full protection they are now beginning to recover. Recent estimates of the humpback population feeding along the California, Oregon, and Washington coasts are about five thousand whales. This population has been growing at about 8 percent per year since the international whaling moratorium in the 1980s but is still considered endangered and depleted under the Marine Mammal Protection Act. Ship strikes and entanglements in fishing gear are the most common anthropogenic threats to these whales. Ocean noise pollution from ships and sonar is also a concern.[20] Central California north and south of the Golden Gate, and the northern Channel Islands, are feeding hotspots for humpbacks.[21]

Male humpback whales have been called "the jazz singers of the sea." Humpback songs are unique among whales because of their musical structure, with repeated phrases and themes, and variations that suggest improvisation, as in jazz music.[22] Moving across a wide sound spectrum from extremely low to very high frequencies, one humpback song can last for thirty minutes and be repeated for a whole day. The phenomenon of humpback whale songs was first recognized by biologist Roger Payne,[23] who thought that what he called the "exuberant, uninterrupted rivers of sound" might have the potential to motivate whale conservation if more people heard them. They have been called "the songs that saved the whales."[24] In the late 1960s Payne began distributing recordings of humpback songs to musicians and composers. One of those was Judy Collins, who took an old traditional whaling ballad, "Farewell to Tarwathie," and created a duet with a humpback from one of his recordings.[25] Her song resonated strongly with me and many others at the time, and I played it in my university ecology and conservation classes for many years, trying, I guess, to sneak in a message about the compatibility of science and emotion.

As I was watching the humpbacks feed that morning in Monterey Bay, I was thinking about a fascinating scientific paper I'd read recently—an analysis of humpback whale songs recorded by a hydrophone placed nine hundred meters below us by the Monterey Bay Aquarium Research Institute. The author of the paper, Miriam Hauer-Jensen, used the traditional method of analyzing the structure of humpback songs: listening to them and categorizing the sound "units" according to familiar descriptions of human and other animal sounds. The fun part of the article for me is the terms she used to describe the sounds in the songs:

> The most popular unit type was the moan, followed by gurgle, grunt, shriek, cry, groan, etc. In the 20151207 song, even though gurgle was the most popular unit type, it only made up about 24% of the song, further proving the complexity within one song. The results helped us answer some questions about the evolution of humpback song and patterns. From 2015 to 2016, there was an overlap of six unit types: cry, groan, gurgle, moan, purr, and shriek. From 2016 to 2017, there was an overlap of three unit types: gurgle, moan, and shriek.[26]

Even among "the jazz singers of the sea," apparently, the music evolves. Dorsey, Gillespie, Coltrane, Mingus, George . . . ?

Because only males sing these songs, they are assumed to play a role in courtship and mating; they have been likened to the songs of male nightingales, which seem to play a role in both courtship and territorial defense in those birds. But that hypothesis doesn't quite seem to fit with humpbacks, and the research to date leaves the purpose of humpback jazz something of a mystery still. "To truly understand the function of these songs would require further analysis on the behavior of humpback whales alongside their vocalizations," says Hauer-Jensen. Maybe they are calling out into the galaxy for extraterrestrial help in saving the planet?

∼

As a final example, let's turn to the blues. Blue whales, that is. Humpbacks may be the jazz singers of the sea, but blue whales may still be singing the blues, at least in their struggle to recover to preexploitation population levels. According to whale expert John Calambokidis and his colleagues, "Unlike other baleen whale species in the eastern North Pacific whose populations have increased, such as fin, humpback, and gray whales, blue whales have not shown signs of recovery from whaling over the last 20 years."[27] The most recent NOAA Fisheries stock assessment for blue whales in that region estimates a total population of around two thousand whales and notes the "observed lack of a population size increase since the early 1990s." This stock is listed as endangered and depleted for federal management purposes. Vessel strikes are considered the major anthropogenic threat, but there is some debate about whether that is the cause of the lack of apparent recovery of the species since commercial whaling ended.[28]

Monterey Bay, and the national marine sanctuaries to the north and south that are included in the Golden Gate and Channel Islands Biosphere Reserves, are among the most biologically important feeding areas for blue whales on the US Pacific Coast. A research study in Monterey Bay discovered that these blues are singing some interesting songs. They apparently call out to other blue whales to come and take advantage of episodes when summer winds cause intense upwelling that brings cold, nutrient-rich water to the surface and triggers blooms of plankton and blue whale food species like krill and anchovies.[29]

Migrations of large marine mammals like whales (and elephant seals) raise intriguing questions about long-distance flows of energy and nutrients in ecosystems—and call into question the sustainability of the massive flows of energy, food, and other resources that are now commonplace and viewed as normal within the global human economic system. The scale of those human resource transfers is vastly greater than those of marine mammal migrations. It is ecologically aberrant and not likely to be ecologically sustainable.

Many whale species, such as the grays, humpbacks, and blues just mentioned, make long seasonal migrations of thousands of miles between high-latitude summer feeding grounds and often food-deficient, low-latitude breeding areas. The ecological explanation for the evolution of these migrations is not completely clear. They are energetically costly—so why wouldn't whales just stay around their summer feeding areas to mate and calve during the winter season? One idea is that the warmer and less stormy waters at lower latitudes in winter may help whales, especially mothers and calves, conserve energy and pay back the energy cost of seasonal migrations. Another hypothesis is that they move to warmer waters to facilitate the molting of their skin and maintain skin health.[30] And still another hypothesis is that whales migrate to areas with fewer killer whales and a reduced risk of calf predation to give birth. But some whale ecologists "are not convinced that the threat of killer whale attack could provide the impetus for what is (or at least was, prior to the advent of global industrial whaling) arguably the largest seasonal movement of animal biomass on Earth."[31]

❧

The morning after watching the orcas hunt sea lions just off the mouth of Elkhorn Slough, I was in a kayak on that slough. The twin smokestacks of the Moss Landing Power Plant again loomed overhead, a local landmark. A brilliant sun shone today in contrast to yesterday's leaden gray, and this was Earth Day 2022.[32] What better way to spend Earth Day could there be than among sea otters? They were common in the first mile of the slough, afloat on their backs, resting, grooming, diving, playing, feeding, and nursing pups. As the northwest wind came up in the early afternoon and the tide started to run in, it was hard work paddling down the slough. I paddled hard past small groups of otters, four or five together sometimes, and then drifted back up the slough among them. They were rollicking and rolling, wrestling and nuzzling—mostly just playing now, it seemed. There was lots of vocalizing too; they were clearly very social and were having a good time. Sometimes one would give a loud "mew! mew!"—almost catlike—and another would call back and then sprint toward the caller to wrestle in the water some more.

It's lucky that there are sea otters left to see. Once, an estimated 150,000–300,000 sea otters ranged around North Pacific coasts from Kamchatka to Baja California, but during the Fur Rush, which preceded the much more well-known California Gold Rush by decades, at least 99 percent of sea otters were killed. Of the approximately two thousand otters that survived this slaughter, most were found in the Aleutian Islands and Alaska. They were thought to be extinct in California, but in 1914 a group of fewer than fifty were rediscovered off the coast of Big Sur.[33] They apparently survived there because of the difficulty of marine access for otter hunting along that rugged coast. Otters slowly expanded their range from that Big Sur population over the decades. Now they have been seen south to about Point Conception, just west of Santa Barbara, and north to Pigeon Point, north of Santa Cruz, but their range expansion has slowed and almost stopped. Their population in California is now estimated to be around three thousand otters. They have recolonized only about 13 percent of their historic range, and their population is far below the sixteen thousand that the California coastline is estimated to be able to support.

Sea otters don't have blubber like whales, elephant seals, and many other marine mammals but rely on their amazing air-trapping fur for insulation. They have the densest, finest fur of any mammal, more than eight hundred thousand hairs per square inch, or about as many as on six human heads. Otters need to spend a lot of time grooming their fur to keep it dry and oiled so it traps air for insulation. The sea is cold where most otters live, and in addition to their insulating fur, they also need a high metabolism to generate body heat. They eat a lot, about 25 percent of their weight per day.[34]

That soft fur was the cause of the near demise of the sea otter. The use of otter fur became fashionable in China in the mid-1700s, launching an era of hunting and trade. Otter pelts were exchanged for tea, silk, porcelain, and other exotic Chinese trade goods. Otters were hunted intensively until they were nearly wiped out in the first decades of the 1800s. Russian fur traders and their conscripted Aleut hunters were especially efficient. The Russians established a southern anchor on the California coast for their fur trade in 1812, at Fort Ross, about nine miles north of present-day Jenner at the mouth of the Russian River.

Sea otters are thought of as mainly inhabitants of outer-coast kelp-forest ecosystems. That was a major habitat for this species and was where their remnant populations survived. Research in the Aleutian Islands in the 1970s demonstrated that sea otters are a keystone species in kelp forests. A paper by James Estes and John Palmisano, titled "Sea Otters: Their Role in Structuring Nearshore Communities," was published in *Science* in 1974, just five years after Robert Paine had first used the term "keystone species" to describe the role of the ochre seastar, *Pisaster ochraceous*, in structuring Pacific intertidal ecosystems.[35] Estes and his colleagues soon showed that removal of otters could trigger a "trophic cascade" in which the sea urchin population exploded, gobbled up all the kelp, and flipped the ecosystem into an "alternate stable-state."[36] Many giant kelp forests along the Pacific Coast have suffered that fate since sea otters became locally extinct, the alternate stable-state becoming what have been called "urchin barrens."[37]

Recent research has expanded our understanding of the ecological role of sea otters in an intriguing direction. It suggests that the image of them among both the public and most scientists as outer-coast, kelp-forest specialists is too narrow. It turns out that sea otters were probably as much or more at home in quiet estuarine waters as on stormy outer coasts, but their early extermination from estuarine habitats, where it would have been easiest to hunt them, created a "skewed baseline" for understanding their ecological niche.[38]

In the 1970s, descendants of the Big Sur sea otters began to appear in Elkhorn Slough, and by the 1990s they were common there. There are now more than one hundred otters living in the slough, and the population shows signs of reaching the carrying capacity of the habitat. Estuaries have several benefits for otters, including less stressful conditions for temperature maintenance than on the outer coast, which may be especially important for mothers and pups, and as a refuge from predation by killer whales and sharks.

The recolonization of Elkhorn Slough by otters revealed that they act as keystone species there, as in kelp beds, but through a different influence on the food web. Before the otters showed up, eelgrass beds in the slough were struggling under algal overgrowth caused by nutrient overload from the fertilizer washing off nearby truck farms. But with otters, the eelgrass became healthy again. Why? Careful research showed that otters ate crabs that ate the smaller creatures that grazed the algae from the eelgrass; with fewer crabs, the grazers proliferated and cleaned the overgrown eelgrass, and it thrived once again.

Archaeological evidence from shell middens along central California estuaries shows that sea otters were once common in those habitats and were hunted by Native peoples for thousands of years, apparently sustainably. Otter bones have been found at Drakes Estero on Point Reyes, Elkhorn Slough, and Morro Bay; at one midden by San Francisco Bay they were the most abundant mammal remains.[39]

The current southern sea otter recovery plan does not include estuaries as target habitats in otter recovery, but this recent research on their historic use of estuaries suggests that it should. An otter population growth model for San Francisco Bay based on the Elkhorn Slough research estimated that the bay alone could support about 6,600 sea otters, more than double the entire 2018 California population. Drakes Estero, in an area of the Point Reyes National Seashore designated as wilderness, would be another prime candidate for sea otter reintroduction, and Tomales Bay could be another possibility.

Why haven't otters spread farther north and south in the century since they were found at Big Sur? The main factor seems to be predation by young white sharks, which kill dispersing otters. Shark predation seems to be why sea otters haven't already made it the short distance up the coast from Elkhorn Slough and into San Francisco Bay, or around Point Conception and over to the Channel Islands, where they were once abundant. Restoring otters in estuarine habitats, where they are safe from predation by sharks or killer whales and where their populations could grow, might help them leapfrog the high-predation zones of the outer coast and more rapidly recolonize their historic range.

In 2020, Congress directed the US Fish and Wildlife Service to "study the feasibility and cost of reestablishing sea otters on the Pacific Coast of the contiguous United States." The feasibility assessment report made a number of recommendations for "next steps" in a sea otter restoration program; one recommendation was for experimental reintroductions in estuaries.[40]

The lesson emerging from sea otter research in Elkhorn Slough and other

California estuaries is similar to that from whales: as populations rebound to preexploitation levels and historic habitats are restored and recolonized, the incomplete or even distorted picture we may have had of their range and ecological niche because of the skewed baseline created by devastating exploitation is being corrected. The lesson is also similar to that from the Salmon River estuary in the Cascade Head Biosphere Reserve, where restored estuarine habitats were shown to be highly important to recovering Oregon Coast coho salmon.[41]

~

Monday, October 18, 2021. It was a beautiful sunny morning at Santa Barbara Harbor when I arrived just before noon to meet Sean Hastings, whose job title is "resource protection coordinator" for NOAA's Channel Islands National Marine Sanctuary. Sean was my point of contact to learn more about the Channel Islands Biosphere Reserve. He has worked for NOAA with the marine sanctuary here for twenty-five years and coauthored the 2016 periodic review required by the UNESCO MAB Programme that enabled this biosphere reserve to continue as part of the international network. We met in front of the Santa Barbara Maritime Museum facing the harbor and went around the corner to order fish tacos for lunch. This is a "working waterfront," and as we ate, local commercial fishermen would stop to greet Sean and chat about things. His office is at the harbor, and it was obvious that he had his finger on the pulse of what was going on offshore.

Ship strikes endanger whales, and efforts to reduce this threat are occurring in the national marine sanctuaries that are part of both of California's coastal biosphere reserves, where whales congregate to feed during the summer upwelling season. In Southern California, large vessels such as container ships, car carriers, and tankers—about 4,500 ships per year—use the ports of Los Angeles and Long Beach, which together account for approximately 30 percent of all US imports and exports.[42] A large proportion of this ship traffic passes through the Santa Barbara Channel between the northern Channel Islands and the mainland, using a two-mile-wide ship freeway in the middle of the channel designated by the International Maritime Organization.

The Channel Islands are an important seasonal feeding area for endangered blue, fin, and humpback whales,[43] all federally protected by the Marine Mammal Protection Act, the Endangered Species Act, and the National Marine Sanctuaries Act from any killing (or "take"), incidental or otherwise. Nevertheless, it is estimated that about nine blue, ten fin, and five humpback whales are killed by vessel strikes in the area during the summer feeding season each year.[44]

Whale deaths aren't the only problem with the ship traffic in the Channel Islands area. Air quality is another. These ships burn some of the dirtiest fossil fuels on the planet; emissions from ship traffic sometimes push ambient air quality in the area into the bad zone, and California air quality control districts have supported an initiative that at first sounds incongruous, called "Protecting Blue Whales and Blue Skies." Created with NOAA's Channel Islands National Marine Sanctuary, the program's website describes it as

> a partnership for cleaner air, safer whales, and a quieter ocean . . .
> a voluntary Vessel Speed Reduction (VSR) Program along the
> coast of California which incentivizes companies to incorporate
> sustainable shipping practices across their global supply chain. By
> creating seasonal and predictable slow speed zones, this program
> helps companies protect endangered whales, reduce fuel use and
> regional greenhouse gas emissions, and improve air quality and
> human health outcomes.[43]

Sean called the Channel Islands Biosphere Reserve a "laboratory" for this initiative; it has served as the site of scientific research on the several dimensions of the problem—the reduction of ship-whale strikes, air pollution, and underwater noise. Eighteen global shipping lines now participate in the program, which also operates in the national marine sanctuaries in the Golden Gate Biosphere Reserve (Greater Farallones, Cordell Bank, and Monterey Bay National Marine Sanctuaries).[44]

The program's website provides a table of hopeful statistics, and it clearly has had some positive results. For example, NOAA is monitoring underwater sound in five national marine sanctuaries, including Channel Islands and Monterey Bay,[45] and a study based on this monitoring, titled "Underwater

Noise Mitigation in the Santa Barbara Channel through Incentive-Based Vessel Speed Reduction," was published in 2021 in the prestigious journal *Nature Scientific Reports*. The authors concluded that "commercial shipping is the dominant source of low-frequency noise in the ocean. It has been shown that the noise radiated by an individual vessel depends upon the vessel's speed. This analysis highlights how slowing vessel speed to 10 knots or less is an effective method in reducing underwater noise emitted from commercial ships."[46] Container ships are loud, "louder than a rock concert," Sean said. Since whales communicate and navigate using sound, ocean noise pollution is likely having an effect on their behavior and survival, but the science about it is still evolving. The research from Monterey Bay discussed above, on the vocalizations that blue whales use to call their family and friends to dinner, suggests one possible effect: it's hard to hear the dinner call with a container-ship rock concert blaring.

But despite some optimism on the noise reduction and air quality fronts, the results of reducing ship speed may still fall short for whale safety. A study a few years ago of the behavioral responses of blue whales in the Channel Islands area concluded that they don't really know how to react in the presence of large ships to avoid being struck. They don't seem to turn away, and they make a shallow dive only about half the time when they sense a ship approaching.[47] Perhaps it's no wonder that these huge creatures don't react more appropriately; they never had to deal with that kind of threat before in their evolutionary experience. Research published in 2022, "Evaluating Adherence with Voluntary Slow Speed Initiatives to Protect Endangered Whales," found that

> while average speeds of large vessels have decreased across the years studied, cooperation with voluntary 10-knot speed reduction requests has been lower than estimated to be needed to reduce vessel-strike related mortality to levels that do not inhibit reaching and maintaining optimal sustainable [whale] populations. Voluntary VSR [vessel speed reduction] approaches may be insufficient to achieve cooperation levels needed to significantly reduce the risk of vessel strike-related mortality for these federally protected whales. Mandatory regulations in the southern Califor-

nia Bight may maximize benefits to whales, and costs to industry accrued by slowing down vessels in these areas are minimal.[48]

Mandatory, rather than only voluntary, ship-speed reductions may be needed, but it would be better yet to simply keep ships and shipping lanes away from seasonally important feeding areas for whales. A small positive step in that direction was recently taken by the International Maritime Organization, which manages global shipping routes. In November 2022, the IMO accepted recommendations from NOAA and its partners to expand the "area to be avoided" by large ships around the northern Channel Islands and adjusted the boundaries of the traffic separation scheme in the Santa Barbara Channel to reduce overlap with important whale feeding areas.[49]

But for me, the issue comes back to a phrase used in describing the goal of the "Protecting Blue Whales and Blue Skies" program: to "incentivize companies to incorporate sustainable shipping practices across their global supply chain." Slowing down current container ships is a tiny step in the right direction, but it is like a Band-Aid on a deep wound. The real long-term solution to the dead whales, dirty air, and noisy ocean problem is to create a sustainable human economy that does not involve long-distance global trade in basic resources—a bioregionally based, ecologically sustainable global economic system. Do I want my (1) underwear, (2) running shoes, (3) lightbulbs, (4) ballpoint pens, (5) cell phone, (6) shower curtain, and you name it, to have to come on a container ship from Asia? No! There is no reason that they should have to; they all could be manufactured perfectly well in the United States, or even just in California. In an ecologically sustainable economy, none of the items listed above, or many, many others, would come from other continents via container ships.

Let's listen to the whales calling and singing to us and quiet the oceans from the ultraloud throbbing of container ship engines that perpetuate ecologically unsustainable and maladaptive global flows of energy and materials. Let's start on a voyage home to a quieter, healthier planet. They say the sea is cold, but it is full of hot blood that deserves the sound-space to conduct its ancient conversations, which predate our noisy self-absorbed chatter by eons.

10

The Chumash Channel and Its Islands

When animals were still people, Falcon and his two cousins started out one day to go fishing. They talked and paddled, talked and paddled, and before they knew it, they were closer to Santa Cruz Island than to the mainland and it was getting late. We'd better spend the night on the island, or the wind might catch us and kill us, they thought. The people there on the island saw the canoe approaching, and the chief invited the boys to come ashore. The boys were Eagle's nephews, and they were very handsome. The girls gathered and there were many of them, but the three prettiest were Otter, Duck, and Wildcat.

—María Solares, "The Island Girls," circa 1915[1]

WHEN SPANISH EXPLORER Juan Rodríguez Cabrillo sailed into the Santa Barbara Channel in 1542, he found a thriving Indigenous maritime culture living along the coast and on the Channel Islands. The Spaniards were especially impressed by the large seagoing canoes. One major coastal village had so many canoes on the beach that Cabrillo called it "pueblo de los canoas." The Chumash name of the town was humaliwo, "where the surf sounds loudly"; now the place is called Malibu, echoing the Chumash name, and is known as a surfing mecca. Farther west along the coast Cabrillo noted a village where canoes were being manufactured, and he therefore called it Carpinteria (meaning "carpentry") in Spanish; the modern city, between Ventura and Santa Barbara, is still called Carpinteria.

Cabrillo had encountered what has been called a culture of "complex hunter-gatherers" that managed to support one of the densest populations of any nonfarming group of Native Americans at the time Europeans arrived. Chumash society was more complex and sophisticated than many other hunter-gatherer cultures in many ways. Traits associated with this sociopolitical complexity included permanent settlements of considerable size; storage of large amounts of food, such as acorns and fish; environmental manipulation, especially the use of fire, to promote desired species; occupational specialization; social hierarchy; extensive political and economic alliances; complex technologies; and intensive regional trade facilitated by shell-bead money manufactured primarily on the islands.[2]

The *tomol*, perhaps the most technologically sophisticated watercraft in Indigenous North America, was the keystone technology of the society and economy of the Chumash. It linked the marine and terrestrial ecology of the culture, enabling regular cross-channel travel for social, economic, and ceremonial purposes, and for trade of foods, raw materials, and finished products. From the mainland, foods such as edible seeds, animal skins and furs, and milkweed and dogbane fibers for making twine were traded for island specialties such as soapstone, redwood driftwood for making tomols, otter pelts, finished products of marine mammal bone and shell, and shell beads.[3] A map in the Santa Barbara Maritime Museum shows the network of tomol routes that knitted this trade together. A coastal route—surely the safest and most regular—served Chumash settlements from Point Conception in the west, along the Gaviota Coast to present-day Santa Barbara, Ventura, and Oxnard, and past Point Mugu to Malibu. Routes to the four northern Channel Islands left Ventura and Oxnard and went to Anacapa and Santa Cruz Island and then west to Santa Rosa and San Miguel. According to the map, there was a route across the western mouth of the channel from Point Conception to San Miguel Island, which must have required great knowledge and skill to navigate safely. Trade across an ecoregion with both terrestrial and marine components may have enabled the development of the advanced hunter-gatherer society the Spanish encountered half a millennium ago.

The production of shell beads for trade focused on Santa Cruz Island, and these came to be used as a form of money throughout the area. The word *chumash* originally meant "makers of shell-bead money," and Santa Cruz Island, the hub of the production of shell beads, was called mi'chumash, "the place where they make shell-bead money," throughout the region—except by the inhabitants of the island themselves, who called it limuw, "in the ocean." So, the name "Chumash" given to the Indigenous communities of the California Bight and islands is something of a misnomer; it is an "exonym"—a generic name given by outsiders that is not used in the communities by the people themselves.[4]

The tomol is a type of sewn-plank canoe found only among the Chumash and the Tongva, their neighbors just to the south. It is not known when the Chumash invented or acquired this sewn-plank canoe technology, which is a unique boat type on the Pacific Coast.[5] Similar sewn-plank canoes are known in Polynesia, and some people have proposed that the Chumash learned how to make tomols from Polynesian voyagers who visited the Channel Islands, perhaps up to several thousand years ago.[6] The nearest Indigenous seagoing canoes on the Pacific Coast were used by groups living north of Cape Mendocino, almost five hundred miles north, such as the Yurok of the lower Klamath River, who carved dugouts out of single redwood logs. Boats made of bundles of tule, the giant wetland sedge (*Schoenoplectus acutus*), were used by Central Valley tribes and those of the San Francisco Bay Area, but it seems they were not used in the Chumash Channel. The oldest human remains found on the Channel Islands are around thirteen thousand years old, and even then, with sea levels much lower than today, the distance between the islands and the mainland was five miles or so, so the first humans on the islands must have had some type of seaworthy watercraft.

Redwood was the preferred wood for tomols, although Douglas-fir or pine was sometimes used. Although the nearest redwoods grow just south of San Francisco Bay, the California Current often carried redwood logs that washed out of Northern California rivers to the shores of the outer northern Channel Islands. The Chumash name for what is now called Santa Rosa Island was wi'ma, "driftwood," apparently because it was a prime location for finding redwood for tomol building.

~

I had read and heard about the Chumash tomol before visiting the area in October, and I wanted to learn more and see these boats up close. My first chance came at the Santa Barbara Museum of Natural History, where the first attempt to revive the traditional design and methods of tomol building is displayed. It now sits just below the ceiling in a dimly lit room displaying other artifacts of Chumash culture. The feeling was of a sad, dried fish out of water. But the story of this particular tomol is inspiring, reaching right to the roots of the restoration and revitalization of Chumash culture and language.

One of the lessons from the Cascade Head Biosphere Reserve in Oregon is that "people matter," and this forlorn tomol links with a wonderful example of a person whose life made a difference in our ability to understand and revitalize some of Chumash culture. Fernando Librado, who also used his Chumash name Kitsepawit, was born in 1839 at Mission San Buenaventura to parents from Santa Cruz Island who had been moved to the mission some twenty-five years earlier.[7]

The last Chumash tomols were being built in the 1850s. Librado had seen the process as a young man and also heard descriptions from older Chumash who had been members of the canoe-building and paddling guild called the "Brotherhood of the Tomol." Librado became one of the most important linguistic and ethnographic informants of anthropologist John P. Harrington (more on him in a moment). Harrington persuaded Kitsepawit to build a tomol for display at the Panama-California Exposition, which was held in San Diego from 1915 to 1917 to celebrate the opening of the Panama Canal. Working from memory, Librado directed the construction beginning around 1912, when he was seventy-three years old. He did not attempt to use only traditional methods and tools. Harrington recorded the process in scrupulous notes. This is the canoe now displayed at the Santa Barbara Museum of Natural History.

Harrington's notes and Librado's tomol were the foundation for the modern era of tomol building and voyaging. In 1976, the Santa Barbara Museum of Natural History and the Quabajai Chumash Association of the Coastal Band of the Chumash Nation used them to build a full-sized tomol named *Helek* (*Falcon* or *Peregrine Falcon* in Chumash), which was tested at sea around several of the northern Channel Islands. At the same time, the Brotherhood of the Tomol was reconstituted. Many more tomols and cross-channel voyages have followed.

Kitsepawit's accomplice in capturing the last memories of tomol technology was an American anthropologist, John Peabody Harrington (1884–1961).[8] "Few scholars can claim to have saved an entire culture from historical oblivion. John Peabody Harrington was one of those," wrote Brian Fagan in his book *Before California*.[9] Harrington couldn't have done his work without his Chumash informants, of course, so they deserve much of the credit. Harrington grew up in California and began undergraduate studies at Stanford University in 1902, majoring in anthropology and classical languages. He took a summer class at UC Berkeley from Alfred Kroeber, the first graduate student and protégé of Franz Boas, who was just beginning his lifelong study of California Indians.[10] "Kroeber's lectures electrified Harrington," Fagan wrote, and Harrington began *his* lifelong study of the languages and cultures of Southern California, focusing especially on the Chumash. Anthropologist Richard Applegate notes that

> for Harrington, the preservation of the Chumash languages was
> a labor of love which bordered on obsession. He did most of his
> work between 1912 and 1922, when there were still some flu-
> ent speakers of Chumash left. Although it had been well over a
> century since the arrival of the missionaries, a few of Harrington's
> informants were able to recall a great deal of what they had heard
> of the old people and their ways. In particular, Maria Solares of
> Santa Ynez and Fernando Librado of Ventura furnished valuable
> linguistic and ethnographic information.[11]

Harrington's "labor of love which bordered on obsession" also made possible the reconstruction of something much less tangible than the tomol: the worldview of the Chumash. Based on Harrington's diligent ethnographic recording of the stories, legends, and myths of his Chumash informants, Thomas Blackburn attempted to do that in his book *December's Child*, as I'll discuss in another essay, "The View from Limuw."

~

I mentioned seeing the tomol built by Librado/Kitsepawit at the Santa Barbara Museum of Natural History to a Chumash contact, Diego Cordero, who, it turned out, was a tomol paddler himself. Tomols are sea creatures, he said; they are stranded and sad if not in or near the ocean. I asked him where I could see a modern, living tomol, perhaps even one that had been involved in the crossings to the islands that I'd read about and seen in videos.

"Go to Arroyo Burro," Diego said.

So I went on a quest to Arroyo Burro Beach, a Santa Barbara County park. West of the parking lot and beach access at this tucked-away and locally popular little spot was the Watershed Resource Center; on its public deck were a series of photos and informational signs about the recent history of tomol building and voyaging. On the ground level, in a securely fenced area, a large dark tomol rested on a trailer, as if ready to be pulled to the beach and slide off into the water. I guessed its length to be about thirty feet. The inlaid design on its bow, what looked to me like a golden dolphin in a ring of leaping dolphins, must have signified its name, but I couldn't find pictures or other information to identify this tomol.

Poking around a little more on the ground level, I saw the snout of another tomol peeking out from under the supports of the Watershed Resource Center, its length pushed under the raised foundation of the building above for protection. The inlaid design of abalone shell on her bow identified this tomol as the *Elye'wun*, or *Swordfish*.

The *Elye'wun* (the apostrophe in Chumash words represents a glottal stop sound, as in "uh-oh" in English) was built in 1997 by the Chumash Maritime Association and was the first tomol to be owned by the Chumash community itself in over one hundred years. In September 2001, the *Elye'wun* was paddled from Ventura Harbor to Scorpion Anchorage on the eastern end of Santa Cruz Island—the site of the old Chumash village of swaxil. The 21-mile voyage took ten hours. Since then this ceremonial voyage has been repeated almost every year. The National Park Service's Channel Islands National Park and NOAA's Channel Islands National Marine Sanctuary, the two main federal managers in the Channel Islands Biosphere Reserve, were very supportive of the first tomol crossing to the islands and have been ever since.[12] The Chumash Maritime Association continues to focus on building, maintaining, crewing, and voyaging with traditional tomols.

I wish I could have seen *Elye'wun*'s sleek length lying back there in the darkness, but I could imagine it, and it gave me goosebumps. *Elye'wun* embodies the adaptiveness and resilience of human cultures in the Channel Islands ecoregion, potentially reaching back to the time of the first human encounters with North America at the end of the last Ice Age.

≈

Six distinct Chumash dialects, some so different as to perhaps qualify as separate languages, were identified at about the time Spanish Catholic missions were established in the California Bight.[13] The missions themselves may have acted as hubs for consolidation of those dialects, as people were moved from surrounding areas to the five missions founded in Chumash territory—San Buenaventura, Santa Barbara, Santa Ynez, La Purisima, and San Luis Obispo. I imagine these linguistic distinctions as something like the differences between Spanish, Portuguese, and Italian, which have some level of mutual intelligibility. Perhaps this local linguistic divergence is similar to that among the Pueblo peoples of northern New Mexico where I grew up. Within a forty-mile radius, nine different Pueblo communities speak dialects of the Tewa, Tiwa, and Towa languages. Several Chumash languages were well documented in the unpublished field notes and wax-cylinder recordings of John P. Harrington.

The Santa Ynez Band of Chumash Indians is the only federally recognized Chumash tribe, but according to several Chumash contacts there are thirteen or fourteen "sort-of-organized bands." They said that these were not some sort of "ancient traditional thing," but that Chumash society was more like a mosaic of interacting communities than some superorganized political system, with the diversity of Chumash dialects and languages reflecting that.

Chumash languages are generally placed in a language family that was called Hokan by Alfred Kroeber and Edward Sapir, members of the first generation of Franz Boas's students of linguistics and ethnography. "It is a 'language isolate,' a technical term meaning that the Chumashan family has no known or well-established close relatives among other languages; in California, it is a true language isolate as it is not related to any other language or language family in the state," according to anthropologist Dr. Terry L. Jones.[14] This explanation reminds me of some of the "language isolates" in Africa, where there are pockets of ancient languages in which "click" sounds are common. They are often associated with "relict" hunter-gatherer cultures like the rainforest Pygmies of the Congo Basin, the Hadza of northern Tanzania, and the San of the Kalahari. They were apparently washed over by the Bantu languages of the agricultural cultures that spread east from West Africa, and then south and west until their agriculture collided with the agriculture-inhospitable Kalahari in southwestern Africa. Could the Chumashan and other Hokan languages be a parallel to the click languages of Africa? Perhaps they carry forward the language of the maritime peoples who arrived on the Channel Islands during the last Ice Age.

The last native Chumash speaker was Mary Yee, who spoke Barbareño; she died in 1965. It is frankly quite remarkable that these languages survived among native speakers for so long after Spanish missionization, and that thanks to Harrington and his Chumash consultants, they were documented well enough to allow Chumash linguists and language revitalization activists to bring them back to life today, albeit without the rich cultural milieu in which they functioned.

Given the malleability and evolution of languages, and the current lack of Chumash native speakers,[15] it is probably not possible to know for sure how words flowed over and gave meaning to this place. But humans have been speaking, storytelling, and singing across the landscapes and seascapes of the Chumash Channel for a very long time.

∼

The surprisingly early date of evidence for human occupation of the Channel Islands (thirteen thousand years ago or more) has led to a tidal wave of interest in how the first people got to the Americas. For many decades the paradigm among paleoanthropologists was that people first walked across the Bering land bridge that connected Asia and North America when sea levels were much lower, traveled south through a long "ice-free corridor" between continental ice sheets, and rapidly spread out across the Americas.

A characteristic type of spearpoint first unearthed near Clovis, New Mexico, gave the name to this culture. But more recent discoveries, including early evidence for humans on the Channel Islands, challenge this "Clovis First" hypothesis. A large extended academic family of paleoarchaeologists and anthropologists is now finding evidence for another possibility: human colonization of the Pacific Coast by maritime cultures with seagoing watercraft along what has been called the "kelp highway,"[16] after the ubiquitous coastal kelp forests that hug the northern Pacific Coast from Hokkaido to Baja California. A recent popular article in the *Atlantic* by Ross Anderson, titled "The Search for America's Atlantis," tried to summarize some of the current excitement and research.[17]

More than 2,800 archaeological sites are found on the five islands that make up Channel Islands National Park, according to Dr. Kristin Hoppa, the park's archaeologist. This is a very high density of archaeological sites, reaching back a very long time, and archaeology here has the potential to rewrite our theories of how humans first reached the Americas. Archaeological sites on the Channel Islands generally have excellent stratification—layering that provides a sequential time record—because burrowing mammals like gophers that mess it up are not found on the islands, not to mention the general lack of development, which has bulldozed, dug up, and built over many archaeological sites on the California mainland.[18] Environmental archaeologist Douglas Kennett notes that "the offshore islands of California are particularly important because they contain the longest and best-preserved archaeological sequences available for study along the west coast of North America."[19] The scientific value of the unique island species of "California's Galapagos" is one thing; but the value of the archaeological sites on these islands in helping us understand better the cultural evolution and adaptation of humans here is another unique scientific resource that must be recognized and conserved.

Relatively few of the thousands of archaeological sites on the Channel Islands have been investigated using modern scientific methods, and the biggest challenge is that many of the most informative sites may now be underwater. When humans first settled on the islands during the last phase of the Ice Age, the four northern Channel Islands of today were one large island because sea level was much lower, and so coastal villages of ten thousand years ago are now underwater somewhere around the coasts of the modern islands. Underwater archaeology of the sort needed to find and excavate such sites is in its infancy, although some attempts are beginning.[20]

The long archaeological record on the islands is a unique and valuable resource for understanding the human-nature relationship in this place. The middens of the Channel Islands allow ecologically inclined archaeologists to examine how humans have harvested from and lived in the unique natural ecosystems here over many millennia. One value of understanding that is to compare them with us. We are clearly not in balance with the resources of the ecosystems we inhabit—were they?

It was long fashionable to view pre-Columbian Indigenous cultures as ecologically sensitive and in "harmony" with their natural environments. Is that romantic view true? Archaeological evidence from the Channel Islands can inform that discussion, but it is complicated. The evidence shows that the ancestral Chumash changed island ecosystems by introducing dogs, foxes, mice, and probably other organisms; by reducing sea otter populations and thereby causing trophic cascades in nearshore marine ecosystems; and by regularly using fire to maintain the grasslands where they harvested many roots, bulbs, and other plant foods. However, Dr. Jon Erlandson, whose career-long research has helped assemble this evidence, told me that "we have always stressed that such impacts pale in comparison to the rapid ecological devastation that followed European colonization."[21]

In fact, Erlandson and his colleagues take the long record of human habitation on the Channel Islands as a message of hope. In a paper titled "Island of Hope: Archaeology, Historical Ecology, and Human Resilience on California's Tuqan Island,"[22] they argue that the Island Chumash "survived and thrived" despite sometimes dramatic natural geographic and ecological changes—including climatic warming, rapid sea level rise, and shrinking land area—from the late Pleistocene until the arrival of Europeans and the Holocene. They write that "the story of Island Chumash persistence, adaptability, and resilience, along with the continuing recovery of island ecosystems under the management of federal agencies and the Nature Conservancy, provides lessons of hope for modern island and coastal communities threatened by similar processes today."

~

I mentioned at the beginning of this essay that "trade" of resources across the Channel Islands ecoregion may have enabled the population growth and sociopolitical complexity—and perhaps the ecological resilience—of Chumash peoples. But "trade" is an ecologically fraught proposition. There are very few examples of species other than humans that move "resources" of either nutrients (i.e., food) or energy over significant geographic distances or from one ecosystem or ecoregion to another. Whales, as I discussed in the previous essay, may do this, but on scales much smaller than that of our current globalized economic system.

Tomol routes, both ancient and modern, slice at right angles across the container-ship superhighway that now passes through the Chumash Channel—as if symbolically challenging the very idea of such globalized trade. Digital cryptocurrencies threaten to become the new global shell-bead money, much of it produced by "miners" with electricity-gobbling banks of computers. Neither of these modern trends seems likely to be ecologically sustainable or resilient.

What we have already learned from research in the Chumash Channel Islands Biosphere Reserve, and what more we can learn in the future, will help us better understand what is required to create a sustainable, resilient human-nature relationship—to "live in place," in the phrase of Peter Berg and Raymond Dasmann—before it is too late.

11

The View from Limuw

Sky Snake, the people are too noisy! I want to sleep. I whisper to them,
shhh, children, it is time to be quiet. It is time to rest, it is time to sleep.
But do they listen to Earth Mother? No.
   —Hutash, the Earth Goddess[1]

THE INDIGENOUS INHABITANTS of the island called it limuw, "in the ocean." A prosaic but apt geographic name for the place. The name has a very matter-of-fact, here-and-now implication. It is where Hutash created the first humans.

But the Spanish who explored the Chumash Channel and its islands beginning in the sixteenth century and colonized the area with their string of forts and missions beginning in the late 1700s named it La Isla de la Santa Cruz (The Island of the Holy Cross). The story behind the origin of the Spanish name is that when Sebastián Vizcaíno visited the island in 1602, one of the padres with the expedition lost his staff, which was topped by an iron cross, in the Chumash town of xaxas—located at what is now called Prisoners Harbor. When a ship from the Portolá expedition revisited the island in 1769, the cross was returned—supposedly having been safeguarded for almost two centuries by the Chumash inhabitants. The Spaniards apparently considered this rather miraculous and so gave their name, now anglicized as Santa Cruz Island, to that place in the ocean.

The contrasting names span and exemplify worldviews half a planet apart: from the worldview of the deserts and myths of the Middle East, carried by the Spanish (the monotheistic beliefs of the Judeo-Christian tradition), to the equally ancient Indigenous worldview of a culture that arrived in these islands from Asia more than thirteen thousand years ago.

~

"What's in a name?" Juliet asked (in her soliloquy overheard by Romeo in act 2, scene 2 of Shakespeare's *Romeo and Juliet*). "That which we call a rose by any other name would smell as sweet." We can use her words to open a discussion of a question that anthropologists and linguists have been pondering for more than a century: How deeply are language, perception, and thought entwined in our ultraverbal species? *Would* a rose by any other name smell as sweet?

Some Inuit and Yupik (sometimes called "Eskimo") languages have been said to have fifty or more words for different varieties of snow. Can an English speaker distinguish even half a dozen kinds? This claim is somewhat debatable—perhaps based on the way very different languages name and describe things—but the general observation that Arctic Indigenous peoples are much better at describing snow than we are is beyond debate. On the other hand, the Tupian family of languages (some seventy languages centered in the western Amazon basin) don't distinguish the colors blue and green, calling both *oby*. And the Japanese word *aoi* can name either blue or green. Forests and mountains can look *aoi* to a Japanese speaker, but so can the sea or the sky. Linguists call this phenomenon "colexification"—naming more than one "thing" with one word. But are colexified phenomena actually perceived as different things by the speakers of the languages whose words don't distinguish them? Can speakers of Japanese or Tupi distinguish the multifold colors of green and blue that English names: lime, sage, olive, emerald; sky, navy, cobalt, teal, turquoise, indigo?

Franz Boas, the founding father of American anthropology, cut his ethnographic "teeth" when he went to Baffin Island in 1883 to live for a year among the Inuit. His explanations of how their language was linked with their environment inspired many of his students and other anthropologists, lending support to the hypothesis that language, through both its vocabulary and grammatical structure, shapes its speakers' perceptions and view of the world.[2] Boas's students Edward Sapir and Benjamin Whorf proposed that language can limit—or expand—how we see and think. This was called the principle of "linguistic relativity" because it was seen as having cultural implications similar to those of Einstein's theory of relativity for the physical world.

Roots of this idea reach back to the early nineteenth century, when Wilhelm von Humboldt, the pioneering German linguist, stated that "the diversity of languages is not a diversity of signs and sounds but a diversity of views of the world."[3] Wilhelm was the elder brother of Alexander von Humboldt, the great German explorer-scientist, himself a cultural-relativist thinker, who inspired pretty much all of the founding thinkers of American environmentalism and nature conservation and . . . oh my gosh, we are going down a rabbit hole into a wonderland of fascinating historical connections between worldviews and environmentalism that would take three or four more stories to do justice to, so I have to say no, I'm not going there right now!

∾

On another level below simple perception, at the level of "meaning," words are the vehicles for transporting worldviews. We could ask, paralleling Juliet, "What's in a worldview?" Would the world through every such lens look the same?[4]

According to Matthew Vestuto, a Chumash language scholar, "Our language contains our philosophical outlook from a long, long, long time ago. You can't understand our culture, really, through the lens of English or Spanish . . . you need to know the language."[5] Vestuto and Dr. Kristin Hoppa, the park archaeologist at Channel Islands National Park, have worked together on an initiative to map and revitalize Chumash place names on the islands as a way of advancing our understanding of the cultural significance of the area; they have described it as "navigating cultural landscapes through ethnographic place names."[6]

A similar initiative in Anchorage, Alaska, the Indigenous Place Names Project, has placed signs at thirty locations throughout the city that present and explain the Native place names for those locations.[7] In a recent article in the *Washington Post* titled "We Are Still Here," Melissa Shaginoff, an artist of Athabaskan and Paiute ancestry who is associated with the project, explained her view of its purpose: "It's very much digging deeper than just renaming a place. It's about this sort of reclamation of an incredible, incredibly old and relevant information system that is Indigenous languages. Our language is the most perfectly designed language for that space, for that area, and there's so much knowledge embedded in that."[8] It's a bold claim: that an Indigenous language is culturally evolved and adapted to "fit" a place or an ecosystem, much as a species or subspecies that inhabits a place is adapted to it because of natural selection by ecological and evolutionary forces.

$\approx$

And so we come to the view from limuw, the name for the largest of the California Channel Islands in the language of its most recent non-European inhabitants.[9] It's time to try to dig deeper, like linguistic archaeologists, into language and myth to seek the roots of the Chumash worldview as it was before Spanish contact and colonization.

Worldviews—how we think and feel about our place in nature—shape our individual and collective behavior, and thus the effect we humans have on the ecosystems and the biosphere we inhabit. My research on the history and ecology of the Cascade Head Biosphere Reserve led me to three general conclusions, or "lessons," as I called them in the title of my book about the place. One lesson was that "worldviews matter" because of their influence on our planet and ourselves.[10]

The "worldview" of a culture—a direct translation of the German word *Weltanshaung* that first described this concept—is expressed through its language, through stories invented, retold, and passed down the generations, perhaps with cultural "mutations," and selection and rejection of those new bits and pieces to create a better fit between the human cultural worldview and the real natural world.

Our history turns again to John Peabody Harrington, the anthropologist who recorded most of what we know about Chumash language and culture from his interviews with Chumash elders. In the previous essay, "The Chu-

mash Channel and Its Islands," I sketched Harrington's biography. Archaeologist Brian Fagan highlighted a key influence on Harrington: "While taking a summer class at the University of California, Berkeley, he came under
the influence of Alfred Kroeber, then working on his encyclopedic study of
California Indians. Kroeber's lectures electrified Harrington. Almost immediately, he became obsessed with Indian languages and ethnography."[11] Harrington's academic pedigree lies firmly within the academic family tree of
Franz Boas and his students Edward Sapir and Benjamin Whorf, and he is
clearly aligned with their hypothesis of linguistic relativity.

And then we turn to Thomas C. Blackburn, whose 1975 book, *December's
Child: A Book of Chumash Oral Narratives*, compiled many of the stories, legends, and myths recorded by Harrington and then "abstracted" postulates or
elements of the Chumash worldview from the narratives.[12] I've never seen
an attempt to reconstruct a worldview from ethnographic texts like this before, although perhaps it has been done and I'm ignorant of those efforts. I'm
impressed!

Blackburn defines worldview as "the explicit and implicit beliefs held by
a society about the nature of man, the universe and of man's relations to the
universe and his fellow man"—similar to how I conceive it. He goes on to
say that

> within this general frame of reference two major types of postu-
> lates or basic assumptions can then be distinguished that appar-
> ently provide the members of the society with criteria for choos-
> ing between alternative courses of action. Existential postulates
> are statements about the nature of things, the what and how of
> existence, while normative postulates are concerned with desirable
> states and goals, with what "should be" rather than with what "is."
> Existential and normative postulates are for the most part mutu-
> ally consistent and reinforcing: in fact, one set should logically be
> derivable from the other through careful analysis.[13]

As far as "the nature of things," the Chumash saw themselves as part of
what Blackburn calls a "personalized universe," in which the natural environment, including "plants, animals and birds, celestial bodies, and various

natural forces are all part of the social universe to which man belongs, and their activities and interests may vitally affect the course of human events."[14] Furthermore, within that eco-social universe, the members "share reciprocal rights and responsibilities with respect to one another and comprise the membership of a structured community reinforced by bonds of kinship and mutual dependency." This sounds like John Muir, who frequently talked about plants and animals as people and as his kin, or Aldo Leopold writing about the "biotic community."

Another existential postulate of the Chumash worldview, says Blackburn, is the "assumption of negative-positive integration." Thus, "good and evil are not mutually exclusive categories, nor is the sharp dichotomy between the two, familiar to Western society, of any great relevance to daily life."[15] As a consequence, because positive and negative elements are present in all phenomena, "the universe is considered both dangerous and unpredictable . . . full of dangers that one can only hope to avoid through a judicious combination of knowledge and prudence."[16] This echoes the yin and yang ideas of Chinese Taoism (or Daoism, in the official modern Chinese pinyin romanization system).

And still another postulate about the nature of reality identified in the Chumash worldview concerns space and time; this one leans in a decidedly relativistic, Einsteinian direction. Blackburn writes that "subjective time in the realm of the sacred may be quite different than that experienced by man, or it may be virtually meaningless to any structured reality," and "normal spatial parameters can, with sufficient power, be transcended."[17] Chumash shamans (like those of other Eurasian and American Indigenous cultures) were thought to be able to travel rapidly in time and space to gather intelligence about the forces affecting or likely to affect the here and now.

A final existential postulate is the "assumption of a dynamic equilibrium of oppositions." This one is a relative of the aforementioned "assumption of negative-positive integration" but emphasizes the dynamic effects of that yin-yang integration. According to Blackburn, "For the Chumash, the great forces of nature are in a constant state of balanced opposition to one another, with none possessing an ultimate superiority that might irrevocably alter the proper condition of dynamic equilibrium that should normally prevail in the universe."[18]

The contrast between these existential postulates of the Chumash worldview and the Western worldview is stark. In one culture we see a unified, nondual, material-spiritual world; in the other a dualistic, material-spiritual dichotomy. One pictures a world of immanent gods and powers; the other a lone transcendent God. In one world humans and all creatures are interrelated and equal; in the other, humans are favored and given domination over all others. For one culture, time is relativistic and cyclical; for the other, it is linear and historical. In one worldview, good and evil are seen as inseparable—perhaps creative—partners; in the other worldview it's a war between God and Satan, good and evil.

After laying out the "how is the world constructed," existential elements of the Chumash worldview, Blackburn turns back to the body of stories, legends, and myths collected by Harrington from his Chumash informants for a look at their ethical or normative elements, listing thirteen specific postulates. A sampling of Blackburn's names for these values yields knowledge, prudence, self-constraint, moderation, reciprocity, industriousness, pragmatism, and etiquette. To my modern ear, these sound like the ethical values and norms of a humble, hardworking, communitarian culture—almost the antithesis of our arrogant, acquisitive, individualistic society today.

∾

The first of a chain of what would eventually become twenty-one missions in California was established in 1769 in San Diego by the Franciscan priest Junípero Serra. Five missions in Chumash territory, the first at San Luis Obispo in 1772 and the last at Santa Ynez in 1804, rapidly destroyed the fabric of Chumash culture economically and politically.[19] The missions, each with a church and priests as well as forts and soldiers, were supposed to be economically self-supporting enterprises, and they immediately injected an Old World, European agricultural system into the previously nonagricultural, complex hunter-gatherer society of the Chumash. Chumash were lured to the missions with gifts of cloth, trinkets, metal tools, and cheap glass beads—which quickly devalued their shell-bead money—and were conscripted for labor on the mission farms. Old World crops like wheat, barley, and maize, and fruits like apples, pears, and peaches were introduced, and Old World livestock—sheep, cattle, pigs, and horses—grazed, trampled, and degraded the rich wild ecosystems that had provided the Chumash with food for thousands of years. Mission enterprises produced European-style goods such as tallow, candles, soap, hides, leather, wool, and blankets for trade mainly with other Europeans and Euro-Americans.

Barely over half a century after the first mission had been established in Chumash territory, Chumash society basically collapsed. Was it really that fragile? Since it lasted so long, it is hard to imagine that it was, but under the horrendous assault it faced from Old World diseases, technologies, and worldviews, it is all the more surprising that any elements of Chumash culture survived. "Guns, germs, and steel" is a common formulation of the forces that destroyed so many Native American societies, derived from the title of the best-selling, prize-winning book by Jared Diamond, *Guns, Germs, and Steel: The Fates of Human Societies*, published in 1997. Certainly, guns helped Spanish soldiers enforce the conscription of Chumash people, and their population was certainly dramatically reduced by European diseases to which they had no previous exposure, and so no acquired or evolved immunity. But Erik Davis, author of *The Visionary State: A Journey through California's Spiritual Landscape*, has reformulated Diamond's phrase slightly, but significantly, to describe the triple threat brought by the Spanish to the Chumash as "guns, germs, and God."[20]

∽

At a bend in Highway 154 as it climbs toward San Marcos Pass in the Santa Ynez Mountains above Santa Barbara, I turned sharply up Painted Cave Road, dutifully following the verbal orders from the assertive but gentle female voice guiding me from Google Maps on my iPhone. The road was steep and winding and at the switchbacks gave wonderful views over Santa Barbara and the Chumash Channel. In a narrow, dark canyon there was a tiny pullout where only a few cars could park, and a sign by the road identified the place as the Chumash Painted Cave State Historic Park.[21] A metal cage covered the cave mouth to protect its pictographs from vandals. In the late afternoon shade of the canyon the cave itself was pitch black, and no paintings were visible. At first I resigned myself to a wasted trip, but then I thought of my camera and its flash and tried taking a few flash photos into the cave, aiming randomly. Scrolling through the images, I saw that one of them had caught an edge of some bright designs—I was suddenly seeing the invisible. With more attempts I slowly corrected my aim into the dark and in the photos was able to see what my eyes couldn't see directly and immediately. Vibrant mysterious spoked wheels and swirling suns seemed to be the dominant motif. So what is the worldview represented there? How do those images hint at it? What do they mean?

I thought of a passage from Erik Davis's book *The Visionary State*: "One message of California's rock art seems clear: humanity's most fundamental sacred space is nature itself . . . and the extreme cleavage between architecture and the natural landscape . . . the sharp divide of all our built sacred architecture, may ultimately reflect our longing for the sort of Paleolithic intimacy that once characterized our relationship to the ordinary world."[22]

According to Chumash language scholar Matthew Vestuto, Harrington's informant Fernando Librado (Kitsepawit) is recorded as saying, "I've always believed what the old ones told me when I was a child, that the world is God. When they translated 'Dios' or God to Chumash, they used the word *hesup*, meaning 'this world.' So, our concept of god was a little larger . . . or more grounded."[23]

∾

The dominant Western worldview of human supremacy stems from the biblical creation myth of Genesis 1:27, shared by the Middle Eastern monotheisms (Judaism, Christianity, and Islam), which pictures "man" created in the image of "God," assumed to be the pinnacle of value in the universe and charged with "dominion" over all of nature. This kind of anthropocentric monotheism is not a common worldview; it is an outlier among the diverse spiritual, religious, and philosophical traditions documented by anthropologists. The Western human-supremacist worldview has often been viewed as the deep root cause of our current ecological crisis (for example by Aldo Leopold, Lynn White Jr., Gary Snyder, and Eileen Crist) over a span of more than fifty years.[24]

The humans-dominant dogma of Genesis evolved (culturally) among sparsely populated pastoral tribes wandering the relatively harsh and unproductive ecosystems of the Middle East, who fought for water and grass with other tribes, each believing that its own god was on its side. As the human population exploded with the invention of irrigated crop agriculture in that region, tribes banded into kingdoms and empires, still fighting for scarce natural resources; the humans-dominant worldview still worked as a tool for land and resource competition. Later cultures and empires of the Mediterranean world, the Greeks and Romans, refined this worldview still further as a political instrument. Their offspring cultures colonized most of the planet from Portugal, Spain, Holland, and England, and European technology and alien diseases allowed the anthropocentric human-supremacist worldview to overwhelm many locally adapted worldviews around the globe, especially perhaps in the New World.

The Western worldview can be seen as the cultural equivalent of an alien invasive species—picture prickly pear cactus or rabbits in Australia, for example—taking over previously diverse, locally adapted worldviews because of its competitive ability. In the process of European colonization, much of the delicate cultural evolution of worldviews that had adapted humans to the diverse ecoregions of the biosphere was lost (along with the languages that carried them), just as so much biological evolution has been and is being lost as biological species become extinct. The Western human-supremacist worldview has been highly "fit" at conquering and colonizing the planet. The erstwhile "success" of the anthropocentric worldview now threatens our own species with potential extinction. That worldview has become highly maladaptive and needs to be replaced.

Worldviews are the result of cultural evolution. Parallel in some fundamental ways to biological evolution, the process of cultural evolution depends on cultural variation—cultural "mutations," if you will—that are replicated and selected within a particular socioecological environment. Over time, new combinations can arise; the cultural equivalent of introgressive hybridization (discussed in earlier essays) can even play a role and hasten this process. Cultural evolution, like biological evolution, is creative. Cultural evolution can create new worldviews. And we need that to happen now.

Two sources of raw material for this urgently needed cultural evolution are available. The old worldviews, or fragments of them that managed to survive the invasion of the Western worldview, are one source. Indigenous worldviews are as unique and valuable—and as worthy of conservation and restoration—as endangered biological species. The other source is an important cultural "mutation" that arose within the Western tradition itself: science. Of particular importance in shaping emerging science-based worldviews is the science of evolutionary ecology, which clearly places humans on a tiny branch of the huge evolutionary family, at the same evolutionary "level" at this point in time with all our relatives, from viruses and bacteria to beetles, mushrooms, bats, and ants—and not "higher" or "lower" than any of them.

If biosphere reserves are to be laboratories for improving and healing the human-nature relationship, they must experiment with solutions to not only the short-term, proximate causes of the problem, but also the deeper, fundamental root cause—the now globally dominant, human-supremacist Western worldview.

Could biosphere reserves be laboratories for restoring or developing ecocentric worldviews, and nuclei from which they could spread and expand? My optimistic view is "yes." In my work as an international ecological consultant, I've had the opportunity to work in thirty-five biosphere reserves in seventeen countries around the world. Although each is unique, they all face similar kinds of challenges and provide lessons for all the others. In several of them I have found examples of indigenous, non-Western, ecocentric worldviews and have seen evidence that those can influence human behavior and practices that affect the environment. For example, in the Middle Zambezi Biosphere Reserve in northern Zimbabwe, my research showed that traditional Shona spiritual values have protected areas of "sacred" forests.[25] In the Sierra Nevada de Santa Marta Biosphere Reserve in northern Colombia, several Indigenous ethnic groups have mapped the area from the perspective of their cultural worldview. They aim to raise awareness about traditional sacred sites and how they could guide plans and policies that would benefit "all beings in nature . . . so that balance is maintained on earth, life is preserved and there is a true harmony between: cold and heat, day and night, winter and summer, life and death, man and nature and man with man."[26] This work has also already begun in the Channel Islands Biosphere Reserve. These and many other examples give me hope that biosphere reserves can not only help us understand and address the proximate causes of the ecological crisis we've created, but also address the deep root cause of our problem, our human-supremacist worldview.

~

I've heard about Point Conception since I was in high school, when I first attended a marine science camp in Oregon and read *Between Pacific Tides*, the "bible" of Pacific intertidal ecology by Edward F. Ricketts. After flowing south along the Pacific Coast from Alaska, the cold California Current passes Point Conception, sweeps past the Channel Islands, and goes farther offshore, allowing a countercurrent of warm water from the south to flow up past Southern California into the Southern California Bight. The change in water temperature creates a marine biological divide and influences onshore ecosystems as well. But I never had the chance to go to Point Conception until now. The Nature Conservancy's new Dangermond Preserve[27] lies just north of the Santa Barbara (Chumash) Channel along the Gaviota Coast and turns north at Point Conception toward San Luis Obispo and Big Sur. TNC's stewardship manager at the preserve, Moses Katkowski, took me to see that place I had always wanted to see on a glorious mid-October day.

For the Chumash, Point Conception, called humqaq, was one of the most sacred places in their homeland. Here, according to their mythology, was the jumping-off point for the souls of the dead on their journey to the afterworld across the ocean, šimilaqša. They made their way here to this point and departed to the western heaven. María Solares of Santa Ynez, one of Harrington's main informants, told him that "three days after a person has been buried the soul comes up out of the grave. Between the third and fifth days it wanders around the world, visiting the places it used to frequent in life."[28] On the fifth day after death, it goes to humqaq, which Solares said is a "wild and stormy place. In ancient times no one ever went near humquq," only to a great shrine nearby. Below the cliffs of the point is a pool where the spirit of the dead person bathes and paints itself, said Solares. "Then it sees a light to the westward and goes toward it through the air, and thus reaches the land of šimilaqša." One version of the story[29] says that when the dead souls reached humqaq, ravens pecked out their eyes, and they groped on the ground until they plucked golden-orange poppies, which they put into their empty eye sockets so they could find their way to šimilaqša. When they arrived there, the poppy eyes were replaced with blue-green abalone shell.

When my time comes, I'll be ready for the journey. Just imagine! To see the world anew through eyes of nacreous blue!

~

When I first came across references to the Chumash story "Crossing the Rainbow Bridge," it struck me as a parable for our time, this time of humans on Earth. Here's the story:

The first human people were made by Hutash, the Earth Goddess, on lim-uw, the place now called Santa Cruz Island. Life was kind of hard for them, until they got fire from Hutash's husband, Sky Snake—the Milky Way—who had a tongue like a lightning bolt. One day he decided to give them a gift and he licked the ground with his tongue and started a fire. The people learned to tame this fire and things were a lot easier. They could cook food and keep warm in the winter, and their villages started to get bigger and bigger . . . and life was so much easier they spent more time having more and more babies. But Hutash was getting annoyed. Limuw was getting crowded, and the noise the people made was keeping her awake at night. She decided some of them would have to leave the island and move to the mainland, where no human people were living in those days. To get them over there she made a bridge from a rainbow that went from the top of the highest peak on the island, now called Mount Diablo, to a high peak near what is now called Carpinteria. She sent some people over the Rainbow Bridge to settle on the mainland and told them not to look down while crossing over, because it was a long way down and they might get scared and fall off. But sure enough, some of the people were curious and didn't follow Hutash's instructions, and they looked down and fell off into the channel. Hutash felt bad about that, so she turned them into dolphin people and they didn't die.[30]

Since first hearing this story, I have become aware of differences of opinion among Chumash scholars about its source and authenticity. The fact that it was not recorded by Harrington from his informants makes some of them skeptical, but others attribute it to authentic sources.[31] In any case, this story is such an eloquent parable for our planetary predicament that if the Chumash were not its source, somebody would have to invent it. Greg Sarris, a writer of Miwok and Pomo heritage from Sonoma County, California, has done something like that, channeling the tone and wisdom of his culture in a delightful book of modern fables, *How a Mountain Was Made*.[32]

We can invent new stories, legends, and myths as needed to motivate and guide us. Worldviews are living, evolving, adaptive cultural creations, not dead dogmas fixed in the past.

The Rainbow Bridge legend is an apt metaphor for "Earth Island" now. We humans have bred ourselves up to population of eight billion on Island Earth. Thanks to Sky Snake, we evolved our control of fire into technologies that in a couple of centuries have allowed us to burn up all the energy that was stored in ancient ecosystems over millions of years. Yes, we've now had a happy time of burning and breeding, but there are way too many of us and we have changed the climate of our little island planet. Not to mention the noise!

Where will we go to escape the ecological problems of our own making? Where will Hutash, the Earth Goddess who created us, send us on a new Rainbow Bridge? To colonize Mars, another planet on the "mainland" of our solar system? Or perhaps farther afield, to other planetary systems around other stars in our galactic neighborhood?

I'm not counting on it. On those journeys we are bound to look down . . . and we will then realize that there is no other place for us than this tiny island called Earth anywhere in the universe, so we have to live here, if anywhere, and take care of it.

12

Coyote's Basket

*It is said that Coyote was sitting atop Sonoma Mountain when he de-
cided to create the world and people—but that is part of the big story
of the Mountain and we are getting ahead of ourselves.*
—Greg Sarris, from *How a Mountain Was Made*, 2017[1]

IT WAS HUMMINGBIRD WHO FIRST brought fire to the world. The Bad-
ger People didn't want to share it, so Eagle sent Hummingbird to steal fire
for Everyone. With his bravery, intelligence, and quickness, Hummingbird
succeeded ... but as he was passing it to the People waiting on top of Mount
Umunhum, the flame singed his throat—which is why hummingbirds have
red throats today.

Umunhum. The name of this mountain means "hummingbird" in five
different Ohlone dialects, including the Mutsun dialect spoken by the Indigenous people of the southern Santa Clara Valley and Monterey Bay areas.
The word, when spoken, is said to sound like a hovering hummingbird.[2]

≈

From Los Gatos you drive south, up, up, up, the steep road winding up
canyons, slopes, and ridges to the summit of Mount Umunhum. The huge,
ten-story concrete cube, painted tan, with strange vent hoods emerging here

and there on the walls and a single mirrorlike door of stainless steel on the north side is still standing on the high point of this sacred mountain. It was the base of one of the largest rotating military radar antennae ever built, a spinning dish of metal that looked like it had been assembled from a giant's erector set. It could look hundreds of miles out over the Pacific horizon for approaching Soviet bombers during the Cold War.

The Almaden Air Force Station was part of a West Coast early-warning network that was supposed to protect us from nuclear attack. Established in 1957, the radar system was decommissioned in 1980, when nuclear missiles and satellite early-warning systems made it obsolete. For more than two decades more than one hundred military personnel and their families lived and worked on top of Mount Umunhum. Dozens of buildings housed equipment, and there were living quarters, a commissary, food services, and recreational facilities that included a bowling alley and swimming pool. A sister radar station was built on top of Mount Tamalpais, north of the Golden Gate in Marin County.[3]

The peak is now within the Sierra Azul Preserve, more than nineteen thousand acres of protected lands managed by the Midpeninsula Regional Open Space District.[4] The summit was opened to the public in 2017 after a decade-long effort to remove abandoned military buildings, clean up the site's hazardous materials, build a parking lot and trails, and restore the summit for public access.

Mount Umunhum is the fourth highest peak in the Santa Cruz Mountains, at 3,486 feet. The San Andreas Fault runs close along the west side; the fault bent a bit to the west here, creating the forces that thrust up this peak and its neighbors. Serpentine rock outcrops on the summit, as it does along the fault just west of Mount Tamalpais, and supports a sky-island rock garden ecosystem of plants and animals that can tolerate the toxic soil, wind, sun, and dryness.

Other prominent peaks around San Francisco Bay are visible on a clear day from here: Mount Hamilton to the east; Mount Diablo to the north; and Mount Tamalpais to the northwest. Each of these mountains was considered sacred to Native peoples in the Bay Area, places "where the human spirit interacts with the universe."[5] In his book *Before California*, archaeologist Brian Fagan wrote: "The ancient Californian worldview combined the physical with the mythical. . . . Each human group had its own vision of the world, which almost invariably began atop the highest peak in their territory. . . . Here the Creator and other powerful gods lived, and here the world was created."[6] In designing trails and interpretive facilities at the summit, the Open Space District worked with the Amah Mutsun Tribal Band of Ohlone to create a circular ceremonial space as a way of acknowledging its significance to their culture.[7]

There was some debate about demolishing and removing "the cube," as the giant radar's base building was called. The Open Space District wanted it removed, but apparently it had some local fans; Santa Clara County officials designated it a historic structure, preventing its demolition. It will now sit here on this sacred mountain for millennia, a tombstone of the Cold War era and landmark of the Anthropocene. It's a perfect reminder, a metaphor perhaps, for the different worldviews of the Ohlone and other Bay Area peoples and our own; a reminder of how far we are from a healthy, sustainable relationship with the planet. The massive concrete cube is truly otherworldly and surreal sitting on the sacred summit of Hummingbird Mountain. A monument to the evolution of a species gone dangerously off track on a dangerously maladaptive, dead-end road. A monument to human tribalism run amok, to fear and competition between human tribes living even on different continents, whose scientists stole the nuclear fire of the sun and brought it to Earth.

∼

More than three hundred thousand people lived in what is now called California when the first Europeans passed or stopped along its coast beginning almost five hundred years ago. These Native peoples had been here for more than thirteen thousand years and spoke an estimated sixty to eighty different languages.[8] Their traditional ecological knowledge and sophisticated environmental management techniques supported the densest populations of Native Americans at the time of first contact with Europeans even without true agriculture. "They survived because they lived in edible landscapes where many different foods were there for the taking," a cornucopia resulting from California's geographic and ecological diversity, according to Brian Fagan. "California . . . has always been a palimpsest of edible land-scapes . . . a kaleidoscope of potential diet."[9] The San Francisco Bay bioregion itself supported a remarkable diversity of Native cultures—Ohlone, Miwok, Pomo, and others—for thousands of years before the arrival of Europeans. The cultural diversity was intimately linked with the region's rich biological diversity.[10]

The archaeological record shows that around 2500 BCE, many of these diverse California Native cultures suddenly "altered course quite inde-pendently of one another in a subtle paroxysm of economic, political, and social changes."[11] This cultural realignment remained relatively stable for the next four thousand years, until European contact. What happened? These cultures took up serious acorn processing; their food economy changed; they stopped moving as widely across the landscape and settled in more per-manent villages; and their economic and political relations with neighboring groups changed.

Okay, but why? The archaeological record again suggests an answer: pop-ulation growth. "What happens, however, if the number of people living off these edible landscapes rises slowly but surely, until they begin to exceed the carrying capacity of their homelands?"[12] They begin to eat less-favored foods, like acorns, Fagan argues in *Before California*. Because of their tannin content, acorns required a time-consuming process to make them edible. Most precontact California peoples must have eaten acorns occasionally, but they were less favored than other wild plant foods like seeds and tubers be-cause they took so much more work to process.

Fifteen species of oaks are found in California, with at least several spe-cies in most places. Oaks have a seed production strategy called "masting," in which they produce an abundant crop of acorns only every two or three years. This is thought to be an evolutionary strategy for limiting the pop-ulations of acorn-consuming species. But some of those, like acorn wood-peckers, scrub jays, and humans, figured out how to store acorns. California Indians stored acorns for up to two years in large storage baskets inside their dwellings or in woven granaries, giant baskets on stilts or platforms, to keep them off the ground and protect them from moisture and rodents. Families would travel to masting oak groves to harvest acorns for a few weeks each fall and then transport loads of acorns back to villages for storage and processing.

Removing the tannin from acorns to make them edible was the most la-bor-intensive part of the operation. They had to be cracked to remove their shells, winnowed to remove the inner membranes, and then pounded using a mortar and pestle. The crushed acorn flour was sifted and then leached in water, using one of several methods to remove the bitter tannin. The leached acorn meal could then be made into a kind of bread or used as a base in soups and stews. The whole process took lots of time and skill; it was generally women's work. By the time Europeans arrived, acorns provided as much as half the dietary calories of many groups.[13]

Another alternative for feeding more people would have been for these ancient post-population-boom cultures to start farming maize and beans like their neighboring tribes along the Colorado River and in the Desert South-west. These California peoples certainly knew about agriculture, but even though acorn harvesting and processing was a lot of work, it was easier than farming. It also left natural ecosystems more intact, and so better able to pro-vide ecosystem services that agricultural ecosystems could not. The lack of agriculture in most of pre-Columbian California left a long-term legacy of biodiversity and more intact ecosystems there than in many other parts of North America. Agriculture has certainly been the main cause of the loss of biodiversity during the last ten thousand or so years since the often-touted "agricultural revolution," as species-rich natural ecosystems were converted to crop fields and livestock pastures around the world—but not in California.

We have been taught to think of agriculture as a giant leap for human-kind, but it really may have been a desperate last-ditch effort by previously perfectly contented hunter-gatherer cultures to feed their burgeoning popu-lations. Hunter-gatherers may have been perfectly happy until they had too many babies. Anthropological studies of living hunter-gatherers have shown that they spend far less time on subsistence activities than farmers. After all, it's much easier to harvest wild grasses, fruits, and roots and to hunt wild an-imals than to dig up the dirt; plant, tend, and sometimes irrigate crops; and take care of feeding and breeding domestic animals. Even the California In-dians may have been perfectly happy to eat other wild foods besides acorns until they had too many babies.

The hypothesis that seems to emerge from the long-term archaeological record is that population growth drove many Indigenous cultures in California to an ecological economy based on acorns, which in turn led to the social and political situation encountered at the time of European contact. When the Spanish arrived in California they found "a jigsaw [puzzle] of tribelets, a bewildering array of small political and social groups."[14] When the first trained anthropologists like Alfred Kroeber encountered these Native peoples, they didn't really have ways of describing the social order they observed. Kroeber pointed out that "political life in ancient California was so different from that in other parts of North America that one needed an entirely new model."[15] He argued that the term "tribe," used for other American Indian societies, was meaningless in California—tribes were much larger social and political units, he said, and they didn't exist here. He coined the term "tribelet" for the smaller-scale, more local social structure of California Native communities instead.[16]

Tribelets were autonomous, self-governing, independent village communities. They were often extended families or groups of families, people who shared a common history, culture, and language. Each had deep relationships with its local environment. Kroeber estimated that there had been as many as five hundred tribelets in California, with between one hundred and five hundred people in each. More recent estimates suggest there may have been a thousand of these tribelets.[17]

As in the Chumash area, languages reflected this small-scale social and political organization. There were, for example, eight different Ohlone language groups in the Bay Area: Karkin, Chochenyo, Ramaytush, Tamien, Awaswas, Mutsun, Rumsen, and Chalon.[18] The contemporary legacy of this Indigenous cultural diversity is complicated and sometimes contentious. The state of California's Native American Heritage Commission, tasked with documenting the current state of California's tribes, lists eleven "affiliated tribes" in the Ohlone (sometimes called Costanoan) cultural region on the San Francisco Peninsula and east and south of the bay.[19] The commission's "Digital Atlas of California Native Americans" notes that "cultural affiliations are self-reported by Tribes," and access to the online map requires acknowledgment of a disclaimer says, "The geographical information displayed in the Atlas is not for use in determining locations of cultures, boundaries or people for recognition, consultation or any other legal or policy purpose."[20] This reflects the sensitivity of the issues of tribal identity and territory, for which there are good reasons, given the uncertain status of many Native communities in the aftermath of the horrendous history of their colonization, dispersal, and destruction.[21] The eleven self-organized Ohlone groups recognized by the commission include many that have petitioned the Department of the Interior for federal recognition as tribes, which could bring benefits of all kinds—not the least of which, in an economic sense, is the authority to open a casino. Attempts to restore tribal sovereignty have sometimes led to disputes, however; one example is that between the Tamien of the Los Gatos area and the Muwekma of the East Bay.[22]

Kroeber's early ethnographic and linguistic work came at about the same time that botanists like Alice Eastwood (remember Alice?) were scouring Bay Area habitats to document and conserve uniquely adapted species and subspecies of manzanitas and other plants that were quickly disappearing because their habitats were being lost. Linguists and ethnographers like Kroeber, John P. Harrington, and Jaime de Angulo were searching for the last speakers of the Native languages of California to record and document their uniquely adapted cultures and worldviews before it was too late. This effort has been called "salvage" linguistics and ethnography and was spearheaded by Franz Boas, Kroeber's professor and mentor, and another student of Boas, Edward Sapir. Human languages, like whale songs, are not often treated as an aspect of biodiversity, but of course they are: they would not exist without living creatures and their behavioral diversity, so they are by definition part of biological diversity. The efforts of Kroeber, Harrington, and de Angulo, like those of Eastwood, were all efforts to salvage and conserve the rich biodiversity of California.

~

Among the anthropologists engaged in cultural conservation in California, Jaime de Angulo is especially intriguing to me, an enigmatic and colorful countercultural character who eventually became a linguistic anthropologist and left his unique mark on the California scene from San Francisco to Carmel, Big Sur to Berkeley, and far beyond. De Angulo was born in Paris in 1887 to wealthy Spanish parents but fled Europe at age eighteen. He cowboyed a while in western Colorado, went briefly to Honduras, and then arrived in San Francisco on the evening before the great 1906 earthquake. His life story is so improbable and adventurous that it would be challenging to find anything like it.[23] His daughter, Gui de Angulo, wrote a biography of her father titled *The Old Coyote of Big Sur*; Andrew Schelling explored his poetic and philosophical peregrinations in *Tracks along the Left Coast: Jaime de Angulo and Pacific Coast Culture*. De Angulo is the epitome of the countercultural "gold rusher" that California attracted over many decades. I've mentioned others in earlier essays, including Alan Watts and Gary Snyder. California is a rich landscape of ferment and experiment. Andrew Schelling distills de Angulo's life this way:

> He was one of the first to bring into his life what I consider the primary characteristics of Pacific Coast culture, art, and scholarship. I'll list some of these. The encounter with wilderness. The search for primitive mind. A sharp investigation into what language is and how it works. A deep spiritual hunger, lonely, eccentric, keenly unorthodox, alert to Asian and Native California traditions. Anarchist pacifist politics. In more recent years, bioregional writers have gone to his writings, with their emphasis on nature literacy, watershed consciousness, and reinhabitation. Bioregional people also use his writings in their search for initiatory rites and folkloric tales indigenous to their specific regions, and in the empirical search for lifeways that tread lightly on the land.[24]

De Angulo focused his early linguistic work on the Achumawi, or Pit River Indians, in northeastern California. Alfred Kroeber and his academic colleagues at Berkeley recognized de Angulo's talent for languages but are said to have criticized his ethnographic method of "going native"—hanging out and drinking with old men who still spoke their Native languages. *Rolling in Ditches with Shamans*, as the title of a book about him has it.[25] Franz Boas and Edward Sapir, on the other hand, respected de Angulo highly.

Part of the fascination for me is his touchpoints with other places in my life: he was a cowboy in Colorado in 1905, he did genetics research at Stanford University in 1913, and in 1924 and 1925 he was involved in the arts-and-Indians scene in Taos, New Mexico, near where I grew up among the northern Rio Grande Pueblos. In Taos, he hobnobbed with people like D. H. Lawrence, invited Carl Jung to visit and served as his translator, and hung out with the old men of the pueblo, learning their language and listening to their stories.

In 1948 de Angulo was diagnosed with cancer. Living in Berkeley at the time, he somehow found the stamina to record a series of radio broadcasts called *Old Time Stories* on KPFA, Pacifica Radio, in 1949 and 1950 before his death in 1950. Twenty-two of those broadcasts, reedited and produced by his daughter Gui de Angulo in 1991 from Pacifica Radio Archives recordings and labeled "Indian Tales," are available online.[26] His book with that title, *Indian Tales*, published posthumously in 1953, is described as "a fictional synthesis of myths learned from various California Indians."[27] Listening to these recordings, I close my eyes and am sitting around a smoky campfire somewhere in the California hills, listening. His accent, his inflection, his frequent use of Native words, his style of storytelling—it's spellbinding!

≈

"Basketry . . . reached in California a very high state of perfection," wrote Samuel A. Barrett, a UC Berkeley ethnographer, in a 165-page treatise titled "Pomo Indian Basketry," published in 1905. He wrote, "The California Indians taken together had a very great variety of materials, forms, methods of manipulation, and ornamentation of basketry. Among no other California people was there so great a variety in basketry as among the Pomo."[28] Alfred Kroeber was also impressed with the Indigenous basketry of California, especially of the Pomo, about which he published an article in the *American Anthropologist* in 1909. "In the matter of weaves it appears that the Pomo are anomalous in California in practising an unusual variety of technical processes," he wrote.[29]

Pomo baskets were part of a special exhibition I visited at the de Young Museum in Golden Gate Park, *Jules Tavernier and the Elem Pomo*, touring from the Metropolitan Museum of Art in New York.[30] Tavernier (1844–1889) was a French artist who painted landscapes and Native American subjects in the American West, including California and Hawaii, in the 1870s. His richly detailed painting of a Pomo dance in an underground roundhouse at Clear Lake, made in 1878, was the central focus of the exhibition, but it provided a perfect springboard for a discussion of Pomo history and cultural resilience, especially the artistry of their baskets, more than thirty of which were displayed along with Tavernier's paintings.

Oh, the baskets! Just looking at them you can feel the sophistication of the culture that made them. They embodied a long, long dialogue—thousands of years—with the ecosystems of this place. So beautiful, and so sad. I was entranced by this exhibit.

Among many older baskets on display were several made recently by Clint McKay, a noted contemporary basketmaker of the Dry Creek Rancheria Band of Pomo and Wappo Indians in Sonoma County, including several miniature coiled baskets, one decorated with quail topknot feathers. Such very small coiled baskets have been called "gift baskets" and were presented at times of birth, marriage, and death, and used by shamans during rituals of healing and burial.[31] They are often decorated on the outside with bird feathers, the quills of which are woven into the warp, leaving the feathers on the outside of the basket in colorful patterns: red from woodpeckers, yellow from meadowlarks, and black from blackbirds, for example. "Our lives as Pomo people revolve around baskets," Clint McKay said. "Those baskets and those roots that we use, those are the roots that bind me to my ancestors. The most precious gift we can give somebody as a Pomo person, besides ourselves, is a basket."[32]

In a video produced in conjunction with the exhibition, McKay and Sherri Smith-Ferri, a PhD historian and scholar of California Indian basketry who is of Pomo and Coast Miwok ancestry, engage in a deeply thought-provoking discussion of Pomo basketry that probes its links with traditional culture, ecology, spirituality, and worldviews. At one point in the video, Smith-Ferri expresses her opinion that unless we can heal the human-nature relationship on a large scale, "I think we might not be around too much longer." But she explains how basketry is a model or metaphor for the kind of work needed for human-nature healing: "All of the relationships you [as a traditional basketmaker] have with the environment to be able to do that work, [those relationships are] a model for today's world, an older model for today's world that is one I think the world needs."[33] She says she is optimistic because "when I look around, I see a lot of cultural revitalization going on in

Pomo country, and basketry is central to that, just as it's always been central to our lives."

Baskets distill the essence of Pomo and other California Native cultures and "allow us to go beyond the basket into the meaning of the basket, allow us to see the basket not as an item in and of itself only, but as the focal point or gathering place for a cluster of ideas which may derive from some of the most important philosophical perspectives in the experience of a group of people . . . [and] assume the status almost of living things—dream-inspired poetic entities of mind and mythology."[34]

Stories are baskets, and baskets are stories. Baskets weave the deep roots of the worldview of the people together. The warp, the foundation, of the worldview-basket is made of the nature of things—existential postulates about why things are the way they are; the weft weaves in the normative postulates—ethical lessons about how to behave in the world to achieve desirable states and goals.

≈

Tule boats were the Indigenous watercraft of the Central California Coast, its estuaries, and inland wetlands from Bodega Bay to Point Conception, where the unique Chumash sewn-plank tomol canoe appeared for a short span of coast. Tule boats then reappeared around the entire Baja Peninsula and in the Sea of Cortez.[35] Sometimes called tule "balsas," after the Spanish word for "rafts," tule boats are essentially canoe- or kayak-shaped baskets: baskets designed to carry people over water. They are constructed from bundles of tule, *Schoenoplectus acutus*, a giant sedge common in California wetlands. This is the plant after which the tule elk is named; that endemic subspecies of elk once thrived in wetland habitats throughout the state. Tule can grow more than ten feet tall and has stems an inch or so in diameter with air-filled, closed-cell tissue something like flexible styrofoam. By binding bundles of tule together, sometimes around rigid wooden members, builders made boats that looked something like inflatable kayaks.

One of the first pictures of a tule boat to reach European eyes was painted in 1816 by Louis Choris, a Ukrainian artist who accompanied a Russian expedition to the Pacific under the command of Otto von Kotzebue. The ship spent a month in San Francisco Bay; Choris's painting shows two paddlers and a passenger crossing choppy waters in a tiny tule boat.[36]

As with the Chumash tomol, tule boats have served as a focal point in the revitalization of Native culture and pride among the Ohlone, Miwok, Pomo, and neighboring groups in the Bay Area. One striking example was a tule-boat journey to Alcatraz Island taken in 2019 to mark the fiftieth anniversary of the occupation of the island.[37] From November 1969 to June 1971, a group called Indians of All Tribes occupied Alcatraz to protest US government policies that took aboriginal land away from them and aimed to destroy their cultures.[38]

In the Monterey area, Linda Yamane, of Rumsen Ohlone descent, has been making both baskets and tule boats for three decades. She has constructed over thirty of these boats, which is one aspect of her work to educate people about the Ohlone and their ecologically sustainable culture. One of her tule boats is on display at the Monterey Bay Aquarium during the summer season, and another at Santa Clara University's de Saisset Museum.[39] In the East Bay, various Ohlone groups have organized tule boat-building workshops and events, facilitated by the East Bay Regional Park District, which manages Coyote Hills Regional Park. Coyote Hills protects an important archaeological site, a 2,400-year-old Ohlone village and shell mound among wetlands near the east end of Dumbarton Bridge.[40] And in Marin County, basketmaker and tule-boat builder Charles Kennard has led boat-building workshops and constructed models that are on display at various locations.[41]

≈

The Ohlone Way: Indian Life in the San Francisco–Monterey Bay Area, by Malcolm Margolin, published in 1978, found an audience hungry for more information about the Indigenous cultures of the area. It was named by the *San Francisco Chronicle* as one of the hundred most important nonfiction books of the twentieth century. Its author, the founder of Berkeley-based Heyday Books (in 1974), described how he came to write the book: "I saw a need for a book about Indian life in the Bay Area, and I thought there wasn't very much to know about it. I thought these were a kind of simple people who ate acorns and hunted deer and led a simple life . . . sort of like Paleolithic hippies or something." But as he began to research and write the book, he got deeper and deeper into the story, meeting anthropologists, archaeologists, historians, and Ohlone descendants, and began to see how rich and complex Ohlone culture really was—and how different from the society around him.[42] Margolin came to have "a keen, deeply felt desire to know, something bordering on urgency," what our culture could learn from those old Ohlone ways about the meaning and purpose of our lives and how we should live them now.[43]

> The Ohlones were very different from us. They had different values, technologies, and ways of seeing the world. These differences are striking and instructive. Yet there is something that lies beyond differences. For as we stretch and strain to look through the various windows into the past, we do not merely see a bygone people hunting, fishing, painting their bodies, and dancing their dances. If we look long enough, if we dwell on their joy, fear, and reverence, we may in the end catch glimpses of almost forgotten aspects of our own selves.[44]

What was Margolin really trying to say in *The Ohlone Way*? I think it was "We've lost something; they had something we've lost." That's what made it such a popular book, almost a cult book. It resonated. People were feeling they'd lost something. People were seeking what that was, and how to get it back. Margolin helped them look back to a possible source of how to find meaning in the San Francisco Bay bioregion—the Ohlone bioregion.

Gary Snyder was echoing Margolin's thoughts, I think, in *The Practice of the Wild* (1990), when he wrote: "Our immediate business, and our quarrel, is with ourselves. . . . Human beings themselves are at risk—not just on some survival-of-civilization level but more basically on the level of heart and soul. We are in danger of losing our souls. We are ignorant of our own nature and confused about what it means to be a human being."[45] He could have been thinking of the Ohlone, or most other Native American cultures, when he wrote:

> The little nations of the past lived within territories that con-

formed to some set of natural criteria. The culture areas of the major native groups of North America overlapped, as one would expect, almost exactly with broadly defined major bioregions. . . . In the old ways, the flora and fauna and landforms are *part of the culture*. The world of culture and nature, which is actual, is almost a shadow world now, and the insubstantial world of political jurisdictions and rarefied economies is what passes for reality. We live in a backwards time. . . . There are tens of millions of people in North America who were physically born here but who are not actually living here intellectually, imaginatively, or morally.[46]

Snyder cites Alfred Kroeber's 1947 study, which I cited previously, as support for his view of Indigenous bioregionalism. And then he points us toward the future, and a book by Kroeber's daughter, Ursula K. Le Guin, *Always Coming Home*, published in 1985. Snyder calls it "a genuine teaching text . . . a re-imagining of the robust wisdom of our earlier ways . . . a meditation on what it means to be human."[47]

Ursula Kroeber Le Guin's imaginative future-fiction derives from her grounding in the anthropological world of her parents. Her mother, Theodora Kroeber, was also an anthropologist, most known for her book *Ishi in Two Worlds: A Biography of the Last Wild Indian in North America* (1961). In that book, Theodora Kroeber presents the story of Ishi, the last known member of the Yahi people of Northern California, who "startled the Modern World by accidently wandering into it from the Stone Age"[48] in 1911. He was taken in, supported, and studied by her husband and his colleagues in Berkeley.

In the opening sentence of *Always Coming Home*, Ursula Le Guin places us in an imaginative future past, immediately challenging our sense of time: "The people in this book might be going to have lived a long, long time from now in Northern California." Le Guin characterized the book as "a collection of fictional ethnographic material created about a people living in a valley in California in the far future." Her imaginary Kesh people live in a postapocalyptic time, long after global, industrial society has collapsed—although there is no historical knowledge of the exact cause of that apocalypse. We learn about the Kesh from the observations of Pandora, a fictional anthropologist of the future. "The difficulty of translation from a language that doesn't yet exist is considerable," she says, "but there is no need to exaggerate it."[49]

The "Serpentine Codex" of the Kesh people is a text that "provides a compact summary of the structure of society, the year, and the universe, as perceived by the people of the Valley." Everything, living and dead; past, present, and future, exists in two moieties, according to the Codex: The Houses of the Earth, and The Houses of the Sky. Le Guin fleshes out this universe with stories with evocative titles: "The Bright Void of the Wind"; "How to Die in the Valley"; "The Life Story of Flicker of the Serpentine of Telina-na."[50]

She seemed to be imagining the future almost as in a vision from a Native American vision quest—a countercultural, anthropology-inspired future that provides a striking contrast to the global political and technological vision of the also thought-provoking future-fiction novel *The Ministry for the Future*, by Kim Stanley Robinson (2020).

～

One day Old Man Coyote was bored, and so he decided to have some fun and make a basket. A *big* basket, round like an acorn storage basket, only much bigger and rounder. He gathered all the materials he needed—willow shoots, sedge root, bulrush root, redbud bark, and lots of other secret materials he knew about—and started weaving it. He wove his tracks into the pattern to give a hint who'd made it. When it was finished, he put everything People would need, forever, into the basket. And then he put the basket by the trail to see what would happen.

Sure enough, along came some People, and when they saw the big basket they said, "Hey? What's this?" They knew it was a basket, but they had never seen any basket this big before. Then they said, "What good is it? What can we do with it?" When they looked inside and saw that it had everything they needed, they said, "We can live in it!" So they did. All the People moved into that basket: Plant People, Fish People, Bird People, Animal People, and the Two-legged People who chatter so much—everyone!

Well. Old Man Coyote had put everything We the People would need into that basket, but he never imagined that there would someday be so many of us, and some of us would invent needs that Coyote could never imagine we needed! Pretty soon he began to hear lots of fighting and arguing in the basket. And before long some of his strongly woven strands began to tear, and the basket got holes in it, and some of the People who went in together got thrown out through the holes! Just imagine!

Well, again. Old Man Coyote wasn't really surprised. He's not surprised at anything, of course. Being a Trickster, he just wants to try something and see what will happen—which is why he put the big basket by the trail that day when he was bored in the first place. But . . . Coyote was a bit sad anyway, seeing that his gift basket had become the place for a big fight among the People. That's why you sometimes hear him crying and singing to himself at night.

Some people, mostly scientist-types among the two-leggeds, now call Coyote's basket the "biosphere." But it's really just Old Man Coyote's big basket. You can tell by the design of his tracks that he wove into it.[51]

13

Circling the Mountain

Who can leap the world's ties
And sit with me among the white clouds?
— Han Shan, ninth century CE
(translation by Gary Snyder)[1]

BEFORE SETTING OFF TO WALK up and around Mount Tamalpais, we chanted the last line of the Heart Sutra where the two-plank bridge crossed the trickling flow of Redwood Creek in Muir Woods on this summer solstice, in a second year of drought:

Gate, Gate, Paragate, Parasamgate, Bodhi Svaha!

The Heart Sutra, a fundamental teaching of Mahayana and Vajrayana Buddhism, has at its heart the idea that nothing exists separately by itself but is only a node of being in an interconnected, interdependent universe. The phrase "dependent co-arising" is often used to translate this fundamental concept—*paticca samupadda* in Pali, the ancient language of the Buddhist canon. Thich Nhat Hanh, the Vietnamese Zen Buddhist teacher who has done so much to explain the Zen worldview for the West, calls it "interbeing." Robert Aitken, an American Zen teacher, has called it "the harmony of universal symbiosis." The basic idea is that there are no divisions, no dualities, no boundaries; if you look hard enough you will see only connections, relationships.

A small group of us were following the route taken by Gary Snyder, Allen Ginsberg, and Philip Whalen in October 1965 in their circumambulation of Mount Tamalpais, which rises just north of the Golden Gate, the highest point near San Francisco. The walk around Mount Tam was started by Snyder and his Beat-Buddhist friends as a way of re-creating a type of ritual pilgrimage, common in Asia, to give "sacred" meaning to their local mountain and landscape in California. The circumambulation practice took root, and now on every equinox and solstice a dedicated group walks the same route and chants the same sutras and incantations at the designated places they chose. Snyder described that first walk around the mountain in his prose poem "The Circumambulation of Mt. Tamalpais." Whalen gave his version in a shorter poem.[2]

After a thousand-foot climb up onto Dipsea Ridge, we came to the first station of the ten traditional places for stopping and chanting, an old, gnarled live oak growing out of a rock that its roots have split. We chanted the mantra to Chanda Maharoshana, Great Lord of Heat, which is also the last stanza of Snyder's old poem "Spel Against Demons," giving a sense at the beginning of this walk that it was, to Snyder and friends, a kind of purification ritual. "Live Oak Tree-Out-of-Rock" did feel like an appropriate power center—Whalen called these "shrines"—for introducing us to the mountain.

The next station was a ring of boulders where the Dipsea Trail crosses the ridge, "Ocean Overlook." Whalen's poem says they made an "Address to the Ocean"; Snyder's says, "Looking down a canyon to the ocean—not so far." We looked down on a sea of bright fog, and Eric and Johnny blew conchshell trumpets. We knew the ocean was there even if we couldn't see it.

After the tradition of the circumambulation became established, Gary Snyder was asked whether he thought it was important to retain the same stations and the same Hindu and Buddhist chants. He answered, "I see no reason to consider those particular chants as absolute or even necessary. I have advised people to use the idea of 'stations' in their own way—feel what they feel, stop at other points where they feel drawn to it, and use it as a moment of mindfulness."[3]

Okay, pay attention! Be mindful!

thrush songs filling steep woods
trail wet with Doug-fir fog drip
warmth through top of cloud layer
smell of fog-moistened grass
half blue half fog at Tree-Out-of-Rock
ocean invisible under fog at Ocean Overlook
into redwood shade
fat turd-colored slug on the trail
thimbleberries red-ripe
coyote scat

Up through Douglas-fir forest to Pantoll Camp, across the busy road and on up across slopes of golden grasses, trail snaking over serpentine ridges raked by fog, to "Bay Tree Glade," a shadowy grove of bay laurels surrounding a rocky knoll. On to "Serpentine Power Point," past Rock Spring. Lunch at Potrero Meadows, then up past Rifle Camp and along the North Side Trail. Mind melding with legs, legs with landscape, breath and brain endorphin feedback loop of long walking. Almost pure groves of madrone along the trail just before Inspiration Point. From there, Snyder wrote: "Looking down on Lagunitas. The gleam of water storage in the brushy hills. All that smog." And later, from the summit: "All about the bay such smog and sense of heat. May the whole planet not get like this."[4]

We circled the summit below the lookout, taking in views of the bay and the city, and then plunged down steep trails to reach Muir Woods again, shafts of setting sunlight penetrating the cathedral of redwoods, the crowds of the day gone home.

≈

What are the roots of this mountain-circling walk I'd just experienced? Gary Snyder encountered a version of the Asian mountain-circumambulation tradition—called kaihōgyō in Japanese,[5] "circling the mountain"—when studying Zen in Kyoto in the 1950s. Mount Hiei, only slightly taller than

Mount Tamalpais, rises northeast of that city. The temple of Enryaku-ji, the seat of Tendai Buddhism in Japan, was founded on Mount Hiei in 788 CE. Dōgen Zenji, founder of the Soto school of Zen, trained there as a young monk. Throughout Japan a syncretic spiritual practice of mountain walking had developed, widely practiced by *yamabushi*, or "mountain monks," but Mount Hiei became especially famous for what have been called its "marathon monks," who walk up to marathon distances each day for one hundred or more days (and some even one thousand times over the course of seven years!), practicing walking meditation and stopping to offer prayers at shrines and other sacred places.

Snyder had first seen Muir Woods and Mount Tamalpais as a boy when visiting his aunt in the Bay Area. He returned and explored the Tamalpais trails in 1948 during a Labor Day camping trip with his girlfriend from Reed College.[6] After college, hitchhiking to Indiana to start graduate school in anthropology in 1951, he picked up a copy of D. T. Suzuki's *Essays in Zen Buddhism*, first published in 1949. Suzuki's book was the first accessible and comprehensive treatment of Zen in English. Snyder later recalled that through Suzuki's *Essays* he first saw the relationships among Taoism, Buddhism, and Chinese Tang dynasty poetry.

> The convergence that I really found exciting was the Mahayana
> Buddhist wisdom-oriented line as it developed in China and
> assimilated the older Taoist tradition. It was that very precise
> cultural meeting that also coincides with the highest period of
> Chinese poetry—the early and middle Tang Dynasty Zen masters
> and the poets who are their contemporaries and in many cases
> friends—that was fascinating.[7]

After one semester in Indiana, Snyder spent the summer as a fire lookout in the North Cascades of Washington State, where he taught himself to do zazen, and then went to UC Berkeley in the fall of 1952 to study oriental languages, with the idea of both translating Tang poets and studying Zen in Japan. It was there he met Allen Ginsberg, many other poets of the "San Francisco Renaissance," and Jack Kerouac, who would later make "Japhy Ryder," the oh-so-hip Beat-Buddhist-mountaineer, the protagonist of his barely fictionalized novel *The Dharma Bums.* In the spring of 1956, Snyder and Kerouac shared a little cabin above Mill Valley they called "Marin-an" before Gary went to Japan to study Zen in Kyoto, and they hiked together on Mount Tam's trails. Between 1956 and 1968 Gary lived in Japan and traveled occasionally back to California, where he settled permanently in 1968. It was during one of his return visits to California, in 1965, that the first circumambulation of Mount Tamalpais took place. In early 1967 Snyder was back in San Francisco again for the "Gathering of the Tribes for a Human Be-In," held in Golden Gate Park. As a spin-off from that event, Snyder, Ginsberg, and enthusiastic local organizers put out an invitation in a Haight-Ashbury newspaper for a public circumambulation of the mountain. More than seventy people showed up for the walk on February 10, 1967.[8]

Snyder met Alan Watts soon after he arrived in Berkeley in 1952—he apparently sought him out at a talk Watts was giving. Watts, born in 1915 in England, was a key figure in explaining the Zen worldview to an American audience and making it accessible to us today. His biography is complicated and convoluted. Watts became interested in Chinese and Japanese art and culture at a young age and began to study Buddhism seriously in his teens. He published his first book, *The Spirit of Zen*, in 1936 when he was twenty-one, and in the same year he attended the World Congress of Faiths in London, where he met D. T. Suzuki. In 1951 he moved to San Francisco to join the American Academy of Asian Studies, where he taught and served as director until 1957. Always interested in promoting and popularizing Zen and other Asian thought, Watts gave many talks and lectures, and it was at one of those that he met Gary Snyder. In 1953 he began making a weekly broadcast on a local Berkeley radio station, KPFA, as a volunteer and attracted a large and dedicated following; his broadcasts continued until 1962. He was a prolific author, with over two dozen books published during his lifetime, and many more published posthumously. His collection of personal essays, *Cloud Hidden, Whereabouts Unknown: A Mountain Journal*, was published in 1972, a year before his death. The title is taken from a ninth-century Tang poem by Chia Tao, "Searching for the Hermit in Vain," and alludes to his walks and wanderings on Mount Tamalpais from his home at Druid Heights, near Muir Woods:

I asked the boy beneath the pines.
He said, "The Master's gone alone
Herb-picking somewhere on the mount,
Cloud-hidden, whereabouts unknown."[9]

∾

I grew up in the mountains of northern New Mexico, looking across the Rio Grande Valley from Los Alamos to the peaks of the Sangre de Cristo Range. The air was so clear and transparent that I could imagine myself invisible; only the landscape existed. In retrospect, I think it was the landscape and atmosphere that led me to some kind of innate resonance with the Zen view, a view that reaches beyond words or concepts.

My old paperback copy of *The Way of Zen* by Alan Watts, copyright 1957, lists a price of $1.95 on the lower righthand cover. I was in high school when I bought the book in the late 1960s, probably at a hippie bookshop some of my friends and I used to frequent on Canyon Road in Santa Fe. I can't remember why I might have been inspired to buy it, but maybe it was because I had been introduced to Japanese haiku poetry by my high school English teacher. I really liked the distilled, imagist aesthetic of haiku, and I knew that somehow haiku and Zen were related.

Zen is a worldview as starkly different from the Western worldview as can be imagined. The first sentences of *The Way of Zen* describe it as "a way and a view of life which does not belong to any of the formal categories of modern Western thought. It is not religion or philosophy; it is not a psychology or a type of science."[10] If we can use terms from the English language to describe Zen, we might call it a "psychological practice" or "observational practice." The term "philosophy" isn't quite right. Most people's connotation of "religion" is of an organized community of believers in some worldview—but if we took religion to mean what its etymological roots suggest, a "binding back," Zen could be that: a "binding back" to our true nature, our spontaneous, wild mind. Zen practice, evolved through many millennia in Asia, is designed to help its practitioners find that original, untamed mind.

Words are the vehicles for transporting worldviews. The worldview of a culture—a direct translation of the German word *Weltanshaung* that first described this concept—is expressed through its language. Watts emphasized this relationship to language in *The Way of Zen*, saying that language can reflect "differences in the basic premises of thought and in the very methods of thinking."[11] English, Watts wrote, is grammatically structured such that "things," named by nouns, create "actions," which are named by verbs. But reality isn't all, or always, that simple. Consider, he says, what happens to your "fist" when you "open" your hand. The supposed thing disappears before your very eyes because it was really an action in the first place.

Watts says that "a great number of Chinese words do duty for both nouns and verbs—so that one who thinks in Chinese has little difficulty in seeing that objects are also events, that our world is a collection of processes rather than entities."[12] I'd read the same thing long ago about the Navajo language. This echoes the Buddhist idea of *paticca samupadda*, "dependent co-arising" or "interbeing." Other scholars of Taoism, and Chinese Ch'an and Japanese Zen Buddhism, have argued that the Chinese language enables ways of thinking and perception that facilitate this worldview. "The Chinese written language has a slight advantage over our own, and is perhaps symptomatic of a different way of thinking," wrote Watts.[13]

Worldviews—how we think and feel about our place in nature—shape our individual and collective behavior, and thus the effect we have on ecosystems. A root cause of the ecological crisis is the human-supremacist worldview that now underlies and impels the current global economic and geopolitical system. A sustainable and resilient long-term future for the human species will require more than technological and managerial changes. To motivate the needed economic and geopolitical transformation and heal the human-nature relationship, we need a new, ecocentric worldview to replace the currently dominant anthropocentric worldview.

Zen is an example of such an ecocentric worldview, the kind of worldview humans need to save our species from its self-destructive hubris and turn us from the trajectory toward extinction that we are currently on. The San Francisco Bay Area is where Zen first took root in America. Like a sharp samurai sword cutting into Western anthropocentrism, Zen helped motivate the Californian cultural and environmental rebellion here, from the Beats of the 1950s to the beginnings of the environmental movement of the 1970s and beyond.

~

California has long pulled, and provided a home for, people seeking a new life. The kelp-highway voyagers from Asia coming south along the North American coast at the end of the last Ice Age. Spanish soldiers and priests probing up from Mexico seeking land and converts to the Christianity of the Old World. American gold rushers hoping for a quick fortune, looking for an escape from the constrictions of the pre–Civil War East. Okies fleeing the Depression and Dust Bowl, sun seekers, orange growers, oilmen, film stars. Beatniks, poets, visionaries. Environmentalists. All had visions of a new way of thinking and living: freer, happier, more in tune with nature. "Go West, young man!" is a phrase attributed to Horace Greeley, New York newspaper publisher and editor, in 1865, just at the end of the Civil War. Lots of social evolution and change has been cooking in California for decades, centuries, millennia. And so, no wonder the San Francisco Bay would provide a landing point, welcoming committee, and springboard for Zen in America.

And also no wonder that this non-Western worldview would appeal to some of the seekers of cultural meaning in the decade or so following World War II. In the preface to *The Way of Zen*, Watts wrote: "We are in a state of considerable confusion.... The various wisdoms of the West, religious, philosophical, and scientific, do not offer much guidance to the art of living in such a universe, and we find the prospects of making our way in so trackless an ocean of relativity rather frightening."[14] Watts was sympathetic to those seekers, some called the Beats, and was one of them in many ways. The Beats and their successors the "hippies" have been labeled "countercultural," but Californian woodblock artist and historian Tom Killion, in an interview with the Mill Valley Historical Society, says that description isn't quite right.[15] Like generations of seekers of new lives and opportunities in California, they were actually solidly in the main current of rebellion against the constraints of the old European- and Atlantic-oriented East Coast culture of the United States—and all of Western culture, really. From the gold rushers to the Depression and Dust Bowl refugees of John Steinbeck's novels, from the "dharma bums" to the "ecotopians," California has always been its own kind of cutting-edge culture.

∾

Matthew Davis, who took part in the first organized circumambulation of Mount Tam in 1967 and was an organizer and leader of the regular repetitions of this ritual walk on the solstices and equinoxes that began in the mid-1970s, compiled his thoughts and memories in the 2006 book *Opening the Mountain*. "Walking around the mountain," he wrote, "I feel I am in contact, and in sacred relationship with this ground, this valley, the mountain, the sky above and the bay and ocean around. Never mind the Internet, I am receiving all manner of information from the wind and clouds, the rains and streams, the birds and sky."[16] Davis developed a logo for announcements about the walk and described it as

> a shaded mountain silhouette with a dotted line looping around it, one end pointed to show the clockwise direction. This circular line came back to the beginning of the oval but not quite aligned with it, arriving on a higher level. The idea was that people making the walk come back to the same place they started, and they have been changed by the day's experience so that the same place seems different. It is different in who-knows-how-many subtle ways besides the obvious change of sunlight angle.[17]

After eleven hours of walking, a bit sunburned and knees aching, we came back through the deep redwood twilight of Muir Woods to the two-plank bridge where we'd started in the morning. Once again, we chanted the last lines of the Heart Sutra.

Gate, Gate, Paragate, Parasamgate, Bodhi Svaha!

"Gone, gone, gone beyond, gone beyond beyond, to awakening!"

14
Wild Mind

It is in vain to dream of a wildness distant from ourselves. There is none such.

— Henry David Thoreau, Journal, August 30, 1856[1]

WHEN WE STARTED THE circumambulation of Mount Tamalpais in Muir Woods, an old sanctuary of American nature conservation named for and dedicated to John Muir, I didn't realize how fitting that was. In retrospect I think Muir's spirit must walk and chant with every group that follows this practice.

For Muir, mountains had a special, spiritual power. "Muir's journals reveal an intense, ecstatic joy in his mountain rambles," says Raymond Barnett in his 2016 book, *Earth Wisdom*.[2] Barnett notes that mountains have been considered "sources of health and vitality for several millennia in China, cosmic pillars where the qi energy of earth contacts that of heaven, thus creating nodes of power. Being on a mountain permits you to connect with this qi energy."[3] Muir must have felt something similar. In his book *My First Summer in the Sierra*, describing the summer of 1869, Muir wrote, essentially as from his journal:

> September 7. Left camp at daybreak and made direct for Cathedral Peak ... up the heavily timbered slope forming the south bound-

ary of the upper Tuolumne basin, along the east side of Cathedral Peak, and up to its topmost spire, which I reached at noon.

"No feature, however," Muir continued,

> of all the noble landscape as seen from here seems more wonderful than the Cathedral itself, a temple displaying Nature's best masonry and sermons in stones. How often I have gazed at it from the tops of hills and ridges, and through openings in the forests on my many short excursions, devoutly wondering, admiring, longing! This I may say is the first time I have been at church in California, led here at last, every door graciously opened for the poor lonely worshiper. In our best times everything turns into religion, all the world seems a church and the mountains altars."[4]

Muir was raised in a very strict and conservative Christian family. His father, Daniel, held the harsh view of Scottish Calvinism that "everyone is born corrupt and sinful, predestined for hell, with no hope of redemption except that given by God to a select, undeserving few," according to Muir biographer Donald Worster.[5] Daniel Muir took out his dark view of God's will on his son, with overwork and frequent beatings on their Wisconsin homestead. It isn't hard to understand young John's delight at finally escaping from that worldview to the free, nonjudging, beautiful world of the mountains of California, which he called the "Range of Light." Muir's journals, articles, books, and letters are full of statements that leave no doubt about his abandonment of the Christian worldview in which he was raised.

One pillar of Muir's evolving worldview was that "all creatures on the planet are related in kinship, with humans but one part of the whole."[6] The evening of September 7, 1859, after his ascent of Cathedral Peak, Muir wrote that he

> camped beside a little pool and a group of crinkled dwarf pines; and as I sit by the fire trying to write notes the shallow pool seems fathomless with the infinite starry heavens in it, while the onlooking rocks and trees, tiny shrubs and daisies and sedges, brought forward in the fire-glow, seem full of thought as if about to speak

aloud and tell all their wild stories. A marvelously impressive
meeting in which every one has something worth while to tell.[7]

He placed himself squarely and tenderly into the present moment and made
himself part of a multispecies biotic community of equals.

From his solo climb of Mount Ritter to riding out a windstorm at the
top of a tree to see what it felt like, or surviving a blizzard on top of Mount
Shasta by alternately toasting one side of his body and the other over a volca-
nic steam vent, Muir's adventures in the wilderness sometimes seem reckless
and his survival almost superhuman. Out of it all he found a joyous participation in life, meaning, and the wholeness of nature.

There is a striking parallel in Muir's self-chosen encounters with the
forces of nature and the vision quests so common across Native American
cultures, and even with more widespread traditional shamanic practices that
spanned Asia and Native America. The worldview Muir eventually developed was much more congruent with those of the former Native American
inhabitants of California than with the worldview of the Euro-American
society in which he lived. For Native Americans, and for Muir, landscapes
are spiritual and sacred, and nonhuman species are kin. Perhaps because he
had slept with the spirits of the Indigenous inhabitants of the place so many
nights alone in the wilderness they experienced, Muir channeled their vision
and ecocentric worldview. Anyone who could accuse Muir of not understanding or honoring America's Indigenous peoples hasn't understood his
philosophy at its depth.[8]

∼

The American nature conservation movement is built on a long history of
positing and recognizing a spiritual dimension to nature. Henry David Thoreau, his mentor Ralph Waldo Emerson, John Muir, John Burroughs, Gary
Snyder, and many, many others in between were adamant in their arguments
for the spiritual value and meaning of "wildness," "wilderness," "Nature," and
the "sublime." Their rebellion against a sterile, desacralized view of nature
was inspired by the great German explorer and geographer Alexander von
Humboldt (1769–1859).

Humboldt was the most popular, widely read scientist of his day, and we are finally coming to realize what a profound influence he had on science, nature conservation, and art. He was an inspiration to natural scientists like Charles Darwin, Alfred Russel Wallace, Asa Gray, and Louis Agassiz; ethnographers and anthropologists like Prince Maximilian of Wied-Neuwied and Franz Boas; nature writers like Ralph Waldo Emerson, Henry David Thoreau, John Muir, and John Burroughs; and artists like George Catlin and the many landscape painters of the Hudson River School such as Thomas Cole, Frederic Edwin Church, Thomas Moran, and Edward Bierstadt.[9]

Besides being an explorer and scientist, Humboldt was a moral and political activist. He wanted to make the world a better place. His thought touched on philosophical and ethical questions about the relationship of ecology and society, and his followers continued seeking answers to those questions. Over more than a century, Humboldt's acolytes were slowly piecing together a new, ecological worldview that combined science, aesthetics, philosophy, and spirituality. It was a slow but coherent cultural rebellion against the Western, Manifest Destiny, anthropocentric worldview of the America of their times. They were rediscovering or re-creating—from scientific, ancient, and Asian sources—the aboriginal worldviews of America, in which nature was spiritual and sacred. Muir was part of that rebellion, not a lone pioneer.

Humboldt's unified-field "cosmos" worldview had in turn been influenced by Johann Wolfgang von Goethe (1749–1832), the great German Romantic poet, novelist, playwright, and scientist. Humboldt first met Goethe in 1794, and for the next several years they engaged in periodic bouts of intense scientific and philosophical experimentation and debate.[10] Goethe's philosophy had in turn been influenced by that of seventeenth-century Dutch (but Portuguese-Jewish) philosopher Baruch Spinoza (1632–1677).[11] Spinoza has also been credited as a source of "deep ecology"[12] through his influence on Norwegian philosopher Arne Naess, whose 1973 article "The Shallow and the Deep, Long-Range Ecology Movement" first described the deep-ecology philosophy. Through that philosophical phylogeny, via Spinoza and Humboldt, deep ecology (à la Naess) circles back to the roots of American nature conservation.

My working definition of deep ecology is that it is a worldview (a phi-

losophy of existential and normative postulates) derived from the proper-
ties of ecological systems. According to Naess, deep ecology is defined by
"rejection of the man-in-environment image in favour of the relational, to-
tal-field image." He also said that deep ecology views "organisms as knots
in the biospherical net or field of intrinsic relations."[13] A "biospherical net"
sounds suspiciously like the Buddhist metaphor of the jeweled Net of In-
dra,[14] a depiction of a world of "dependent co-arising" or "interbeing," which
I mentioned in the previous essay, "Circling the Mountain." So maybe the relations among these ideas also circle eastward around the mountains to Asia.

~

Let's bring Jaime de Angulo (discussed in a previous essay), that "old
coyote" as his daughter called him, back into the conversation for a minute.
He had a lot to say about the ideas we're considering here. In 1920, Alfred
Kroeber hired de Angulo to teach two summer courses at Berkeley (Jaime
had met Kroeber through his then girlfriend, and later his wife, Lucy S. Free-
land, who was a graduate student of Kroeber's). One course was called "The
Mental Functions in Primitive Culture." Most social scientists at the time,
including anthropologists, held a Eurocentric view of the progressive evolution of culture, although some, like Kroeber and other students of Franz
Boas, were beginning to bring a broader view of cultural relativism to their
discipline. But de Angulo was the vanguard of an even deeper relativism. He
thought that "modern, civilized humans have advanced in certain rational
and technological ways, but have discarded a range of skills and intelligence
conserved by so-called primitive people."[15] Andrew Schelling quotes from de
Angulo's book on psychology and religion among the Achumawi, the California culture he studied perhaps most deeply, on this topic. Although they
rapidly acquired the outward trappings of Euro-American civilization, de
Angulo wrote:

> Why expect that the cut of their trousers would make them change
> their mentality? It remains that of Paleolithic man. The experience
> of the Achumawis simply proves that Paleolithic man would have
> learned to make use of our material civilization in a few years: this

demands only the use of reason. . . . But reason does not constitute all thought, it is only one compartment (of which we civilized people have been forced to exaggerate the importance), and in all the rest of the psychic domain primitive thought is oriented differently from ours. Could it be that we have simply lost something without suspecting it?[16]

Schelling notes that de Angulo was far ahead of his time in recognizing that "tribal people hold a full ecosystem of the mind, it is the rationalist Modern world that has shrunk."[17]

~

My studies in graduate school focused on ecological and behavioral genetics and evolution, and I have always had a strong interest in how those topics relate to my own species. So perhaps it's no surprise that I agree with de Angulo. My hypothesis is that our unique, hypercultural minds are the product of at least a few million years of evolution. The agricultural revolution, when humans began to domesticate wild species rather than just hunt-and-gather them to eat, began in various parts of the world some ten or twelve thousand years ago—an eyeblink in evolutionary time. The period before the invention of agriculture has been named the Paleolithic, and the one after it the Neolithic—the "Old Stone Age" and the "New Stone Age." Evolution certainly hasn't had time to change the deep genetic structure of our minds since agriculture was invented, but cultural evolution, running at a much faster pace, has shaped our technology, language, culture, and worldviews. Our mind structure is certain to be fundamentally the same as that of our Paleolithic ancestors, genetically shaped by our evolution over a period a hundred times as long as the mere ten millennia of the Neolithic. Our original mind—the innate way we perceive, feel, understand, and interpret our personal experience of nature—must be Paleolithic. We may have put on trousers, as de Angulo describes the superficial adoption of modern dress by the Achumawi, and we may eat crops and animals produced in agricultural ecosystems, text on cell phones, drive electric cars, and travel into space, but our minds are still as they have been for perhaps a few hundred thousand years, at least.

Claude Lévi-Strauss (1908–2009), the French ethnologist and anthropologist, explained his view of the situation in his 1962 book, *La pensée sauvage*. The title has been translated to English as *The Savage Mind*, but that rendering is controversial because, as Lévi-Strauss explained, the book was about "neither the mind of savages nor that of primitive or archaic humanity, but rather mind in its untamed state as distinct from mind cultivated or domesticated." A new translation with the title *Wild Thought* seems to better reflect the intent of the original French title.[18] In the first chapter of the book, titled "The Science of the Concrete," Lévi-Strauss emphasizes the extensive and precise ecological knowledge of traditional cultures around the world.

∼

Alan Watts pointed out that Zen—the Japanese pronunciation of the Chinese ideograph "Ch'an"—is firmly rooted in Chinese Taoism, as much as or more than in Buddhism (although the deeper roots of those two ancient Asian traditions probably reach the same Paleolithic bedrock). "The West has no recognized institution corresponding to Taoism," Watts says.[19] "Taoism concerns itself... with the understanding of life directly, instead of in the abstract, linear terms of representational thinking."[20] This way of thinking, Watts argues, differs "startlingly from our own ... for that very reason [it is] of special value to us in attaining a critical perspective upon our own ideas."[21]

David Hinton, a translator of classical Chinese poetry, argues in his book *China Root: Taoism, Ch'an, and Original Zen* that Ch'an began during the Tang dynasty of ninth-century China as an intellectual and cultural rebellion. Ch'an practice was seeking to recapture the feeling and experience of immediacy and wholeness of the Paleolithic human mind and to overcome the alienation of humans from the world that resulted from the agricultural revolution and its modus operandi of humans taking control of wild nature.

> Humankind's primal wholeness began to fade during the Paleolithic.... But that incipient separation eventually became a rupture in agrarian Neolithic culture, when people began settling into villages (permanent enclaves separate from the landscape) and began controlling "nature" in the form of domesticated plants and animals: a detached instrumentalist relationship to the world.[22]

If our Paleolithic, nondual, ecocentric, original mind is indeed deeply embedded and innate because it evolved into us as our foundation for relating to experience, it must somehow still be accessible to us. Zen (Ch'an) practitioners may have found a method to uncover it from under the debris of millennia of Neolithic cultural and linguistic constructions—the words and concepts under which it is buried. So, how do we uncover and discover our original wild minds? Zen, in Japan at least, developed two major practice pathways for that psychological archaeology, both aiming for the same thing. Both were brought ashore in the United States, but the Soto Zen tradition, emphasizing zazen, or "just sitting," landed most strongly in the San Francisco Bay Area through the work of Alan Watts and Shunryu Suzuki. The other school, Rinzai Zen, emphasized the rigorous practice of studying and "solving" koan—a kind of mental puzzle or riddle without an answer, meant to jolt the mind out of its ruts.

"What happens if we dismantle all of our human conceptual constructions, all of the explanations and assumptions that structure consciousness and orient us and define us as centers of identity?" asks David Hinton. "This dismantling is the adventure of Ch'an [Zen in Japanese] Buddhism, and its primary revelation is the larger self or 'original nature' that remains after the deconstruction."[23] Shunryu Suzuki wrote in the prologue to his 1970 book, Zen Mind, Beginner's Mind, that

> for Zen students the most important thing is not to be dualistic. Our "original mind" includes everything within itself. It is always rich and sufficient within itself. You should not lose your self-sufficient state of mind. This does not mean a closed mind, but actually an empty mind and a ready mind. If your mind is empty, it is always ready for anything; it is open to everything. In the beginner's mind there are many possibilities; in the expert's mind there are few.[24]

The bottom line would be that language and its constructs can get in the way of nondual, holistic perception and experience, of what Suzuki Roshi called "beginner's mind."

Both Watts and Hinton have emphasized that however unfamiliar this observational and conceptual practice may be to Westerners, it is universal, natural, and accessible. Both point out how congruent Zen is with some aspects of modern science and culture. It "represents such a remarkably contemporary worldview," wrote Hinton. "It is secular, and yet deeply spiritual. It is thoroughly empirical and basically accords with modern scientific understanding . . . and it is what we now call 'deep ecology,' meaning it weaves human consciousness into the 'natural world' at the most fundamental level. In fact, the West's separation of 'human' from 'nature' is entirely foreign to it."[25]

~

So, what should we do if we accept the argument that "deep ecology" is a new spiritual-scientific path, a new worldview to re-place humans in nature? Snyder, in his poem "The Revolution in the Revolution in the Revolution,"[26] proposes that if "civilization is the exploiter"—"civilization" meaning the contemporary world of post-agricultural-revolution population growth and concomitant global economic systems and governance structures—then "nature" is the exploited "class," and the leadership of the "party" (which will lead the way to a solution) goes to "the poets." But then he pushes us deeper inside our minds, our thinking, our worldviews, proposing that

> if the abstract rational intellect
> is the exploiter, the masses is the unconscious
> and the party
> is the yogins

And in that case, he says, the power to change things comes from "the seed syllables of mantras."

That's a complicated thought, Gary . . . it needs an exegesis, perhaps? How about this: in order to fully reinhabit the world of nature we live in and completely depend on for our lives and well-being, we have to change our *minds*. The "revolution" that will change the human-nature relationship is internal. That's because mind is nature, nature is mind, and all are originally, intrinsically, wild.

~

Raymond Barnett found so many parallels with Taoist thought in Muir's writings that he called Muir an "accidental Taoist." Both Taoism and Muir's writings present an "alternative worldview," Barnett says, "an earth-centered, immanent philosophy focused on the here and now of our experiences in life."[27] Sounds like the "beginner's mind" of Zen, or the "wild thought" of Lévi-Strauss, doesn't it?

Based on the evidence from his writings, I think it is safe to posit that Muir essentially arrived at something very akin to a Zen worldview through his own personal explorations of, and experiences in, nature. He found his wild mind through his own experimental brand of observation that was scientific and rational but also emotional, aesthetic, and spiritual at the same time. "I only went out for a walk, and finally concluded to stay out till sundown, for going out, I found, was really going in," Muir wrote in his journal.[28]

The stage was set for him to do so because of his historical time and place: a wild continent only relatively recently colonized by Europeans and their anthropocentric worldview and destructive technologies; a glimpse of nature much less converted and trammeled than anything in the Old World at the time; traditional cultures that still lived in relative harmony with the nonhuman world; and an era of fermentation of new ideas, from science to information about unfamiliar but ancient cultures from Asia. Muir's unique personality and personal history must have played some role also: he was a psychological and emotional explorer with a scientific mind who placed himself as deeply as he could into solitude and wilderness. I think his personal experiences led him to independently rediscover some of the ancient wisdom of the Zen worldview—which is not so surprising, if Zen mind really is "beginner's mind." The hypothesis would be that if humans experience nature deeply and immediately enough, they will eventually uncover their undomesticated mind.

~

Tang dynasty poet Li Po (701–762 CE) wrote that "to refresh our sorrow-laden souls . . . we lay down on the innocent mountain, the earth for pillow, the stars for cover."[29] In 1890, exploring a side fjord of Glacier Bay alone in a canoe, Muir was nearly trapped by ice, and in the middle of a night of dangerous paddling he finally reached a safe spot on the shore above the high tide line. He wrote of that night in his journal:

> My bed was two boulders, and as I lay wedged and bent on their up-bulging sides, beguiling the hard, cold time in gazing into the starry sky and across the sparkling bay, magnificent upright bars of light in bright prismatic colors suddenly appeared, marching swift-ly in close succession along the northern horizon. . . . How long these glad, eager soldiers of light held on their way I cannot tell; for sense of time was charmed out of mind and the blessed night circled away in measureless rejoicing enthusiasm.[30]

Talk about rigorous effort to obtain what Zen practitioners call satori, or "awakening." Muir had paddled through his fear and found himself at home in the Universe.

15

Reinhabiting Our Place
on the Planet

Reinhabitation means learning to live-in-place in an area that has
been disrupted and injured through past exploitation. Simply stated it
involves becoming fully alive in and with a place. It involves applying
for membership in a biotic community and ceasing to be its exploiter.
    —Peter Berg and Raymond Dasmann, "Reinhabiting
    California," 1977[1]

IN LOOKING TOWARD THE FUTURE, I look back to two ideas whose individual and institutional history has been interwoven with the UNESCO biosphere reserve program since its creation, "bioregionalism" and "ecodevel-
opment." It was Ray Dasmann, native son of San Francisco, who was largely
responsible for embedding these concepts into the Man and the Biosphere
Programme. I've traced his influence on the program in the essay "Black Helicopters over Mount Tamalpais." But Dasmann was in "trialogue" during the
1970s with two other influential Californians about these concepts, Peter
Berg and Gary Snyder. Snyder has been part of several earlier essays, but Berg
has not.

Peter S. Berg (1937–2011) settled in San Francisco in 1964 and soon co-
founded the Diggers,[2] a group of radical community activists and street the-

ater performers in the Haight-Ashbury neighborhood; his writings helped prime the city for the 1967 "Summer of Love." Berg became increasingly interested in environmental issues and attended the 1972 United Nations Conference on the Human Environment in Stockholm. "More and more it occurred to me that the most important question to consider was the position of human beings in natural systems," Berg said.[3] He developed and promoted the concept of bioregionalism, speaking and writing about it for the rest of his life, and his passionate interest in living sustainably in place naturally led to his conversations with Dasmann and Snyder. Snyder's anthropological perspective, Dasmann's biogeographic orientation, and Berg's countercultural social views fused in the trialogue among them.

Berg and Dasmann wrote what many people consider to be the defining manifesto of bioregionalism, "Reinhabiting California," an essay published in *The Ecologist* in 1977. (Dasmann had just returned to his native bioregion after seven years in Europe working for the IUCN and with UNESCO to create the MAB Programme and its international network of biosphere reserves.) They called bioregionalism "living-in-place" and described its ecological, economic, and social dimensions:

> A society which practices living-in-place keeps a balance with
> its region of support through links between human lives, other
> living things, and the processes of the planet—seasons, weather,
> water cycles—as revealed by the place itself. It is the opposite of
> a society which "makes a living" through short-term destructive
> exploitation of land and life. Living-in-place is an age-old way of
> existence, disrupted in some parts of the world a few millennia ago
> by the rise of exploitative civilization, and more generally during
> the past two centuries by the spread of industrial civilization.[4]

In "Reinhabiting California," Berg and Dasmann also discussed the political implications of bioregionalism. They argued that bioregions would require their own political and administrative structures to match the ecological realities of the place and develop sustainable economies and cultures. A bioregion "should be a separate state," they wrote, two years after Ernest Callenbach's novel *Ecotopia* had imagined the secession of Northern California, Oregon, and Washington from the United States. At a more local level, they said, counties within states should be redistricted to correspond to watersheds, creating "watershed governments." Furthermore, they wrote that "perhaps the greatest advantage of separate statehood would be the opportunity to declare a space for addressing each other as members of a species sharing the planet together and with all the other species," thereby linking their vision of bioregionalism with a change from a human-centered to an ecocentric worldview.[5]

~

The editors of a 2015 collection of Berg's writings give a succinct summary of his view: "Bioregionalism asks us to reimagine ourselves and the places where we live in ecological terms and to harmonize human activities with the natural systems that sustain life."[6] Let's take a closer look at the economic and social implications of bioregionalism.

To an ecologist, the human species and anything we do are fully embedded in the relationships between living organisms and the other geophysical aspects of our Earth environment. Economics, which describes only a part of human social experience, is thus only one aspect of the ecology of our unique species. Humans don't produce any goods or services except what the Earth environment gives us the energy and materials to produce—in that regard, we're exactly like every other species. Although our biological and cultural evolution launched our species into planetary dominance, we are fundamentally under the same ecological constraints—call them "laws" even—as any other species. We have to play by the ecological rules. There aren't any others.

What would a "green" economy look like? An economy designed by following ecological principles? An economy to help us escape the Anthropocene? An eco-*logical* economy? An ecologically sustainable human economy has to start with fundamental principles of ecology relating to energy, materials, and population.

Let's start at the top, with energy. "Energy is eternal delight," as William Blake wrote; it is what impels everything in the universe, including the biosphere, life, and ecosystems. To figure out what is ecologically normal and sustainable, we merely need to survey the current ecosystems on Earth. All—or at least 99.9999 percent—are powered completely by solar energy. The only exceptions are seafloor geothermal vent ecosystems. Ecological Economy Design Principle #1 is a no-brainer: all ecologically sustainable economies are powered by current flows of solar energy only. All fossil fuels are taboo. Ditto nuclear power.

Second, materials. This is the stuff of which life is made, rather than the energy that makes it. The physical, chemical stuff of life cycles in ecosystems is reused again and again in what are called nutrient, or "biogeochemical" cycles. Our species taps, modifies, manipulates, and amplifies many of the nutrient cycles of natural ecosystems. All nutrient cycles in ecosystems are driven by energy flows, and humans are able to amplify natural cycles either by diverting energy from natural flows or by (nonsustainably) using fossil-fuel energy sources. It is the nitrogen cycle that stands out especially as an Anthropocenic aberration: fossil-fuel-powered nitrogen fixation by humans now equals or exceeds all natural ecological nitrogen fixation. We use natural gas (or other fossil fuels) to chemically capture nitrogen from the atmosphere, and we dump it on our crops as fertilizer. That's only one example. The anthropogenic perturbation of material cycling is fundamentally unsustainable. Ecological Economy Design Principle #2: all ecologically sustainable economies stay within the range of the magnitude of the natural cycling of ecologically significant nutrients.

Finally, population. All large, long-lived species that live or have ever lived on Earth have reached populations of a size that remain relatively stable over long spans of time, fluctuating somewhat according to environmental conditions around their natural carrying capacity, but not growing dramatically or exponentially as the human population has. Ecological Economy Design Principle #3: all ecologically sustainable economies support more or less stable, nonincreasing populations at levels at or below natural carrying capacity.

And those populations don't move around much in natural ecosystems. Significant one-way flows of large numbers of a species across wide geographic ranges don't really happen in nonhuman species and did not even in humans until quite recent times. Now we hear of millions of people fleeing from one continent to another to escape conflict or poverty, and immigration has become a hot-button political controversy around the world. The pressure for emigration and conflict about immigration are the result of the imbalance between the human population and the resources across the planet, and the resulting economic and social conflict that such an imbalance inevitably causes. Human emigration and immigration on a large scale are not sustainable and will diminish to almost nothing when bioregional steady-state economies and governance systems stabilize these human-nature relationships worldwide.

Here's a way of testing the distance between the mainstream "economics-centric" view of human ecology and the ecological view: in any common phrase that uses "economic" as an adjective, substitute "ecological." Let's start with "economic growth"—a phrase ubiquitous nowadays, from the left-most to rightmost of the political spectrum. Try the test: "ecological growth." Ecological growth? It's a bizarre concept. Ecosystems and their component species don't "grow" in any fundamental sense. The energy available to them is constant—the solar flux at that point on Earth's surface. They can change dynamically, in a process called ecological succession, from simpler ecosystems with fewer species that capture less solar energy and store some of it, to mature ecosystems that capture as much energy as possible by photosynthesis and come into balance with the solar flux so that energy capture is exactly balanced by energy loss. Mature ecosystems are "no-growth" steady-state economies. They are more or less sustainable and stable unless an outside disturbance such as a fire, flood, hurricane, volcano, or landslide—an "act of god" in ecological terms—disturbs the system and resets it to a simpler point on the pathway of ecological succession.

What about globalization and trade, one of the big topics in economic discussions these days? One clear fact about ecosystems from an ecological point of view is that they encompass all scales, from local to global. The ecological carbon cycle, for example, is global. On the other end of the scale spectrum, nutrient cycling can take place in a single pond. In general, though, there is no widespread ecological "trade." The basic currencies of the "economy" of ecosystems are energy and materials, and these generally stay put. Most ecosystems are rather local, or at most regional. Local and regional scales of flow and exchange of energy and nutrients are the norm, even in the oceans.

The most dramatic spatial scales of energy and material flows involve bird and mammal migrations that may span continents. Some whale species, discussed in the essay "They Say the Sea Is Cold," are examples. Gray whales carry the energy they store while feeding in the North Pacific in summer to the lagoons of Baja California in winter, but unless they die, they aren't transporting much in the way of nutrients there that would affect the local ecosystem. The passenger pigeon, now extinct thanks to overhunting, may have transported ecologically significant quantities of nutrients between the northern and southern United States during its migrations. Migrating red knots feed and fatten on horseshoe crab eggs in Delaware Bay before flying to the shores of the Arctic Ocean to breed. But these are tiny, tiny fluxes of energy and materials across relatively small spatial scales compared to Earth as a whole. These examples of natural ecological flows are perhaps equivalent to human trade along the Silk Road, or the early spice trade to Europe from the Far East. They are exponentially smaller than the global flows of energy and materials we now consider normal: oil from the Persian Gulf to Asia, Europe, and North America; corn and soy from Iowa to China; wheat from Ukraine to the Middle East and Africa; iron ore from Brazil to China; fertilizer from Russia to Brazil. These current anthropogenic global flows of energy and materials dwarf anything that ever occurred in natural ecosystems. Through an ecological lens, the conclusion is that the globalization and trade that are now considered to be normal and good are ecologically aberrant and unsustainable.

Well . . . deep breath . . . no surprise. It's another no-brainer. The current human economy is not ecologically sustainable. From richest to poorest, all current human societies are ecologically unsustainable because they are violating one or more—usually all three—of these fundamental principles of ecological economics. And the discouraging thing is that we have known this for more than fifty years. You be the judge, but I think we have been losing ground on all fronts (energy, materials, and population), globally speaking at least, for the past half century.

"Can Every Chinese Have a Car?" was the title of an article I remember clearly from the 1970s, but I can't find it on the internet now. The answer from the author—probably some "radical" ecologist like Paul Ehrlich, Hugh Iltis, or their ilk, I suppose—was "Of course not! . . . Unless we want to change the climate of the planet!" As I remember it, our reaction in the United States was "Good thing the Chinese love bicycles and have a one-child population policy." Now, Chinese car production and ownership are surging, and although only about one in five Chinese owns a car, there are more cars in China than in the United States because their population is much larger. In the United States, where four of every five people have a car, there are almost three hundred million cars on the road.[7] Although China is now the largest emitter of climate-warming greenhouse gases, most of the CO_2 already in the atmosphere is because of us (the United States), not the Chinese. But oh! The Chinese, not to mention the whole world, can only be grateful for the period when their country had a one-child policy. Without that, China and all of us would be much deeper in the hole of human population overshoot of the carrying capacity of the planet for our species, and climate change would be much more advanced.

～

What else will an ecologically sustainable society need?

For one thing, a dramatic expansion of wild, natural lands and waters, "untrammeled"[8] by human activities that harm their full ecological functioning (and the full provision of ecosystem benefits they provide for humans and all other species). To get there, large areas that have already been "trammeled" will have to be protected and perhaps passively or actively restored and rewilded—whether they are agricultural landscapes that have been plowed and converted to crops or overgrazed by livestock, or marine ecosystems that have been overfished, had their benthic structure destroyed by dredging or bottom trawling, or had keystone species like sea otters removed, causing trophic cascades that destroyed them. What has been called the "agricultural frontier," the front line in the war with nature, will have to be closed everywhere—no more conversion of wildlands to agriculture. Efforts are already underway to do this in many parts of the world.[9]

Various proposals and initiatives have been made to advance this idea of expanding nature and reducing the human footprint. One that is now commonly mentioned is "30 by 30," a proposal for countries around the planet to designate 30 percent of their lands and waters as some type of natural "protected area" by the year 2030.[10] The Biden administration embraced the

"30×30" target and issued a report about actions for achieving it, *Conserving and Restoring America the Beautiful*, in 2021.[11] California adopted the target and released an outline for action, *30×30 California*,[12] in April 2022. The 30 percent goal represents an increase in the area of land and water under some form of "protection" from harmful human activities but is really only an arbitrary number with no real ecological basis, meant to correspond to a potentially manageable time frame of a decade (2020–2030) to reach it. In his 2016 book, *Half-Earth: Our Planet's Fight for Life*, evolutionary biologist Edward O. Wilson proposed a more ambitious goal with a call for urgent action, but no specific time frame.

Our food system will need to move away from a "meat economy" to one in which a much larger proportion of human protein needs are met by plant proteins and amino acid complementation with those plant proteins (e.g., beans and grains eaten together), especially until population can be dramatically reduced. On my cross-country driving trips, it was very apparent that we are a Meat Nation—from sea to shining sea, most of the visible agriculture is aimed to produce animal feed (corn, soy, sorghum, alfalfa, and wheat) to produce meat, not plant foods.

We need to "design with nature"[13] and create an ecologically stable no-growth economy based on the laws of ecology, as described above. That will require bioregional self-sufficiency in energy and materials, and dramatically reduced global and even national trade. All energy and most food should be produced bioregionally, and there should be a bioregional balance between population and its use of food and other energy.

That will require stabilizing the human population and then in most bioregions reducing it. The total human population needs to be only 20–25 percent of the current global population—approximately two billion humans, maximum. Most people I talk to have a hard time with this one. Although many agree about the goal, they can't imagine it happening in a conscious, controlled way, but only as the result of some apocalyptic event like a nuclear war or a deadly global pandemic. It certainly is hard to see how we can accomplish such a dramatic reduction of the human population, especially relatively quickly. Birthrates have been declining globally as the "demographic transition" works its way through the poorest countries, and the most "developed" ones have aging, shrinking populations—but these are very slow demographic processes. A dramatically smaller human population is ultimately necessary, and if we can't figure out how to make it happen in a controlled way, we are surely setting the stage for some horrible demographic catastrophe in the future. It's clear that the former is the more desirable and human-loving path.

We need to move toward a spatial pattern in which human activities are scattered in a sea of natural ecosystems, rather than the reverse—natural ecosystems embedded in a human-dominated landscape, as now. Ecological connectivity between wild ecosystems needs to increase to maintain biodiversity in the face of, and for resilience to, climate change, and human infrastructural connectivity needs to decline. In general, this will require deurbanization; large cities that parasitize a large region around them, sucking energy and materials into a small area and then exporting the pollution generated there, need to shrink. Deurbanization would not mean spreading people out everywhere. Thirty to fifty percent of a landscape could be conserved as wildlands, with people occupying a network of villages of a size that balances human population and resource demands with the capacity of their immediate bioregion—at least that's the old bioregional vision of Berg, Dasmann, and Snyder. The spatial shift of people away from cities will be much easier when the human population is smaller.

We need much-increased access to nature and to spend more time in nature to allow, promote, and enhance full development of the human potential in its many dimensions—physical, psychological, mental, aesthetic, and spiritual. We evolved in wild nature, and we need it. We need to cultivate our original, wild minds. This is especially true for younger children in our screen-filled virtual world, but also true at all ages. Our mental and physical health will improve and health-care costs decline.

Finally, we need a deliberate shift away from the current dominant, human-supremacist worldview toward an ecocentric worldview. This means we need

- Deliberate critiquing and unteaching of the "human dominion" creation myth of the Middle Eastern monotheisms and the Western human-supremacist worldview that "nature" is a "resource" for the benefit of humans.

• Rediscovery, revival, and restoration of old, autochthonic world-views around the planet, which were largely bioregional and eco-centric everywhere.

• Access to and teaching of other non-Western ecocentric world-views.

• Reinvigoration of the long tradition of "wilderness" thinking in Western and American culture, which is still extremely relevant but not widely understood or appreciated, or completely implemented in practice and policy.

• Renewed development of holistic science-art-spirituality think-ing, and unteaching of the "two cultures" (i.e., science versus hu-manities) myth.

∾

This is serious stuff, designing an ecotopia. This is far, far beyond "tech-no-managerial"[14] tinkering; far beyond incremental adjustments to the human-nature relationship. But it's nothing new. The same need for trans-formation, the same prescription for action, the same vision for a healthy human-nature relationship was clear fifty years ago. In his "Four Changes" broadside in 1969, Gary Snyder laid out nearly the same prescription I've given above. Recognizing the magnitude of the change that would be need-ed, he concluded, "Nothing short of total transformation will do much good. If man is to remain on earth he must transform the five-millennia-long ur-banizing civilization tradition into a new ecologically sensitive harmony-ori-ented wild-minded scientific-spiritual culture."[15] Snyder, poet that he was, also recognized that because of the depth of change in our culture that would be needed, our minds and worldviews would have to change.[16]

I was struck, when reading Eileen Crist's book *Abundant Earth* (pub-lished in 2019, fifty years after "Four Changes"), with the parallel between Snyder's conclusions and hers: "Ending human domination of and domi-nance within the biosphere is the only pathway to resolving the ecological crisis."[17] Crist also wrote: "An immediate turn in the direction of a global ecological civilization is therefore the only real option. It is impossible to foresee what such a civilization will look like; that will be a work in progress for future generations to shape."[18]

Actually, it's not really "impossible" to foresee what such a civilization will look like because it has to be based on fundamental ecological principles, which we know now and which aren't going to change. Eileen Crist and her colleagues at *The Ecological Citizen* have, in their mission statement,[19] laid out some excellent design principles for the ecotopias of the future, and they are quite congruent with what I described above, and with Snyder's "Four Changes."

We *can* imagine the kinds of bioregional, ecologically sustainable societies we must develop if humans are to survive and thrive. It will take decades, if not centuries or even millennia, to remake our worldviews and transform our economic and political systems. We'd better start right away. Biosphere reserves could and should be the nuclei where the transformation begins. In California's Golden Gate and Channel Islands Biosphere Reserves we can begin to see, and better imagine, some of the needed steps toward that transformation.

16
Edging toward Ecotopia

It is so hard to imagine anything fundamentally different from what we have now. But without these alternate visions, we get stuck on dead center. And we'd better get ready. We need to know where we'd like to go.
—Ernest Callenbach, 2008[1]

I BEGAN THESE ESSAYS BY SAYING they were the field notes from my quest to understand what progress we have made in my lifetime toward an ecologically and socially sustainable society. In the previous essays I described example after example of good things done, of successful steps taken toward healing the human-nature relationship, and called attention to stories that clearly demonstrate that individual and group actions can make a difference and influence the course of ecological history.

The question is not whether good things have been done—they have—but whether they are enough, or are happening fast enough. After all the success stories and lessons learned, the overall feeling I have is of relative stasis: of running on a treadmill but not getting anywhere; of "treading water" and not drowning; of swimming in a rip current of our own making and never getting closer to shore; of the boy with his finger in the dike; of bailing a leaky lifeboat with a bucket barely big enough to hold the water leaking into the boat.

∼

I asked almost everyone I talked to in my travels in the Golden Gate and Channel Islands bioregions—scientists, government agency managers, and conservationists—"What about the human future? Are you optimistic? Are you hopeful?"

Their answers ranged widely, sometimes troubling, sometimes inspiring, and always thought provoking.

Perhaps I should start with Paul Ehrlich—who, through his modeling of a socially and politically engaged ecologist when I was a college undergraduate, set a foundation for my whole career. On our drive to Coyote Ridge to look for Bay checkerspot butterflies in April 2022, I asked Paul whether he remembered something he said in a Human Biology Program lecture at Stanford in the fall of 1969, recorded in my freshman notebook: "We know what we need to do, ecologically speaking. But what we don't know how to do is to create the political will to do it."

"Still true. Unfortunately, still true," he said.

The ecological diagnosis of the "disease" and the "prescription" to cure it are still the same. What is sad and dispiriting is that we *still* haven't figured out how to make the needed political, economic, and social changes. Then I asked Paul my big question:

"What about the future—are you hopeful?"

"I'm not interested in hope," he said immediately. "I'm interested in action!"

"So, what should we be doing?" I asked. I think I was expecting a bullet list of "we should do this, this, this, and this." His response surprised me.

"We should just enjoy this life we have," he said.

But before I could process that, he qualified it: "And try to leave the same opportunities to enjoy life to future generations."

That immediately recalled the Native American "seventh generation" principle, codified by the Haudenosaunee (also called the Iroquois), but widespread in many other Native American worldviews as well, that our decisions today should be based on what is good and right not only for us but also for generations far into the future. But even seven generations may be too short a time horizon for an ecological ethic. My European ancestors came to North America three or four generations ago to escape unsustainable political, economic, and ecological systems that were collapsing around them. By then it had been at least two thousand years since there had been a balanced and sustainable relationship between the human population in Europe and the ecosystems of that region—far more than seven generations—and the pressure to explore and colonize the rest of the planet had long been building to explosive levels there.

After undoing the human-nature relationship for so long, we have such a long way to go to reverse the ecological damage we have done and to shrink the human population to a sustainable level that it often seems daunting. But even at his age, Ehrlich is still trying to prod us into taking the appropriate action, despite his off-the-cuff answer to my question about what we should do. In an opinion essay published in June 2022 in *Philosophical Transactions of the Royal Society*, Ehrlich and his coauthors Rodolfo Dirzo and Gerardo Ceballos wrote:

> While concerned scientists know there are many individual and collective steps that must be taken to slow population extinction rates [of nonhuman species], some are not willing to advocate the one fundamental, necessary, "simple" cure, that is, reducing the scale of the human enterprise. We argue that compassionate shrinkage of the human population by further encouraging lower birth rates while reducing both inequity and aggregate wasteful consumption—that is, an end to growthmania—will be required.[2]

~

Stuart Weiss leveraged his experience with the ecology of endangered Bay Area butterflies like the Bay checkerspot and Mission blue, gained in Ehrlich's lab, into a consulting business that designs the habitat conservation plans required by the Endangered Species Act for these listed species—like the first, controversial one at San Bruno Mountain described in an earlier essay. I asked Stu my question: "Are you optimistic about the future? Are you hopeful?"

"On a local scale, yes," he said, ticking off a number of conservation successes in the Bay Area. "We were already at 30 by 30 in '20!" he said, referring to the conservation goal announced by the Biden administration and the state of California to protect 30 percent of the landscape (and seascape) for conservation by 2030. According to Stu, 30 percent of Bay Area lands were already protected in one way or another by 2020. Then he continued with his answer: "On a global scale, no, I'm not optimistic."

Frank Davis, an ecology professor at UC Santa Barbara and director of the La Kretz Research Center at the Sedgwick Reserve near Santa Ynez, confessed that although he personally wasn't very optimistic, he didn't want to convey too much negativity to his students, who were studying ecology because they wanted to solve problems and make the world better. "I find my students leaning toward despair. How do we motivate them to keep going, how can we communicate hope to them?" he asked me. I felt his conflicted confusion. How *do* we convey hope in these times?

I talked with Jon Erlandson, an archaeologist, retired professor, and museum director at the University of Oregon who has spent a long career studying the human and ecological history of the Channel Islands. He said that in the classroom,

> I needed stories of hope to share with my students, and I found much of my inspiration from my experiences on the Channel Islands, witnessing their ecological recovery with my own eyes over the past 45 years. As an anthropologist, I also take hope from the essential ingenuity of the human mind and species—which has allowed us to survive ice ages, global warming, and rapidly rising seas in the past. We've surely made a mess of things, but we must not give up hope, or hard work towards solving the challenges of our day.

Lisa Micheli, executive director of the Pepperwood Preserve, the private nature reserve perched in the oak savanna hills in the wine country north of Santa Rosa, said she thinks social-ecological systems are so complex and so much in flux that good things could happen, and positive outcomes are a real possibility.

That view was surely influenced by her experiences at Pepperwood. Most of the preserve burned twice recently, in wildfires in 2017 and 2019, and now local and state governments are processing and pondering what happened in those wildfires, trying to understand what to do. Research at Pepperwood is weighing in with prescriptions for living with fire in these ecosystems in the face of climate change, and local Indigenous groups are chiming in with ideas about revitalizing traditional fire management practices in the area. Lisa said a new social "mycelium" had formed in response to the fires—using the term for the web of fungal hyphae that reach out through the ground to tap nutrients and synapse with plant roots in mycorrhizal associations as a metaphor for new relationships and conversations among people in the Pepperwood area that the fires stimulated. Lisa's vision of the future seemed to be a sort of phoenix-rising-from-the-ashes outcome to our ecological crisis. Part of hope, for her, she said, is a "faith in the unknown. That leaves room for surprises."

Lisa's view seemed to parallel the answer Daniel Ellsberg, leaker of the Pentagon Papers and later an antiwar and anti-nuclear-weapons activist, gave when asked, in a videoconference a few weeks before he died in June 2023, whether he had hope for the future. Ellsberg said:

> I find hope very easily, and I have real hope—hope that my expectations will prove utterly unfounded! And that's not an idle hope, because it has been true so often in the past! We don't know the future, no one knows with certainty what's going to happen. . . . I don't see any way of getting out [of the mess we're in], not the way we're going, but the fact that I don't see it doesn't mean that there is no way out. . . . My hope is, if you like, the *uncertainty* of events, and the *certainty* that there are people who will do everything they can to avert these terrible events that we are moving toward.[3]

I sipped a cappuccino with Peter Barnes on a chilly, windy day in April at Toby's Coffee Bar in Point Reyes Station. Peter is a writer and social-change entrepreneur who started the Mesa Refuge for writers in 1995 after cofounding a worker-owned solar energy company in San Francisco in 1976, and the Working Assets Money Fund in 1983. His most recent book, *Ours: The Case for Universal Property*, was published in 2021.[4] Peter has promoted the idea of "ecosystem trusts."

"Why not place ecosystems into trusts accountable to future generations, like many land trusts? That is, put them in a legal category that guarantees their protection for future generations." Any watershed—like the Olema Creek watershed that empties into the Giacomini Wetland here at Point Reyes Station, for example—or any other watershed or forest or marine area are possible examples, Peter said. The responsibility of the trusts would be to limit human inputs like pollutants, and harvests like of fish or trees, to sustainable and healthy levels as determined by science, always erring on the side of precaution.

But in spite of Peter's visionary ideas, his take on our future was more somber. "We're in for a long, dark time as we make this transformation," he said. My thoughts flashed immediately to what in our Eurocentric history is often called the "Dark Ages." That period was the struggle—half a millennium or more long—during which the old, indigenous Celtic, Iberian, Germanic, and Norse worldviews were finally overwhelmed by the monotheistic, anthropocentric worldview spreading from the Middle East and Mediterranean. I agreed with Peter that it will likely be a long and very difficult period of many centuries of transformation of worldviews, political systems, and economies before we get to where we need to go if we are to survive as a species.

When I asked Sara Tashker, at the Green Gulch Farm and Zen Center, whether she was hopeful about the human future, she basically said: "Hope isn't something I'm interested in. It's not a Buddhist idea." I interpreted her answer as a reflection of the Buddhist principle of "nonattachment." An emphasis on the results and outcomes of individual actions is a fundamental aspect of the Western worldview, and the word "hope" in English carries that connotation. But Buddhist thought sees this as a flawed understanding of reality. Within a universe of dependent co-arising, if you are "attached" to the results or outcomes of your actions, you are bound to be disappointed. The idea just doesn't fit with the interdependent reality of the world.

~

Is there any room for hope? We have been extremely slow in implementing the changes we know we eventually must make. It seems quite clear that our current political system in the United States is not capable of solving our ecological problems in our own country, and we can't solve problems like anthropogenic climate change without action by every other country also. No political system in the world right now, democratic, authoritarian, or otherwise, seems to work to the extent needed.

Any kind of "hope" that ignores reality won't help. Water does not flow up; it always flows down. Hope that ignores reality won't help the Earth, and it won't help people find meaning in their own lives. And false hope can lead to discounting the future, hedonism, the myopia of individualism.

Many of us have been working as best we know how to heal the broken human-nature relationship. In nooks and crannies, we find small success stories, as many of the essays here have described. Beautiful and inspiring though they are, they are like fingers in the dike, treading water, bailing the lifeboat.

So how much time do we have? It is already too late to do what we knew we needed to do long ago. But at the same time, it is never going to be too late; life on Earth is very resilient and doesn't really need us at all.

I started these essays with an epigraph from Kim Stanley Robinson's future-fiction novel *The Ministry for the Future*: "There is a real situation, that can't be denied, but it is too big for any individual to know in full, and so we must create our understanding by way of an act of the imagination."[5] The meaning of our lives, now, for each of us, lies in what we choose to do, not in the outcome of that. We can't control the outcome, but we can control what we do, and what we do depends on what we can imagine.

Even if it doesn't give me "hope," taking a deep-time perspective on our current situation gives me some solace. The biosphere will be fine, ultimately, no matter what we do. It has survived five mass extinction events already in the 4.5-billion-year history of life, and it will survive the sixth extinction, now being caused by us. In a few tens of millions of years, the biosphere will emerge from this anthropogenic sixth extinction with even more biological diversity than the world our species evolved into.

Whether the human species survives it is another question. I have my doubts, but I love my creative, hypercultural species, and I like to imagine an evolved descendant species of ours carrying through into that posthuman future with some elements of our uniqueness and evolutionary brilliance, but having left our destructive tendencies behind.

When I'm most agitated and angry about our lack of essential ecological action, I often hear the calming voice of Thich Nhat Hanh, the Vietnamese Zen Buddhist teacher; we can "take refuge in Mother Earth," he says, referring to the Buddhist concept of refuge as a condition or place of equanimity, acceptance, reality, and inner peace. "Mother Earth has a lot of patience. She can wait one million years, or ten million years, in order to heal herself. She is not in a hurry."[6] We are part of this co-arising, co-evolving biosphere. She is not in a hurry.

~

One day in June 2021, I hiked to the far northern tip of Tomales Point, the ancient granite finger of the Point Reyes Peninsula that points northwest along the great San Andreas Fault between Tomales Bay and the Pacific Ocean. As I looked across the mouth of the bay, it suddenly struck me that I was looking at North America *over there*, and I had the feeling of being on another continent, waving goodbye as I rode off on the Pacific Plate into the deep time of the future. This was the wild edge, in time and space and imagination. I couldn't stay long; the wind was too strong.

Acknowledgments

THESE ESSAYS ARE BASED ON information and experiences gained with the help of dozens of people—managers of lands and waters that make up the Channel Islands and Golden Gate Biosphere Reserves, scientists, conservationists, Indigenous culture and language activists, nature tourism guides, and other colleagues and friends. My deep gratitude and thanks to each and every one. Quotes or vignettes from field trips and interviews with many of them are found in the essays. I've tried my best to reflect what I learned from them accurately; any errors of fact or interpretation that remain here are mine.

Background research for this book was initially catalyzed by my time at the Mesa Refuge in Point Reyes Station in June 2021. As one of its resident writers focusing on "ideas at the edge," I was graciously supported there by Susan Tillet, Kamala Tully, and Mesa Refuge founder Peter Barnes. My primary point of contact in the Golden Gate Biosphere Reserve was Alison Forrestel of the Natural Resources and Science Office of the Golden Gate National Recreation Area, who enabled my networking with other GGNRA scientists and resource managers. Thanks especially to Michael Chassé, Bill Merkle, and Eric Wrubel. GGNRA's Mia Monroe shared her deep knowledge, enthusiasm, and wealth of contacts, especially for places and people in Marin County and in and around Muir Woods National Monument and Mount Tamalpais; thank you, Mia! I'm indebted to Sara Tashker for a tour of Green Gulch Farm and Zen Center; Charles Kennard for a tour of the basketry garden at the Marin Art and Garden Center; Donna Faure and Heather

Clapp of the Point Reyes National Seashore Association; and Gifford Hartman and fellow Summer Solstice 2021 Mount Tamalpais circumambulators.

Stuart Weiss was my source and guide for butterflies and serpentine grasslands; thanks also to Paul Ehrlich for a memorable field trip and conversation. Nona Chiariello guided me around the Jasper Ridge Biological Preserve and provided historical background about the origins and early days of the Golden Gate Biosphere Reserve.

UC Santa Barbara's Sedgwick and Santa Cruz Island Reserves were my base for information gathering in the Channel Islands Biosphere Reserve in October 2021. I'm grateful to Frank Davis for the invitation to Sedgwick and for introducing me to its ecosystem. Jay Reti, director of the Santa Cruz Island Reserve and Field Station, and director emeritus Lyndal Laughrin facilitated my visit to the island and shared their deep knowledge of its history and ecology. It was wonderful to have my daughter Anya Byers join me as field assistant and hiking companion on Santa Cruz Island. Many thanks to Zoe Keller for her amazing ecological art, *Limuw | Santa Cruz Island*, and for sharing her description of the details behind the work. Thanks also to Karen Flagg, Don Hartley, and Steve Barilotti for information on efforts to restore the Santa Cruz Island bush mallow.

For the Channel Islands Biosphere Reserve my official point of contact was Sean Hastings of NOAA's Channel Islands National Marine Sanctuary. My sincere thanks to Matthew Vestuto for sharing his knowledge of the Chumash language and its revitalization; Teresa Romero, environmental director of the Santa Ynez Band of Chumash Indians for discussions about restoring native plant species of importance in Chumash culture and a tour of their native plant nursery; and Diego Cordero for his knowledge of the revival of Chumash sewn-plank canoes and tomol voyaging. Thanks also to Mark Reynolds, Bill Leahy, and Moses Katkowski of The Nature Conservancy for enabling my visit to the Dangermond Preserve and to Point Conception.

In June 2022, UC Berkeley's Point Reyes Field Station in Olema provided a convenient place to continue my research at the Point Reyes National Seashore, where my stay was facilitated by Alan Shabel, director and manager of the station. At the Pepperwood Preserve near Santa Rosa, Lisa Micheli, Michelle Halbur, Michael Gillogly, and Isabelle Luevano introduced me to the place and their important work. Erika Delamarre shared her impressive knowledge of Monterey Bay's marine mammals as the naturalist on a whale-watching trip.

One important aspect of this work for me has been to piece together and document some aspects of the history of the UNESCO Man and the Biosphere Programme and of the establishment of the Golden Gate Biosphere Reserve; the latter, especially, has not previously been documented. For help with this historical sleuthing, my warmest thanks go to Vernon C. "Tom" Gilbert, who played an important role in this history. His lifelong commitment to the model of conservation represented by UNESCO biosphere reserves is truly inspiring; thank you, Tom! I'm also grateful to several other people who played key roles in the establishment of the Golden Gate Biosphere Reserve and agreed to be interviewed about that history: thanks to Ed Ueber, retired director of NOAA's national marine sanctuaries in the Golden Gate region; Laurie Wayburn, who spearheaded the effort to establish the biosphere reserve; Nona Chiariello and Philippe Cohen, of Stanford's Jasper Ridge Biological Preserve, whose support of the effort was critical in its early years; and Terri Thomas and Daphne Hatch, scientists from the GGNRA whose efforts supported the biosphere reserve at critical moments. William Gregg, John Dennis, and Patrick Mangan also provided some personal insights on this history.

For consultations and fact-checking on various essays I'm grateful to Michael Branch, Peter Brown, Susan Bunsick, Michael Chassé, Alison Forrestel, Gifford Hartman, Sean Hastings, Tim Hogan, Clint McKay, Curt Meine, Dugald Owen, Tom Parker, Robert Michael Pyle, Katherine Renz, Shelley Roberts, Andrew Schelling, Michael Sweeney, Sara Tashker, Peter Thomas, and Harold Wood.

Oregon State University Press recruited two excellent readers, Jon Erlandson and Nancy Steinberg, who reviewed the entire draft manuscript and offered many constructive comments. I am especially grateful to Dr. Erlandson for sharing his deep knowledge of, and perspectives on, the long human history of the Channel Islands. My thanks also to Kim Hogeland and Tom Booth of OSU Press for their help in arriving at a title for the book, not an easy task. Laurel Anderton was the copyeditor for OSU Press; her sharp eyes caught many mistakes and her suggestions helped smooth and clarify my writing in many places. Scott Smiley developed the index for this multidimensional book. Thanks also to Micki Reaman of OSU Press for shepherding the editing, design, and production process.

It was a pleasure to interact with Robin Chandler as she created the imaginative frontispiece drawing that pulls in themes from many of my essays, from serpentine and manzanitas to Mount Tamalpais and California condors. Nora Sherwood produced the sketch maps that orient readers to many of the locations mentioned in the essays.

I also must acknowledge my deep gratitude for ecophilosophical ancestors whose wisdom can continue to help us learn how to reinhabit this planet, especially John Muir, Aldo Leopold, Alan Watts, Shunryu Suzuki, Ray Dasmann, and Gary Snyder. Our fireside conversations are woven into all these essays. Palm to palm!

Notes

Preface

1 Mesa Refuge, "About Us," https://mesarefuge.org/about-us/.
2 Ernest Callenbach, *Ecotopia: The Notebooks and Reports of William Weston* (Berkeley, CA: Banyan Tree Books, 1975).

Introduction

1 Kim Stanley Robinson, *The Ministry for the Future: A Novel* (New York: Orbit, 2020), 41.
2 Bruce A. Byers, *The View from Cascade Head: Lessons for the Biosphere from the Oregon Coast* (Corvallis: Oregon State University Press, 2020).
3 NASA, "Blue Marble – Image of the Earth from Apollo 17," November 30, 2007, https://www.nasa.gov/content/blue-marble-image-of-the-earth-from-apollo-17.
4 Frank B. Golley, *A History of the Ecosystem Concept in Ecology: More Than the Sum of the Parts* (New Haven, CT: Yale University Press, 1993), 57.
5 UNESCO, "Intergovernmental Conference of Experts on the Scientific Basis for Rational Use and Conservation of the Resources of the Biosphere (Paris, France, September 4–13, 1968), Recommendations," https://eric.ed.gov/?id=ED047952; UNESCO, *Use and Conservation of the Biosphere*, Proceedings of the 1968 Biosphere Conference, Paris, France, 1970, https://unesdoc.unesco.org/ark:/48223/pf0000067785.
6 UNESCO, "What Are Biosphere Reserves?," 2021, https://en.unesco.org/biosphere/about.
7 UNESCO, "What Are Biosphere Reserves?"

8   National Park Service, Connected Conservation, "US Biosphere Network," 2021, https://www.nps.gov/subjects/connectedconservation/us-biosphere-network.htm.

9   William Vogt, *Road to Survival* (Boston: Little, Brown, 1948).

10 Fairfield Osborn, *Our Plundered Planet* (Boston: Little, Brown, 1948), quoted from cover of first US edition.

11 Raymond F. Dasmann, *Called by the Wild: The Autobiography of a Conservationist* (Berkeley: University of California Press, 2002), 126.

12 Paul R. Ehrlich, *The Population Bomb* (Berkeley, CA: Sierra Club/Ballantine Books, 1968).

13 Stanley A. Cain, "Preservation of Natural Areas and Ecosystems: Protection of Rare and Endangered Species," in UNESCO, *Use and Conservation of the Biosphere*, 148.

14 Cain, "Preservation of Natural Areas and Ecosystems," 148.

15 Cain, 147.

16 Paul B. Sears, "Ecology—a Subversive Subject," *BioScience* 14, no. 7 (1964): 11, https://academic.oup.com/bioscience/article-abstract/14/7/11/237620.

17 Lynn White, "The Historical Roots of Our Ecological Crisis," *Science* 155 (1967): 1203–1207, https://www.cmu.ca/faculty/gmatties/lynnwhiterootsofcrisis.pdf.

18 Gary Snyder, "Four Changes," in *Turtle Island* (New York: New Directions, 1974), 91–102.

19 Diana Hadley, Jack Loeffler, Gary Paul Nabhan, and Jack Shoemaker, "Four Changes at Age 50: A Celebration on the Environmental Movement's First Manifesto of Contemplative Ecology," Bioneers, 2020, https://bioneers.org/four-changes-by-gary-snyder/.

20 Snyder, "Four Changes," 99–100.

21 Frank Fraser Darling, "Impacts of Man on the Biosphere," in UNESCO, *Use and Conservation of the Biosphere*, 46.

22 Cain, "Preservation of Natural Areas and Ecosystems," 146.

23 Callenbach, *Ecotopia*, 4.

24 Scott Timberg, "The Novel That Predicted Portland," *New York Times*, December 12, 2008, https://www.nytimes.com/2008/12/14/fashion/14ecotopia.html.

1. Evolutionary Ecology on California's Galapagos

1   Charles Darwin, *The Voyage of the Beagle*, annotated and with an introduction by Leonard Engel, Natural History Library Edition (Garden City, NY: Anchor Books, Doubleday, 1962), 378.

2   National Park Service, Channel Islands National Park, "Island Scrub-Jay," 2021, https://www.nps.gov/chis/learn/nature/island-scrub-jay.htm.

3   Daniel R. Muhs, "T.D.A. Cockerell (1866–1948) of the University of

Colorado: His Contributions to the Natural History of the California Islands and the Establishment of Channel Islands National Monument," *Western North American Naturalist* 78, no. 3 (2018), 247–270, https://bioone.org/journals/western-north-american-naturalist/volume-78/issue-3/064.078.0304/TDA-Cockerell-18661948-of-the-University-of-Colorado--His/10.3398/064.078.0304.short.

4 National Park Service, Channel Islands National Park, "Establishing Channel Islands National Park," 2020, https://www.nps.gov/chis/learn/historyculture/park-history.htm.

5 Muhs, "T.D.A. Cockerell," 261.

6 Muhs, 263.

7 T.D.A. Cockerell, "Notes on Some Heliothid Moths," *Entomological News* 21 (1910): 343–344.

8 T.D.A. Cockerell, *Zoology of Colorado* (Boulder: University of Colorado, 1927).

9 Bruce A. Byers, "Colorado Fires and Firemoths," *Frontiers in Ecology and the Environment* 15, no. 1 (February 1, 2017).

10 Todd J. Braje, Jon M. Erlandson, and Torben C. Rick, *Islands through Time: A Human and Ecological History of California's Northern Channel Islands* (London: Rowman and Littlefield, 2021).

11 National Park Service, Channel Islands National Park, "The Pygmy Mammoth," 2020, https://www.nps.gov/chis/learn/historyculture/pygmymammoth.htm; Santa Barbara Museum of Natural History, Earth and Marine Sciences, "Geology, Paleontology, and Marine Science of the Santa Barbara Region," https://www.sbnature.org/visit/exhibitions/54/earth-marine-sciences#:~:text=The%20most%20complete%20Pygmy%20Mammoth,on%20Santa%20Rosa%20in%201994.

12 Torben C. Rick, Jon M. Erlandson, René L. Vellanoweth, Todd J. Braje, Paul W. Collins, Daniel A. Guthrie, and Thomas W. Stafford Jr., "Origins and Antiquity of the Island Fox (*Urocyon littoralis*) on California's Channel Islands," *Quaternary Research* 71 (2009): 93–98, https://www.academia.edu/5774820/Origins_and_antiquity_of_the_island_fox.

13 Jon Erlandson, email to author, July 13, 2023.

14 Paul W. Collins, "Interaction between Island Foxes (*Urocyon littoralis*) and Indians on Islands off the Coast of Southern California: I. Morphologic and Archaeological Evidence of Human Assisted Dispersal," *Journal of Ethnobiology* 11, no. 1 (1991): 51–81.

15 Paul W. Collins, "Historic and Prehistoric Record for the Occurrence of Island Scrub-Jays (*Aphelocoma insularis*) on the Northern Channel Islands, Santa Barbara County, California," *Santa Barbara Museum of Natural History Technical Reports* 5 (2009): 25.

16 Jake Buehler, "Russian Foxes Bred for Tameness May Not Be the Domestication Story We Thought," *Science News*, December 31, 2019, https://www.sciencenews.org/article/russian-foxes-tameness-domestication; Tina

Hesman Saey, "The First Detailed Map of Red Foxes' DNA May Reveal Domestication Secrets," *Science News*, August 6, 2018, https://www.sciencenews.org/article/red-fox-dna-genome-domestication.

17 Joshua M. Akey, Alison L. Ruhe, Dayna T. Akey, Aaron K. Wong, Caitlin F. Connelly, Jennifer Madeoy, Thomas J. Nicholas, and Mark W. Neff, "Tracking Footprints of Artificial Selection in the Dog Genome," *PNAS* 107 (2010): 1160–1165, https://www.pnas.org/doi/10.1073/pnas.0909918107.

18 Nathan B. Sutter, Carlos D. Bustamante, Kevin Chase, Melissa M. Gray, Keyan Zhao, Lan Zhu, Badri Padhukasahasram, et al., "A Single *IGF1* Allele Is a Major Determinant of Small Size in Dogs," *Science* 316 (2007): 112–115, https://www.science.org/doi/10.1126/science.1137045?cookieSet=1.

19 Kathleen Semple Delany, Saba Zafar, and Robert K. Wayne, "Genetic Divergence and Differentiation within the Western Scrub-Jay (*Aphelocoma californica*)," *Auk* 125 (2008): 839–849, https://academic.oup.com/auk/article/125/4/839/5148307.

20 Luke Caldwell, Victoria J. Bakker, T. Scott Sillett, Michelle A. Desrosiers, Scott A. Morrison, and Lisa M. Angeloni, "Reproductive Ecology of the Island Scrub-Jay," *Condor* 115 (2013): 603–613, https://academic.oup.com/condor/article/115/3/603/5152866; T. Scott Sillett, Richard B. Chandler, J. Andrew Royle, Marc Kéry, and Scott A. Morrison, "Hierarchical Distance-Sampling Models to Estimate Population Size and Habitat-Specific Abundance of an Island Endemic," *Ecological Applications* 22 (2012): 1997–2006, https://esajournals.onlinelibrary.wiley.com/doi/abs/10.1890/11-1400.1.

21 Scott A. Morrison, T. Scott Sillett, Cameron K. Ghalambor, John W. Fitzpatrick, David M. Graber, Victoria J. Bakker, Reed Bowman, et al., "Proactive Conservation Management of an Island-Endemic Bird Species in the Face of Global Change," *BioScience* 61 (2011): 1013–1021, https://academic.oup.com/bioscience/article/61/12/1013/389404; Sillett et al., "Hierarchical Distance-Sampling Models."

22 Byers, *View from Cascade Head*, 39–52.

23 Jay Woolsey, Cause Hanna, Kathryn McEachern, Sean Anderson, and Brett D. Hartman, "Regeneration and Expansion of *Quercus tomentella* (Island Oak) Groves on Santa Rosa Island," *Western North American Naturalist* 78 (2018): 758–767, https://bioone.org/journals/western-north-american-naturalist/volume-78/issue-4/064.078.0415/Regeneration-and-Expansion-of-Quercus-tomentella-Island-Oak-Groves-on/10.3398/064.078.0415.short.

24 Collins, "Historic and Prehistoric Record," 39; Jon M. Erlandson, note to author, May 10, 2023.

25 Jon M. Erlandson, Kristina M. Gill, and Mikael Fauvelle, "Responding to Stress or Coping with Abundance?," in *An Archaeology of Abundance: Reevaluating the Marginality of California's Islands*, ed. Kristina M. Gill, Mikael Fauvelle, and Jon M. Erlandson (Gainesville: University Press of Florida, 2019), 13.

26 Kathryn M. Langin, T. Scott Sillett, W. Chris Funk, Scott A. Morrison,

Michelle A. Desrosiers, and Cameron K. Ghalambor, "Islands within an Island: Repeated Adaptive Divergence in a Single Population," *Evolution* 69 (2015): 653–665, https://onlinelibrary.wiley.com/doi/10.1111/evo.12610.

2. The Art of Ecological Restoration on Santa Cruz Island

1 Aldo Leopold, *A Sand County Almanac, with Essays on Conservation from Round River* (New York: Sierra Club/Ballentine Books, 1966), 190.

2 Zoe Keller, *Limuw | Santa Cruz Island*, graphite on paper, 2017, https://www.zoekeller.com/2017-limuw-santa-cruz-island.

3 I have long been interested in the relationship between art and ecology, for several reasons. One is that I'm convinced that the observational and intuitive psychological processes of artists and scientists are very similar. See Byers, "Art and Ecology at the Otis Café," in *View from Cascade Head*, 53–67.

4 Jon M. Erlandson and Todd J. Braje, "From Asia to the Americas by Boat? Paleogeography, Paleoecology, and Stemmed Points of the Northwest Pacific," *Quaternary International* 239 (2011): 28–37, https://www.sciencedirect.com/science/article/abs/pii/S104061821100125X; Michael A. Glassow, comp. and ed., "Channel Islands National Park Archaeological Overview and Assessment," Channel Islands National Park, National Park Service, Department of the Interior, December 2010, https://www.nps.gov/chis/learn/historyculture/upload/Final-Arch-Overview-May-2015.pdf; Braje, Erlandson, and Rick, *Islands through Time*.

5 National Park Service, Channel Islands National Park, "Santa Cruz Island History and Culture," updated June 9, 2016, https://www.nps.gov/chis/learn/historyculture/santacruzisland.htm; Santa Cruz Island Reserve, "History," Natural Reserve System, University of California, Santa Barbara, 2022, https://santacruz.nrs.ucsb.edu/about/history.

6 National Park Service, Channel Islands National Park, "Santa Cruz Island History and Culture"; Santa Cruz Island Reserve, "History."

7 The Nature Conservancy, "Santa Cruz Island," 2023, https://www.nature.org/en-us/get-involved/how-to-help/places-we-protect/santa-cruz-island-california/.

8 Santa Cruz Island Foundation, accessed July 9, 2023, http://www.scifoundation.org/home.aspx.

9 A. Kathryn McEachern, Katherine A. Chess, and Ken Niessen, *Field Surveys of Rare Plants on Santa Cruz Island, California, 2003–2006: Historical Records and Current Distributions*, US Geological Survey, Scientific Investigations Report 2009–5264 (2010), 16, https://pubs.usgs.gov/sir/2009/5264/.

10 Dieter H. Wilken and A. Kathryn McEachern, "Experimental Reintroduction of the Federally Endangered Santa Cruz Island Bush Mallow (*Malacothamnus fasciculatus* var. *nesioticus*)," *Proceedings of the California Native Plant Society Conservation Conference, 17–19 Jan 2009*, (2011), 410, https://pubs.er.usgs.gov/publication/70040720.

11 Wilken and McEachern, "Experimental Reintroduction," 410.

12 McEachern, Chess, and Niessen, *Field Surveys*, 16.

13 Wilken and McEachern, "Experimental Reintroduction," 411.

14 McEachern, Chess, and Niessen, *Field Surveys*, 17.

15 Beesource, "The Honey Bees of Santa Cruz Island," February 24, 2016, https://www.beesource.com/threads/the-honey-bees-of-santa-cruz-island.365408/.

16 Leopold, *Sand County Almanac*, 190.

17 The Nature Conservancy, "Santa Cruz Island."

18 Scott A. Morrison, "Reducing Risk and Enhancing Efficiency in Non-native Vertebrate Removal Efforts on Islands: A 25 Year Multi-taxa Retrospective from Santa Cruz Island, California," *Managing Vertebrate Invasive Species*, Paper 31 (2007), 401, https://digitalcommons.unl.edu/cgi/viewcontent.cgi?article=1030&context=nwrcinvasive.

19 Gillian Flaccus, "Unlikely Hunters Kill Pigs to Spare Santa Cruz Foxes," *Seattle Times*, May 3, 2005, https://www.seattletimes.com/nation-world/unlikely-hunters-kill-pigs-to-spare-santa-cruz-foxes/.

20 Dewey Livingston, "Oral History Interview with Dr. Lyndal Laughrin," University of California Santa Barbara Natural Reserve System, Santa Cruz Island Reserve, May 6–9, 2011, https://www.islapedia.com/images/0/0d/Dr._Lyndal_Laughrin-Dewey_Livingston.pdf.

21 UNESCO, "Golija-Studenica Biosphere Reserve, Serbia," updated January 2021, https://en.unesco.org/biosphere/eu-na/golija-studenica.

22 Peter B. Sharpe and David K. Garcelon, "Restoring and Monitoring Bald Eagles in Southern California: The Legacy of DDT," *Institute for Wildlife Studies, Proceedings of the Sixth California Islands Symposium*, 2003, 323, https://static1.squarespace.com/static/60a6b9c6059cad3139d4d98b/t/615dd25406267602334dd7e4/1633538646204/Sharpe_and_Garcelon.pdf.

23 National Park Service, Channel Islands National Park, "Restoring Balance: Santa Cruz Island" (with videos, 2008), updated December 29, 2017, https://www.nps.gov/chis/learn/photosmultimedia/restoring-balance-santa-cruz-island-long-version.htm.

24 Friends of the Island Fox, "USFWS Announces Recovery of Channel Island Fox," February 12, 2016, http://www1.islandfox.org/2016/02/usfws-announces-recovery-of-channel.html.

25 National Park Service, Channel Islands National Park, "Restoring Balance: Santa Cruz Island."

3. Black Helicopters over Mount Tamalpais

1 Representative Helen Chenoweth, 1995, explaining that armed agents from the US Fish and Wildlife Service were landing in black helicopters on Idaho ranchers' property to enforce the Endangered Species Act, quoted by Paul

Rauber, "Eco-Thug: Helen Chenoweth," *Sierra* magazine, 1996, https://vault.sierraclub.org/sierra/199605/priorities.asp.

2   UNESCO, "Biosphere Reserves: World Network of Biosphere Reserves," accessed July 12, 2023, https://en.unesco.org/biosphere/wnbr. The number of biosphere reserves and host countries continues to grow.

3   Dasmann, *Called by the Wild*.

4   Raymond F. Dasmann, *The Destruction of California* (New York: Macmillan, 1965).

5   Dasmann, *Called by the Wild*; Vernon T. "Tom" Gilbert, interview by the author on the history of US participation in the UNESCO Biosphere Conference, June 9, 2022.

6   Peter Berg and Raymond F. Dasmann, "Reinhabiting California," *Ecologist* 7, no. 10: 399–401, reprinted in Peter Berg, *The Biosphere and the Bioregion: Essential Writings of Peter Berg*, ed. Cheryll Glotfelty and Eve Quesnel (London: Routledge, 2015), 35, http://ndl.ethernet.edu.et/bitstream/123456789/57862/1/Cheryll%20Glotfelty%20_2015.pdf.

7   Dasmann, *Called by the Wild*, 196.

8   Terri Thomas, interview by the author on the history of the establishment of the Golden Gate Biosphere Reserve, August 4, 2021.

9   Sierra Club, "Dr. Edgar Wayburn, M.D.: 1906–2010," accessed July 15, 2023, https://www.sierraclub.org/library/dr-edgar-wayburn-md; Steve Hymon, "Peggy Wayburn, 84; Author and Conservationist," *Los Angeles Times*, March 30, 2002 (obituary).

10 Laurie Wayburn, interview by the author on the history of the establishment of the Golden Gate Biosphere Reserve, September 1, 2021.

11 Ed Ueber, interview by the author on the history of the establishment of the Golden Gate Biosphere Reserve, August 16, 2021. Ed Ueber was a fisheries biologist with NOAA Fisheries who was instrumental in the establishment of three national marine sanctuaries that span the Central Coast of California: Cordell Bank, Greater Farallones, and Monterey Bay National Marine Sanctuaries. As director of those NMSs, two of which are part of the UNESCO Golden Gate Biosphere Reserve, he played a key role in coordinating agencies and stakeholders in the biosphere reserve after its establishment in 1988, working especially with Brian O'Neill of the National Park Service, then superintendent of GGNRA.

12 Nona Chiariello, interview by the author on the history of the establishment of the Golden Gate Biosphere Reserve, April 6, 2022.

13 Philippe Cohen, interview by the author on the history of the establishment of the Golden Gate Biosphere Reserve, September 3, 2021.

14 Gilbert, interview.

15 Cited in Josh Harkinson, "Richard Pombo Rides Again!," *Mother Jones*, January 6, 2010, https://www.motherjones.com/politics/2010/01/richard-pombo-rides-again/.

16 Rauber, "Eco-Thug: Helen Chenoweth."
17 UNESCO, *Statutory Framework of the World Network of Biosphere Reserves,* 2020, https://unesdoc.unesco.org/ark:/48223/pf0000373378.
18 Wayburn, interview.
19 William Gregg, interview by the author on the history of US participation in the UNESCO MAB Programme, June 17, 2022.
20 George Wright Society, "BRInfo: US Biosphere Regions Information Portal," 2023, https://www.georgewrightsociety.org/brinfo.
21 Golden Gate Biosphere Network, accessed July 15, 2023, https://www.goldengatebiosphere.org/.

4. Serpentine and Manzanita

1   William Shakespeare, *Macbeth,* act 1, scene 5.
2   V. Thomas Parker, personal communication to author, September 13, 2022.
3   Susan Harrison, Joshua H. Viers, and James F. Quinn, "Climatic and Spatial Patterns of Diversity in the Serpentine Plants of California," *Diversity and Distributions* 6 (2000): 153–161.
4   California Department of Conservation, "Serpentine: California's State Rock," 2019, https://www.conservation.ca.gov/cgs/Pages/Publications/Note_14.aspx.
5   Hobart M. King, "Serpentine," Geology.com, accessed July 15, 2023, https://geology.com/minerals/serpentine.shtml.
6   National Park Service, Golden Gate National Recreation Area, "Unusual Rock: Serpentinite Outcrops," text of interpretive sign along the California Coastal Trail in the San Francisco Presidio between Langdon Court and Baker Beach, viewed by author April 7, 2022.
7   Susan Harrison and Brian D. Inouye, "High β Diversity in the Flora of Californian Serpentine 'Islands,'" *Biodiversity and Conservation* 11 (2002): 1869, https://doi.org/10.1023/A:1020357904064.
8   Harrison, Viers, and Quinn, "Climatic and Spatial Patterns of Diversity," 154.
9   The history and lore of this traditional, Asian-inspired mountain pilgrimage, started by Gary Snyder and a couple of his Beat-Buddhist friends in 1965, is detailed in the book *Opening the Mountain: Circumambulating Mount Tamalpais; a Ritual Walk,* by Matthew Davis and Michael Scott. It is the subject of a later essay in this book, "Circling the Mountain."
10 The Jepson Herbarium, "*Arctostaphylos montana,*" 2022, https://ucjeps.berkeley.edu/eflora/eflora_display.php?tid=13933.
11 The Jepson Herbarium, "*Hesperocyparis sargentii,* Sargent Cypress," 2022, https://ucjeps.berkeley.edu/eflora/eflora_display.php?tid=89302.
12 Golden Gate National Parks Conservancy, "One Tam," accessed July 15, 2023, https://www.onetam.org/.
13 National Park Service, "Crews Survey Serpentine Barrens on Mount Tam,"

updated December 2, 2019, https://www.nps.gov/articles/crews-survey-serpentine-barrens-on-mount-tam.htm.

14 Rachel Kesel, David Greenberger, Andrea Williams, Michael Sturtevant, and Elizabeth Neill, *Serpentine Endemic Occupancy Project – 2019 Field Season Report*, 2019, https://www.onetam.org/sites/default/files/pdfs/SEOP%20 Report%202019%20CMOT.pdf.

15 V. Thomas Parker, "Diversity and Evolution of *Arctostaphylos* and *Ceanothus*," *Fremontia* 35, no. 4 (Fall 2007): 8.

16 Parker, "Diversity and Evolution," 9.

17 Gregory A. Wahlert, V. Thomas Parker, and Michael Vasey, "A Phylogeny of *Arctostaphylos* (Ericaceae) Inferred from Nuclear Ribosomal ITS Sequences," *Journal of the Botanical Research Institute of Texas* 3, no. 2 (2009): 674.

18 Parker, "Diversity and Evolution," 11.

19 Wahlert, Parker, and Vasey, "Phylogeny of *Arctostaphylos*," 674.

20 Staci E. Markos, Lena C. Hileman, Michael C. Vasey, and V. Thomas Parker, "Phylogeny of the *Arctostaphylos hookeri* Complex (Ericaceae) Based on nrDNA Data," *Madroño* 45, no. 3 (1998): 187; Parker, "Diversity and Evolution," 11; Wahlert, Parker, and Vasey, "Phylogeny of *Arctostaphylos*," 674.

21 Untold Stories, "Alice Eastwood: Pioneering Botanist, Explorer and Naturalist, Lifelong Lover of Flowers and Plants, California Academy of Sciences Curator of Botany," 2019, https://untoldstories.net/1879/01/plant-collector-extraordinaire-alice-eastwood/.

22 University of Colorado Museum of Natural History, "Botany on the Frontier: Alice Eastwood's Collection," May 2008, accessed July 15, 2003, https:// cumuseum-archive.colorado.edu/Research/Objects/may08_eastwood. html. According to this brief botanical biography of Eastwood, "Dr. William A. Weber, curator emeritus of the University of Colorado Herbarium claims, 'the real beginning of the herbarium [at the University of Colorado] was our acquisition of the early collections of Alice Eastwood, Colorado's first resident botanist.'"

23 Untold Stories, "Alice Eastwood."

24 The Jepson Herbarium, "*Arctostaphylos imbricata*, San Bruno Mountain Manzanita," 2022, https://ucjeps.berkeley.edu/eflora/eflora_display. php?tid=13935.

25 V. Thomas Parker, Michael C. Vasey, and Jon E. Keeley, "Taxonomic Revisions in the Genus *Arctostaphylos* (Ericaceae)," *Madroño* 54, no. 2 (2007): 150, https://www.biodiversitylibrary.org/part/169007.

26 Heather L. Lindon, Lauren M. Gardiner, Abigail Brady, and Maria S. Vorontsova, "Fewer Than Three Percent of Land Plant Species Named by Women: Author Gender over 260 Years," *Taxon* 64, no. 2 (2015): 209–215.

27 National Park Service, "Alice Eastwood," updated September 27, 2021, https:// www.nps.gov/people/alice-eastwood.htm.

28 Larry Blakely, "Alice Eastwood," Bristlecone Chapter, California Native Plant Society, updated March 23, 2013, http://bristleconecnps.org/native_plants/

names/eastwood.php, citing Patricia Ann Moore, "Cultivating Science in the
Field: Alice Eastwood, Ynés Mexia and California Botany, 1890–1940" (PhD
diss., UCLA, 1996), 39, UMI 9640244.

29 Jon E. Keeley, V. Thomas Parker, and Michael C. Vasey, "Resprouting and
Seeding Hypotheses: A Test of the Gap-Dependent Model Using Resprouting
and Obligate Seeding Subspecies of *Arctostaphylos*," *Plant Ecology* 217, no.
6 (2016): 743–750, https://www.jstor.org/stable/24751072; Michael
Kaufmann, "Obligate and Facultative Seeders," 2017, https://www.
michaelkauffmann.net/2017/01/obligate-facultative-seeders/; Cheadle
Center for Biodiversity and Ecological Restoration, "Ecology and Diversity
of the Manzanitas," University of California, Santa Barbara, April 5, 2018,
https://www.ccber.ucsb.edu/news-events/ecology-and-diversity-manzanitas;
Michael Kaufmann, Michael Vasey, and Tom Parker, *Field Guide to Manzanitas*
(Humboldt County, CA: Backcountry Press, 2021).

30 Cheadle Center for Biodiversity and Ecological Restoration, "Ecology and
Diversity of the Manzanitas"; V. Thomas Parker, personal communication to
author, September 13, 2022.

31 V. Thomas Parker, personal communication.

32 National Park Service, Point Reyes National Seashore, "After the Vision Fire:
An Educational Trail Guide," accessed July 15, 2023, https://www.nps.gov/
pore/learn/management/upload/firemanagement_visionfire_trailguide.pdf.

33 California Native Plant Society, "Marin Manzanita (*Arctostaphylos virgata*),"
accessed July 15, 2023, https://calscape.org/Arctostaphylos-virgata-().

34 Snyder, "Control Burn," in *Turtle Island*, 19.

35 Alan A. Schoenherr, Robert Feldmeth, and Michael J. Emerson, *Natural History
of the Islands of California* (Berkeley: University of California Press, 1999), 296.

36 In fact, a recent study in Mexico found that gray foxes, to which the island fox
is closely related, are a major seed scarifier and disperser for *Arctostaphylos
pungens*, the pointleaf or Mexican manzanita; see Fabián Alejandro Rubacalva-
Castillo, Joaquín Sosa-Ramírez, José de Jesús Luna-Ruíz, Arturo Gerardo
Valdivia-Flores, and Luis Ignacio Íñiguez-Dávalos, "Seed Dispersal by
Carnivores in Temperate and Tropical Dry Forests," *Ecology and Evolution* 11,
no. 9 (February 9, 2021), https://pubmed.ncbi.nlm.nih.gov/33976775/.

37 Western Neighborhoods Project, "Laurel Hill Cemetery," accessed July 15,
2023, https://www.outsidelands.org/laurel_hill.php.

38 Presidio Trust, "Back from the Brink: For the Last Wild Franciscan Manzanita,"
June 17, 2011, https://www.youtube.com/watch?v=ovTU4FXfB1Q.

39 Daniel Gluesenkamp, M. Chassé, Mark Frey, V. Thomas Parker, Michael Vasey,
and B. Young, "Back from the Brink: A Second Chance at Discovery and
Conservation of the Franciscan Manzanita," *Fremontia* 37, no 4 (2009): 3–17;
Sadie Gribbon, "Presidio's 'Loneliest Plant in the World' Meets Its Match," *San
Francisco Examiner*, February 15, 2018, https://www.sfexaminer.com/news/
presidio-s-loneliest-plant-in-the-world-meets-its-match/article_d306bb51-

d787-57f9-b005-0b4159c735a4.html; KQED, "Restoring San Francisco's Lost Manzanita: Science on the SPOT," January 20, 2011, https://www.youtube.com/watch?v=8SYrYFlb3qs.

40 Parker, Vasey, and Keeley, "Taxonomic Revisions in the Genus *Arctostaphylos*," 150; Presidio Trust, "Back from the Brink," 2011.

41 Peter H. Raven taught at Stanford from 1960 to 1971 and then became director of the Missouri Botanical Garden until his retirement in 2011. He is the coauthor, with Paul Ehrlich, of a seminal paper published in the journal *Evolution* in 1964 that expounded the concept of coevolution, "Butterflies and Plants: A Study in Coevolution." Raven was a proponent of the Golden Gate Biosphere Reserve, and in 2003, after President George W. Bush rejoined UNESCO after a nine-year hiatus, Raven hosted a conference at the Missouri Botanical Garden to once again engage US scientists in the international program, according to Vernon "Tom" Gilbert (personal communication).

42 Harrison and Inouye, "High β Diversity," 1870; Harrison, Viers, and Quinn, "Climatic and Spatial Patterns of Diversity"; Robert H. Whittaker, "The Ecology of Serpentine Soils," *Ecology* 35, no. 2 (1954): 258–288.

43 Parker, "Diversity and Evolution," 8.

5. Butterfly Blues

1 Billie Holliday, December 8, 1957, quoted on "Fine and Mellow," National Public Radio, April 10, 2000, https://www.npr.org/2000/04/10/1072753/fine-and-mellow.

2 Jing Zhang, Qian Cong, Jinhui Shen, Paul A. Opler, and Nick V. Grishin, "Genomics of a Complete Butterfly Continent," preprint posted November 4, 2019, https://www.biorxiv.org/content/biorxiv/early/2019/11/04/829887.full.pdf; genomics is the use of DNA sequencing to elucidate the evolutionary relationships among species.

3 Kevin Whitehead, *Why Jazz? A Concise Guide* (New York: Oxford University Press, 2011), 11.

4 Golden Gate National Parks Conservancy, "Mission Blue Butterfly," 2023, https://www.parksconservancy.org/conservation/mission-blue-butterfly; there are also significant populations in the Marin Headlands.

5 Bette Higgins and Mimi Whitney, op-ed, "The Battle to Save a Mountain," *San Francisco Examiner*, January 10, 1974, San Bruno Mountain Watch Archives, https://www.flickr.com/photos/sbmw/49775230326/.

6 Saskia Solomon, "Little Boxes—Malvina Reynolds' 1962 Song Captured the Mood of the Times," *Financial Times*, January 17, 2022, https://ig.ft.com/life-of-a-song/little-boxes.html; Pete Seeger, "Little Boxes," accessed July 15, 2023, https://ig.ft.com/life-of-a-song/little-boxes.html.

7 Chris Carlsson, "San Bruno Mountain: Historical Essay," FoundSF, accessed July 15, 2023, https://www.foundsf.org/index.php?title=San_Bruno_

Mountain#:~:text=In%20the%20late%201970s%20the%20US%20Fish%20
and,Elfin%20and%20Silverspot%20Butterflies%2C%20the%20SF%20
garter%20snake%29.

8   Frank LaPierre, "Who's Who in the Mountain Controversy," *San Mateo
    Times*, September 10, 1975, San Bruno Mountain Watch Archives, accessed
    July 15, 2023, https://www.flickr.com/photos/sbmw/49775230896/in/
    album-72157670764260637/.

9   Defenders of Wildlife, introduction to *Frayed Safety Nets: Conservation Planning
    under the Endangered Species Act* (1998), accessed July 15, 2023, https://
    defenders.org/sites/default/files/publications/frayed_safety_nets_-_intro.
    pdf; Graham M. Lyons, "Habitat Conservation Plans: Restoring the Promise
    of Conservation," *Environs* 23, no. 1 (1999): 88–92, https://environs.law.
    ucdavis.edu/volumes/23/1/articles/lyons.pdf; Robert M. Pyle, personal
    communication to author, October 6, 2022.

10 San Bruno Mountain Watch, 2022, https://www.mountainwatch.org/; County
    of San Mateo, "San Bruno Mountain State and County Park," 2023, https://
    www.smcgov.org/parks/san-bruno-mountain-state-county-park.

11 Stuart B. Weiss, L. Naumovich, and C. Niederer, *Assessment of the Past 30 Years
    of Habitat Management and Covered Species Monitoring Associated with the
    San Bruno Mountain Habitat Conservation Plan*, prepared for the San Mateo
    County Parks Department by Creekside Science, 2015, available under "30-
    Year Review 2015" at https://www.smcgov.org/parks/san-bruno-mountain-
    habitat-management-approach-projects-documents.

12 National Park Service, "Mission Blue Butterflies," updated April 27, 2020,
    https://www.nps.gov/rlc/pacificcoast/mission-blue-butterflies.htm; National
    Park Service, "Translocation Project Brings Mission Blue Butterflies Back to
    Sweeney Ridge," updated May 18, 2022, https://www.nps.gov/articles/000/
    sfanblog_translocation-project-brings-mission-blue-butterflies-back-to-
    sweeney-ridge.htm.

13 Stuart B. Weiss, "Cars, Cows, and Checkerspot Butterflies: Nitrogen
    Deposition and Management of Nutrient-Poor Grasslands for a Threatened
    Species," *Conservation Biology* 13 (1999): 1478, https://creeksidescience.files.
    wordpress.com/2012/01/weiss_1999_conbio.pdf.

14 Paul R. Ehrlich and Peter H. Raven, "Butterflies and Plants: A Study in
    Coevolution," *Evolution* 18, no. 4 (1964): 586–608, https://onlinelibrary.wiley.
    com/doi/10.1111/j.1558-5646.1964.tb01674.x.

15 Paul R. Ehrlich, "The Population Biology of the Butterfly, *Euphydryaseditha*.
    II. The Structure of the Jasper Ridge Colony," *Evolution* 19 (1965): 327–336,
    https://onlinelibrary.wiley.com/doi/10.1111/j.1558-5646.1965.tb01723.x.

16 John Rawlings, "Native Grass Viewing at Jasper Ridge Biological Preserve's
    Serpentine Grassland," 2008, https://web.stanford.edu/dept/JRBP/plants/
    PDF/SerpentinePrairie.pdf.

17 Susan Harrison, "Long-Distance Dispersal and Colonization in the Bay
    Checkerspot Butterfly, *Euphydryas editha bayensis*," *Ecology* 70, no. 5 (1989):

1241, https://esajournals.onlinelibrary.wiley.com/doi/abs/10.2307/1938181.

18 Weiss, "Cars, Cows, and Checkerspot Butterflies," 1478.

19 Carol L. Boggs, Ward B. Watt, and Paul R. Ehrlich, eds., *Butterflies: Ecology and Evolution Taking Flight* (Chicago: University of Chicago Press, 2003), 1, 6.

20 William Keith, *Sand Dunes and Fog, San Francisco*, circa 1880s, Saint Mary's College Museum of Art, Moraga, CA, https://www.stmarys-ca.edu/museum-art/william-keith-collection.

21 San Francisco Estuary Institute, "Hidden in Plain Sight: The Unique Natural Landscape of San Francisco," accessed July 15, 2023, https://storymaps.arcgis.com/stories/e42ea1a97f4f480b85ffc056734ba14f.

22 Xerces Society for Invertebrate Conservation, accessed July 15, 2023, https://xerces.org/.

23 National Park Service, "Lobos Dunes Boardwalk Guide," 2004; Golden Gate National Parks Conservancy, "Lobos Creek," accessed July 15, 2023, https://www.parksconservancy.org/projects/lobos-creek.

24 The Jepson Herbarium, "*Acmispon glaber* var. *glaber*," 2023, https://ucjeps.berkeley.edu/eflora/eflora_display.php?tid=91825.

25 J. W. Tilden, "San Francisco's Vanishing Butterflies," *Lepidopterists' News* 10, nos. 3–4 (1956): 114, https://images.peabody.yale.edu/lepsoc/jls/1950s/1956/1956-10(3-4)113-Tilden.pdf.

26 Robert Michael Pyle, "The Xerces Story," Xerces Society for Invertebrate Conservation, accessed July 15, 2023, https://xerces.org/xerces-story.

27 Robert Michael Pyle, "Resurrection Ecology: Bring Back the Xerces Blue!," *Wild Earth* 10, no. 3 (Fall 2000): 30.

28 Ken Davenport, "A Concise Update of the Information Provided in *The Butterflies of Southern California* (1973) by Thomas C. Emmel and John F. Emmel," *Taxonomic Report of the International Lepidoptera Survey* 4, no. 7 (May 10, 2004), https://archive.org/details/TREPORT47.

29 Butterfly Identification, "Silvery Blue (*Glaucopsyche lygdamus*)," accessed July 15, 2023, https://www.butterflyidentification.com/silvery-blue.htm.

30 Art Shapiro's Butterfly Site, "*Glaucopsyche lygdamus*," accessed July 15, 2023, https://butterfly.ucdavis.edu/butterfly/glaucopsyche/lygdamus.

31 Stuart Weiss, personal communication to author, November 4, 2022.

32 Revive and Restore, Wild Genomes Awarded Projects, "Xerces Blue Butterfly," accessed July 15, 2023, https://reviverestore.org/projects/wild-genomes/.

33 Dolly Jørgensen, "Reintroduction and De-extinction," *BioScience* 63, no. 9 (2013): 719–720; Curt Meine, "De-extinction and the Community of Being," *Hastings Center Report* 47, S2 (2017), https://www.researchgate.net/publication/318711842_De-extinction_and_the_Community_of_Being; Ben Minteer, "Is It Right to Reverse Extinction?," *Nature* 509 (2014): 261, https://www.nature.com/articles/509261a; Philip J. Seddon, Axel Moehrenschlager, and John Ewen, "Reintroduction of Resurrected Species: A Conservation Translocation Framework for Selecting DeExtinction Candidates," *Trends in Ecology and Evolution* 29, no. 3 (2014): 140–147.

34 T. S. Eliot, "The Love Song of J. Alfred Prufrock," 1915, Poets.org, https://poets.org/poem/love-song-j-alfred-prufrock.

35 Zhang et al., "Genomics of a Complete Butterfly Continent."

36 Ewen Callaway, "Every Butterfly in the United States and Canada Now Has a Genome Sequence," *Nature News*, November 19, 2019, https://www.nature.com/articles/d41586-019-03521-4/.

37 Pamela S. Soltis, "Introgression," accessed July 15, 2023, https://www.sciencedirect.com/topics/biochemistry-genetics-and-molecular-biology/introgression.

38 Gerard Talavera, Vladimir A. Lukhtanov, Naomi E. Pierce, and Roger Vila, "Establishing Criteria for Higher-Level Classification Using Molecular Data: The Systematics of *Polyommatus* Blue Butterflies (Lepidoptera, Lycaenidae)," *Cladistics* 29 (2013): 166, https://www.biologiaevolutiva.org/rvila/Lab/Publications_files/2013_Talavera%20et%20al_Polyommatina_systematics.pdf.

39 Konrad Fiedler, "Ants That Associate with Lycaeninae Butterfly Larvae: Diversity, Ecology and Biogeography," *Diversity and Distributions* 7 (2001): 45–46; Naomi E. Pierce, Michael F. Braby, Alan Heath, David J. Lohman, John Mathew, Douglas B. Rand, and Mark A. Travassos, "The Ecology and Evolution of Ant Association in the Lycaenidae (Lepidoptera)," *Annual Review of Entomology* 47 (2002): 733.

40 Whitehead, *Why Jazz?*, 11.

41 Whitehead, 11.

42 Zhang et al., "Genomics of a Complete Butterfly Continent," 12.

43 Qiaomei Fu, Cosimo Posth, Mateja Hajdinjak, Martin Petr, Swapan Mallick, Daniel Fernandes, Anja Furtwängler, et al., "The Genetic History of Ice Age Europe," *Nature* 534 (2016): 200–205, https://www.ncbi.nlm.nih.gov/pmc/articles/PMC4943878/; Richard E. Green, Johannes Krause, Adrian W. Briggs, Tomislav Maricic, Udo Stenzel, Martin Kircher, Nick Patterson, et al., "A Draft Sequence of the Neandertal Genome," *Science* 328 (2010): 710–722, https://www.science.org/doi/10.1126/science.1188021; Martin Kuhlwilm, Ilan Gronau, Melissa J. Hubisz, Cesare de Filippo, Javier Prado-Martinez, Martin Kircher, et al., "Ancient Gene Flow from Early Modern Humans into Eastern Neanderthals," *Nature* 530 (2016): 429–433, https://www.nature.com/articles/nature16544; David Reich, Richard E. Green, Martin Kircher, Johannes Krause, Nick Patterson, Eric Y. Durand, Bence Viola, et al., "Genetic History of an Archaic Hominin Group from Denisova Cave in Siberia," *Nature* 468 (2010): 1053–1060, https://www.nature.com/articles/nature09710; Aaron B. Wolf and Joshua M. Akey, "Outstanding Questions in the Study of Archaic Hominin Admixture," *PLoS Genetics* 14 (2018): e1007349, https://journals.plos.org/plosgenetics/article?id=10.1371/journal.pgen.1007349.

44 Olga Dolgova and Oscar Lao, "Evolutionary and Medical Consequences of Archaic Introgression into Modern Human Genomes," *Genes (Basel)* 9 (2018), https://www.ncbi.nlm.nih.gov/pmc/articles/PMC6070777/; David Enard and Dmitri A. Petrov, "Evidence That RNA Viruses Drove Adaptive Introgression between Neanderthals and Modern Humans," *Cell* 175 (2018):

360–371, e313, https://pubmed.ncbi.nlm.nih.gov/30290142/; Rachel M. Gittelman, Joshua G. Schraiber, Benjamin Vernot, Carmen Mikacenic, and Mark M. Wurfel, "Archaic Hominin Admixture Facilitated Adaptation to Out-of-Africa Environments," *Current Biology* 26 (2016): 3375–3382, https://www.cell.com/current-biology/fulltext/S0960-9822(16)31267-2; Emilia Huerta-Sánchez, Xin Jin, Asan, Zhuoma Bianba, Benjamin M. Peter, Nicolas Vinckenbosch, Yu Liang, et al., "Altitude Adaptation in Tibetans Caused by Introgression of Denisovan-like DNA," *Nature* 512 (2014): 194–197, https://www.nature.com/articles/nature13408.

6. Making Friends with Fire

1 Snyder, "Control Burn," in *Turtle Island*, 19.
2 National Park Service, Point Reyes National Seashore, "Woodward Fire – August 2020," updated March 17, 2022, https://www.nps.gov/pore/learn/management/firemanagement_woodwardfire.htm.
3 Maritte J. O'Gallagher, Gregory A. Jones, Lorraine S. Parsons, Dave T. Press, Wende E. Rehlaender, Stephen Skartvedt, and Alison B. Forrestel, "2020 Woodward Fire Case Study: Examining the Role of Fire as an Ecological Process in a Coastal California Ecosystem, *Parks Stewardship Forum* 37, no. 2 (2021): 331–340, https://escholarship.org/uc/item/7hg7j88v.
4 Frances Stead Sellers, "Forced from Paradise: Leaving Home after One of America's Deadliest Wildfires," *Washington Post*, July 23, 2019, https://www.washingtonpost.com/graphics/2019/national/paradise-fire-displaced-residents/; Katy Steinmetz, "California's Historic Camp Fire Destroyed Their Home. Now They're Looking for Hope — and Suing Their Utility Company," *Time*, November 30, 2018, https://time.com/5464667/paradise-wildfire-lawsuit-pge/; Zan Romanoff, "As Another Brutal Fire Season Rages, 4 New Books Bring Context and Consolation," *Los Angeles Times*, July 27, 2021, https://www.latimes.com/entertainment-arts/books/story/2021-07-27/on-the-cusp-of-a-brutal-fire-season-a-welcome-new-crop-of-books.
5 US Forest Service, Northern Region, "The Story of Smokey Bear," 2005, https://web.archive.org/web/20100125063452/http:/www.fs.fed.us/r1/centennial/smokey.shtml; Smokey Bear, "Story of Smokey," 2021, https://smokeybear.com/en/smokeys-history/story-of-smokey.
6 Smokey Bear, https://smokeybear.com/.
7 Bryan Daniels, Bootleg Fire Incident Command via AP, accessed July 15, 2023, https://www.reviewjournal.com/news/nation-and-world/weather-helps-but-western-wildfires-grow-2404880/attachment/in-this-photo-provided-by-the-bootleg-fire-incident-command-a-bear-cub-clings-to-a-tree-after-2/.
8 Stephen J. Pyne, *Fire in America: A Cultural History of Wildland and Rural Fire* (Seattle: University of Washington Press, 1982), 164.

9 Wildfire historian Stephen Pyne has been a leader in telling the wildfire story for forty years, from his 1982 tome, *Fire in America*, to his latest book, *The Pyrocene*, published in 2022.

10 Timothy Egan, *The Big Burn: Teddy Roosevelt and the Fire That Saved America* (Boston: Mariner Books, Houghton Mifflin Harcourt, 2010); NPR, "Teddy Roosevelt and the Fire That Saved the Forests," *Fresh Air*, October 29, 2009, https://www.npr.org/2009/10/29/114248029/teddy-roosevelt-and-the-fire-that-saved-the-forests; PBS, *The Big Burn* (film), 2022, https://www.pbs.org/wgbh/americanexperience/films/burn/.

11 County of Marin, "Tamalpais Forest Fire District," 2022, https://www.marincounty.org/depts/fr/divisions/administration/history/1920; Marin Fire History Project, "The Famed Tavern at the Top of Mt. Tamalpais Burned Down in a Spectacular Fire on June 30, 1923," accessed July 15, 2023, https://www.marinfirehistory.org/1923-tavern-of-tamalpais-burns-down.html.

12 Brendan M. Rogers, Jennifer K. Balch, Scott J. Goetz, Caroline E. R. Lehmann, and Merritt Turetsky, "Focus on Changing Fire Regimes: Interactions with Climate, Ecosystems, and Society," *Environmental Research Letters* 15, no. 3 (2020): 030201, https://iopscience.iop.org/article/10.1088/1748-9326/ab6d3a.

13 Christy Avery, *Tomales Bay Environmental History and Historic Resource Study: Point Reyes National Seashore*, 2009, National Park Service, Pacific West Region, https://babel.hathitrust.org/cgi/pt?id=ucl.31822038365995&view=1up&seq=5.

14 Peter M. Brown, Margot W. Kaye, and Dan Buckley, "Fire History in Douglas-Fir and Coast Redwood Forests at Point Reyes National Seashore, California," *Northwest Science* 73, no. 3 (1999): 213–214, http://www.rmtrr.org/data/Brownetal_1999_NWSci.pdf; Dale R. McCullough, *The Tule Elk: Its History, Behavior, and Ecology*, University of California Publications in Zoology 88 (Berkeley: University of California Press, 1969): 209; Betty Goerke, *Discovering Native People at Point Reyes* (Novato, CA: Museum of the American Indian, 2012): 37–41; Sebastian Rodriguez Cermeño and Henry R. Wagner, "The Voyage to California of Sebastian Rodriguez Cermeño in 1595," *California Historical Society Quarterly* 3, no. 1 (April 1924): 14, https://www.jstor.org/stable/25613599?seq=1; Richard Henry Dana Jr., *Two Years before the Mast: A Personal Narrative* (New York: Harper and Brothers, 1840).

15 Bruce A. Byers, Lucía DeSoto, Dan Chaney, Sidney R. Ash, Anya B. Byers, Jonathan B. Byers, and Markus Stoffel, "Fire-Scarred Fossil Tree from the Late Triassic Shows a Pre-fire Drought Signal," *Nature Scientific Reports* 10 (2020): 20104, https://www.nature.com/articles/s41598-020-77018-w; Jon E. Keeley and Juli G. Pausas, "Evolutionary Ecology of Fire," *Annual Review of Ecology, Evolution, and Systematics* 53 (2022): 203–225, https://www.annualreviews.org/doi/abs/10.1146/annurev-ecolsys-102320-095612.

16 Brown, Kaye, and Buckley, "Fire History in Douglas-Fir."

17 Brown, Kaye, and Buckley, 213.

18 R. Scott Anderson, Ana Ejarque, Peter M. Brown, and Douglas J. Hallett, "Holocene and Historical Vegetation Change and Fire History on the North-Central Coast of California, USA," *Holocene* 23, no. 12 (2013): 1797–1810.

19 Anderson et al., "Holocene and Historical Vegetation Change," 1806; R. Scott Anderson, *Contrasting Vegetation and Fire Histories on the Point Reyes Peninsula during the Pre-settlement and Settlement Periods: 15,000 Years of Change* (Flagstaff: Center for Environmental Sciences and Education, and Quaternary Sciences Program, Northern Arizona University, 2005), https://www.nps.gov/pore/learn/management/upload/firemanagement_fireecology_research_anderson_0506.pdf.

20 Brown, Kaye, and Buckley, "Fire History in Douglas-Fir," 214; Anderson et al., "Holocene and Historical Vegetation Change"; Anderson, *Contrasting Vegetation and Fire Histories*; Jon E. Keeley, "Native American Impacts on Fire Regimes of the California Coastal Ranges," *Journal of Biogeography* 29, no. 3 (2002): 303–320, https://onlinelibrary.wiley.com/doi/abs/10.1046/j.1365-2699.2002.00676.x.

21 Anderson, *Contrasting Vegetation and Fire Histories*, 16; Keeley, "Native American Impacts."

22 Brown, Kaye, and Buckley, "Fire History in Douglas-Fir," 214.

23 National Park Service, Point Reyes National Seashore, "After the Vision Fire: An Educational Trail Guide," accessed July 15, 2023, https://www.nps.gov/pore/learn/management/upload/firemanagement_visionfire_trailguide.pdf.

24 Laura Dassow Walls, *Thoreau: A Life* (Chicago: University of Chicago Press, 2017), 171–173.

25 National Park Service, Point Reyes National Seashore, "Fire Ecology – Vegetation Types: Bishop Pine Forests," updated April 26, 2023, https://www.nps.gov/pore/learn/management/firemanagement_fireecology_vegtypes_bishoppine.htm.

26 Constance I. Millar, "Bishop Pine (*Pinus muricata*) of Inland Marin County, California," *Madroño* 33, no. 2 (1986): 123–129; Constance I. Millar, "The Californian Closed Cone Pines (Subsection *Oocarpae* Little and Critchfield): A Taxonomic History and Review," *Taxon* 15, no. 4 (1986): 657–670; Constance I. Millar, Steven H. Strauss, M. Thompson Conkle, and Robert D. Westfall, "Allozyme Differentiation and Biosystematics of the Californian Closed-Cone Pines (*Pinus* subsect. *Oocarpae*)," *Systematic Botany* 13, no. 3 (1988): 351–370.

27 National Park Service, Point Reyes National Seashore, "Fire Ecology – Vegetation Types: Maritime Chaparral," updated April 26, 2023, https://www.nps.gov/pore/learn/management/firemanagement_fireecology_vegtypes_chaparral.htm; National Park Service, "Reflections on the 2020 Woodward Fire: Understanding the Impacts of Fire on Point Reyes Ecosystems," updated September 3, 2021, https://www.nps.gov/articles/000/2020-woodward-fire-impacts-on-point-reyes-ecosystems.htm.

28 National Park Service, Point Reyes National Seashore, "Fire Suppression," updated July 20, 2019, https://www.nps.gov/pore/learn/management/

firemanagement_firesuppression.htm.

29 National Park Service, "Golden Gate Biosphere Network Links People and Places," updated September 2, 2021, https://www.nps.gov/articles/000/goga-biosphere.htm.

30 Audubon Canyon Ranch, "Fire Forward," accessed July 15, 2023, https://www.egret.org/fire-forward/; and "Partnering with You on Land Stewardship," accessed July 15, 2023, https://www.egret.org/good-fire-on-your-land/.

31 Conservation Gateway, The Nature Conservancy, "Indigenous Peoples Burning Network," 2018, https://www.conservationgateway.org/ConservationPractices/FireLandscapes/Pages/IPBN.aspx; Page Buono, "Quiet Fire," *Nature Conservancy Magazine*, Winter 2020, https://www.nature.org/en-us/magazine/magazine-articles/indigenous-controlled-burns-california/.

32 Karuk Climate Change Projects, "Good Fire," accessed July 15, 2023, https://karuktribeclimatechangeprojects.com/good-fire/; Kari M. Norgaard, "Colonization, Fire Suppression, and Indigenous Resurgence in the Face of Climate Change," *YES!* magazine, October 22, 2019; Kari M. Norgaard and Sara Wort, "What Western States Can Learn from Native American Wildfire Management Strategies," *Conversation*, October 29, 2019, https://theconversation.com/what-western-states-can-learn-from-native-american-wildfire-management-strategies-120731.

33 Pepperwood Preserve, accessed July 15, 2023, https://www.pepperwoodpreserve.org; Pepperwood Preserve, "The Burning Question for California Wine Country," July 8, 2021, https://www.pepperwoodpreserve.org/2021/07/08/the-burning-question-for-california-wine-country/.

34 "Wine Country Fires: A Deadly Inferno's First Hours," *San Francisco Chronicle*, accessed July 15, 2023, https://www.sfchronicle.com/bayarea/article/Wine-Country-fires-first-fatal-hours-12278092.php.

35 Ackerly Lab, 2023, https://www.ackerlylab.org/.

7. Séance at Sky Camp

1 Robert Frost, "Mending Wall," in *North of Boston* (London: David Nutt, 1914).

2 Erik K. Cole, "Use of *Cervus elaphus* versus *Cervus canadensis* in Reference to North American Elk (Wapiti)?," July 17, 2020, https://www.researchgate.net/post/Use_of_Cervus_elaphus_versus_Cervus_canadensis_in_reference_to_North_American_elk_wapiti. Eric Cole, of the US Fish and Wildlife Service, explains that despite some academic arguments about the taxonomy of elk, "Management oriented biologists in North America appear to be widely adopting *Cervus canadensis* rather than *Cervus elaphus* as the new convention when referring to North American elk in manuscripts, technical reports, and published peer reviewed articles."

3 E. P. Meredith, J. A. Rodzen, J. D. Banks, R. Schaefer, H. B. Ernest, T. R.

Famula, and B. P. May, "Microsatellite Analysis of Three Subspecies of Elk
(*Cervus elaphus*) in California," *Journal of Mammalogy* 88, no. 3 (2007):
801–808, https://academic.oup.com/jmammal/article/88/3/801/1073029.

4   National Park Service, Point Reyes National Seashore, "Tule Elk:
Return of a Species" 1998, 1, https://www.nps.gov/pore/learn/upload/
resourcenewsletter_tuleelk.pdf.

5   Goerke, *Discovering Native People*, 31–37.

6   McCullough, *Tule Elk*, 209.

7   Goerke, *Discovering Native People*, 37–41.

8   Cermeño and Wagner, "Voyage to California," 14.

9   Dana, *Two Years before the Mast*.

10 Robert H. Schmidt, "Gray Wolves in California: Their Presence and Absence,"
California Fish and Game 77, no. 2 (1991): 80; Michael Ellis, "Ask the
Naturalist: Did Wolves Ever Live in the Bay Area?," *Bay Nature*, May 16, 2016,
https://baynature.org/article/ask-the-naturalist-did-wolves-ever-live-in-the-
bay-area/.

11 National Park Service, Point Reyes National Seashore, "Tule Elk: Return of a
Species."

12 US Congress, "Joint Resolution Providing for Federal Participation in
Preserving the Tule Elk Population in California," Public Law 94-389, August
14, 1976.

13 McCrea Andrew Cobb, "Spatial Ecology and Population Dynamics of Tule
Elk (*Cervus elaphus nannodes*) at Point Reyes National Seashore" (PhD diss.,
University of California, Berkeley, 2010), 13.

14 Dale R. McCullough, Robert A. Garrott, Jay F. Kirkpatrick, Edward O. Plotka,
Katherine O. Ralls, and E. Tom Thorne, "Report of the Scientific Advisory
Panel on Control of Tule Elk on Point Reyes National Seashore," National
Park Service, Point Reyes National Seashore, 1993, 4, https://www.nps.gov/
pore/getinvolved/upload/planning_tule_elk_report_scientific_advisory_
panel_1993.pdf.

15 McCullough et al., "Report of the Scientific Advisory Panel," 34.

16 Cobb, "Spatial Ecology and Population Dynamics," 1–2.

17 National Park Service, *Tule Elk Monitoring and Management at Point Reyes
National Seashore: 2015–2016 Report*, 2018, 3, https://irma.nps.gov/
DataStore/DownloadFile/601983#:~:text=Native%20tule%20elk%20
%28Cervus%20elaphus%20nannodes%29%20at%20Point,Drakes%20
Beach%2C%20and%20in%20the%20Estero%20Road%2FLimantour%20area.

18 Peter Byrne, "Apocalypse Cow: The Future of Life at Point Reyes National
Park," *Counterpunch*, December 11, 2020, https://www.counterpunch.
org/2020/12/11/apocalypse-cow-the-future-of-life-at-point-reyes-national-
park/.

19 Erica Gies, "Unique Elk in California May Be Killed under Controversial
Plan," *National Geographic*, September 30, 2020, https://www.

nationalgeographic.com/animals/article/tule-elk-culled-under-point-reyes-proposal?cmpid=org=ngp::mc=crm-email::src=ngp::cmp=editorial::add=Compass_20210403&rid=5252D779BD5B26BDBB57B7679BE205FE.

20 Jim Coda, "Captive Tule Elk Are Dying in Point Reyes," Sierra Club San Francisco Bay, June 4, 2021, https://www.sierraclub.org/san-francisco-bay/blog/2021/06/captive-tule-elk-are-dying-point-reyes.

21 National Park Service, Point Reyes National Seashore, "Tule Elk at Tomales Point FAQ," updated March 16, 2023, https://www.nps.gov/pore/learn/nature/tule_elk_tomales_point_faq.htm.

22 Marin Conservation League, "Point Reyes National Seashore: Superintendent Kenkel Speaks to the Present and Envisions the Future," *News from Marin Conservation League*, May–June 2022, 4, https://www.marinconservationleague.org/wp-content/uploads/2022/05/MCL-Newsletter-May-June-2022.pdf.

23 National Park Service, Point Reyes National Seashore, "Tomales Point Area Plan," updated June 22, 2023, https://www.nps.gov/pore/getinvolved/planning-tomales-point-area-plan.htm.

24 Point Reyes National Seashore Visitor Center interpretive display on the history of the national seashore, visited by the author in April 2022.

25 New Day Films, *Rebels with a Cause: How a Battle over Land Changed the American Landscape Forever*, 2013, https://www.pbs.org/video/rebels-with-a-cause-g718xi/; National Park Service, "A Bright Star in the Conservation Galaxy: Point Reyes National Seashore," 2022, https://www.nps.gov/articles/000/point-reyes-a-bright-star-in-the-conservation-galaxy.htm.

26 National Park Service, "Bright Star in the Conservation Galaxy."

27 John Hart, *An Island in Time: 50 Years of Point Reyes National Seashore*, 2012, https://johnhart.com/books/an-island-in-time/.

28 Marin Conservation League, "Point Reyes National Seashore," 4.

29 John Muir, "[Statement from John Muir]" (1895), in *John Muir: A Reading Bibliography by Kimes, 1986 (Muir Articles 1866–1986)*, entry 222, https://scholarlycommons.pacific.edu/jmb/222.

30 Curt Meine, *Aldo Leopold: His Life and Work* (Madison: University of Wisconsin Press, 1988); Leopold, *Sand County Almanac*.

31 In one of my favorite books of creative nonfiction, Paul Spencer Sochaczewski described his own visits to many of the places where the British naturalist Alfred Russel Wallace traveled in what are now Malaysia and Indonesia, making observations that led him independently to the discovery of the theory of evolution by natural selection. Comparing Wallace's observations and insights from his journals with his own experiences, Sochaczewski uses the literary conceit of sitting around a campfire with Wallace and mulling over the implications of time and change. It's fascinating and compelling. The book is *An Inordinate Fondness for Beetles: Campfire Conversations with Alfred Russel Wallace on People and Nature Based on Common Travel in the Malay Archipelago* (Singapore: Editions Didiet Millet, 2012).

32 Information on the alcohol preferences of Muir and Leopold is from personal communications with Curt Meine, an environmental historian and biographer of Aldo Leopold, and Harold Wood, who maintains a website of information on John Muir for the Sierra Club.

33 Bruce A. Byers, "Nature's Warm Heart: Following John Muir's Footsteps at Fountain Lake, Wisconsin," August 16, 2016, http://www.brucebyersconsulting.com/natures-warm-heart-following-john-muirs-footsteps-at-fountain-lake-wisconsin/.

34 Wolves are making their way back to California, slowly; it will happen, probably sooner than we think, unless we deliberately stop them. Several packs have established themselves in Northern California, and individuals from these packs are scouting the state. In fact, one was sighted in the mountains of the Los Padres National Forest not that far from Santa Barbara. It's just a matter of time. See Hillary Richard, "Wolves Returned to California. So Did 'Crazy' Rumors," *New York Times*, March 11, 2022, https://www.nytimes.com/2022/03/11/science/california-wolves-misinformation.html#:~:text=The%20%E2%80%9CShasta%20Pack%E2%80%9D%20were%20the,California%20was%20again%20without%20wolves.

8. The Salmon Sermon

1 From Q&A after talk during summer *sesshin*, July 26, 1995, at Sokoji Temple, San Francisco, CA.

2 Prunuske Chatham, Inc., "Coho Return to Green Gulch!," 2023, https://pcz.com/coho-return-to-green-gulch/; Mission Pictures, *Green Gulch Creek Restoration* (film), 2011, https://player.vimeo.com/video/24442302?portrait=0.

3 San Francisco Zen Center, "Green Gulch Farm Long Term Vision and Restoration Plan," 2008, 8.

4 NOAA Fisheries, "Recovery Plan for the Evolutionarily Significant Unit of Central California Coast Coho Salmon," September 1, 2012, https://www.fisheries.noaa.gov/resource/document/recovery-plan-evolutionarily-significant-unit-central-california-coast-coho.

5 National Park Service, "Winter 2020–2021 Coho and Steelhead Spawner Survey Summary," updated September 3, 2021, https://www.nps.gov/articles/000/2020-2021-coho-steelhead-spawner-survey-summary.htm; National Park Service, Pacific Coast Science and Learning Center, *Coho and Steelhead Blog*, updated June 15, 2023, https://www.nps.gov/rlc/pacificcoast/coho-steelhead-blog.htm.

6 Terri Thomas, "Fish Passage and the Power of Water," *News from Marin Conservation League*, January–February 2022, 1, 4–5, https://www.marinconservationleague.org/wp-content/uploads/2022/01/NL-Jan-Feb-22_web_rev.pdf.

7   Byers, *View from Cascade Head*, 50–51.

8   Daniel E. Schindler, Jonathan B. Armstrong, and Thomas E. Reed, "The Portfolio Concept in Ecology and Evolution," *Frontiers in Ecology and the Environment* 13 (2015): 257, https://doi.org/10.1890/140275.

9   Byers, *View from Cascade Head*, 52.

10 John Auwaerter and John F. Sears, "Historic Resource Study for Muir Woods National Monument, Golden Gate National Recreation Area," 2006, 8–10, https://www.nps.gov/goga/learn/management/upload/585_Muir-Woods-Historic-HRS-resource-Report.pdf.

11 Auwaerter and Sears, "Historic Resource Study," 35.

12 National Park Service, "William Kent: Conservationist and Anti-immigrant Politician," updated August 3, 2022, https://www.nps.gov/people/williamkent.htm; Sierra Club, The John Muir Exhibit, "William Kent," accessed July 15, 2023, https://vault.sierraclub.org/john_muir_exhibit/people/kent.aspx.

13 Mick Sopko, "A History of Green Gulch Farm," 2002, http://www.cuke.com/zc-stories/gg-history.htm.

14 Sopko, "History of Green Gulch Farm."

15 Robert Howard, *What Makes the Crops Rejoice: An Introduction to Gardening*, with Eric Skjei (Boston: Little, Brown, 1986); Alan-Chadwick.org, "Alan Chadwick: A Gardener of Souls," accessed July 15, 2023, http://www.alan-chadwick.org/html%20pages/books_articles/what_makes_the_crops_rejoice.html.

16 Micah Van der Ryn, "Sim Van der Ryn: Green Gulch Zen Center, Muir Beach, California," accessed July 15, 2023, http://simvanderryn.com/blank3.

17 Harry K. Roberts, *Walking in Beauty: Growing Up with the Yurok Indians* (Berkeley, CA: Heyday Books, 2022), https://www.heydaybooks.com/catalog/walking-in-beauty-growing-up-with-the-yurok-indians/.

18 Center for Humans and Nature, "Melissa K. Nelson," https://humansandnature.org/melissa-k-nelson/.

19 Rick Fields, *How the Swans Came to the Lake: A Narrative History of Buddhism in America* (Boston: Shambala, 1981, new material 1986), 225–231 (1986).

20 San Francisco Zen Center, "It's Green Gulch Creek, with a Twist," *Sangha News Journal*, December 16, 2014, https://blogs.sfzc.org/blog/2014/12/16/creek-with-a-twist/; Renovation and Restoration, "Green Gulch Creek Restoration," accessed July 15, 2023, https://renovationandrestoration.wordpress.com/creek-restoration-2/; Prunuske Chatham, Inc., "Green Gulch Enhancement Project," 2023, https://pcz.com/project/green-gulch-enhancement-project/.

21 National Park Service, Golden Gate National Recreation Area (GGNRA), "Redwood Creek Watershed Assessment," August 2011, http://npshistory.com/publications/goga/rcwa-2011.pdf; National Park Service, GGNRA, "Muir Beach Restoration," updated September 20, 2018, https://home.nps.gov/goga/learn/nature/muir-beach.htm.

22 National Park Service, GGNRA, "Muir Woods and Redwood Creek Watershed Planning," updated May 31, 2023, https://www.nps.gov/goga/getinvolved/muir-woods-planning.htm.

23 Thomas, "Fish Passage and the Power of Water."

24 Prunuske Chatham, Inc., "Coho Return to Green Gulch!"

25 National Park Service, "Spring 2023 a Record Breaking Smolt Season," updated June 12, 2023, https://www.nps.gov/articles/000/sfanblog_2023-a-record-breaking-smolt-season.htm.

26 Sara Tashker, "Cultivating Soft Earth Mind," Earth Day 2021 dharma talk recorded at San Francisco Zen Center, April 17, 2021, https://www.sfzc.org/teachings/dharma-talks/cultivating-soft-earth-mind-0.

9. They Say the Sea Is Cold

1 D. H. Lawrence, "Whales Weep Not!," in *Last Poems*, 1932, Poets.org, accessed July 15, 2023, https://poets.org/poem/whales-weep-not.

2 Anna Coxe Toogood, "Historic Resource Study: A Civil History of the Golden Gate National Recreation Area and Point Reyes National Seashore," vol. 1, National Park Service, June 1980, 22, 104–105, http://npshistory.com/publications/goga/hrs-civil-history-v1.pdf.

3 William B. Ashworth, "Charles Scammon," Linda Hall Library, Scientist of the Day series, May 28, 2021, https://www.lindahall.org/about/news/scientist-of-the-day/charles-scammon.

4 "Charles Melville Scammon—Naturalist and Hunter on the Pacific Ocean," *The Shelf* (blog), Harvard University, October 24, 2011, https://blogs.harvard.edu/preserving/2011/10/24/charles-melville-scammon-natualist-and-hunter-on-the-pacific-ocean/.

5 Byers, *View from Cascade Head*, 145–146.

6 California Killer Whale Project, "2023 Field Guide," https://www.californiakillerwhaleproject.org/field-guides.

7 Marine Mammal Commission, "Marine Mammal Protection Act," accessed July 15, 2023, https://www.mmc.gov/about-the-commission/our-mission/marine-mammal-protection-act/.

8 NOAA Fisheries, "Species Directory: ESA Threatened and Endangered: Whales," accessed July 15, 2023, https://www.fisheries.noaa.gov/species-directory/threatened-endangered?oq=&field_species_categories_vocab=54&field_species_details_status=All&field_region_vocab=All&items_per_page=25.

9 International Whaling Commission (IWC), "Introduction to Population Status," 2023, https://iwc.int/about-whales/population-status; IWC, "Population (Abundance) Estimates," 2023, https://iwc.int/about-whales/estimate; Easton R. White, Zachary Schakner, Amber Bellamy, and Mridula

Srinivasan, "Detecting Population Trends for US Marine Mammals," *Conservation Science and Practice* 2022(4): e611, https://conbio.onlinelibrary. wiley.com/doi/pdf/10.1111/csp2.611.

10 John Calambokidis, Gretchen H. Steiger, Corrie Curtice, Jolie Harrison, Megan C. Ferguson, Elizabeth Becker, Monica DeAngelis, and Sofie M. Van Parijs, "Biologically Important Areas for Selected Cetaceans within U.S. Waters – West Coast Region," *Aquatic Mammals* 41, no. 1 (2015): 39–53, https:// cascadiaresearch.org/files/Calambokidisetal2015BIAs.pdf.

11 California Killer Whale Project, accessed July 15, 2023, https://www. californiakillerwhaleproject.org/; Cascadia Research Collective, accessed July 15, 2023, https://cascadiaresearch.org/; Happywhale, accessed July 15, 2023, https://happywhale.com/home.

12 Byers, *View from Cascade Head*, 157.

13 NOAA Fisheries, "Gray Whales in the Eastern North Pacific," updated October 7, 2022, https://www.fisheries.noaa.gov/west-coast/science-data/ gray-whales-eastern-north-pacific.

14 California Killer Whale Project, "Orcas," 2021, https://www. californiakillerwhaleproject.org/orcas.

15 NOAA Fisheries, "Critical Habitat for the Southern Resident Killer Whale," updated April 7, 2022, https://www.fisheries.noaa.gov/action/critical-habitat-southern-resident-killer-whale.

16 Nancy Black, "Behavior and Ecology of Killer Whales in Monterey Bay over the Last 30 Years," American Cetacean Society, San Francisco Bay Chapter, webinar, October 27, 2020, https://www.acs-sfbay.org/events/2020/10/27/ nancy-black-behavior-and-ecology-of-killer-whales-in-monterey-bay-over-the-last-thirty-years.

17 NOAA Fisheries, "Marine Mammal Stock Assessment Reports by Species/ Stock," accessed July 15, 2023, https://www.fisheries.noaa.gov/national/ marine-mammal-protection/marine-mammal-stock-assessment-reports-species-stock#cetaceans---large-whales.

18 California Killer Whale Project, "Orcas."

19 Byers, *View from Cascade Head*, 142–143.

20 NOAA Fisheries, "Humpback Whale," accessed July 15, 2023, https://www. fisheries.noaa.gov/species/humpback-whale.

21 Calambokidis et al., "Biologically Important Areas."

22 Miriam Hauer-Jensen, "Analysis of Humpback Whale Songs: Applying the Traditional Method," Summer 2018, https://www.mbari.org/wp-content/ uploads/2018/12/Hauer-Jensen.pdf.

23 Payne first learned about whale vocalizations from William Schevill, a pioneer of marine bioacoustics, when he heard Schevill's recordings made for the US Navy's antisubmarine warfare efforts beginning in World War II; see Sam Roberts, "Roger Payne, Biologist Who Heard Whales Singing, Dies at 88," *New York Times*, June 14, 2023, https://www.nytimes.com/2023/06/14/science/ roger-payne-dead.html.

24 Michael May, "Recordings That Made Waves: The Songs That Saved the Whales," December 26, 2014, NPR, https://www.npr.org/2014/12/26/373303726/recordings-that-made-waves-the-songs-that-saved-the-whales.

25 Judy Collins, "Farewell to Tarwathie," *Whales and Nightingales* album (1970).

26 Hauer-Jensen, "Analysis of Humpback Whale Songs."

27 Calambokidis et al., "Biologically Important Areas," 41–42.

28 NOAA Fisheries, "Blue Whale (*Balaenoptera musculus musculus*): Eastern North Pacific Stock," March 15, 2022, https://media.fisheries.noaa.gov/2022-08/2021-PacBluewhale-Eastern%20North%20Pacific%20Stock.pdf.

29 MBARI: Monterey Bay Aquarium Research Institute, "Sound Reveals Giant Blue Whales Dance with the Wind to Find Food," October 5, 2022, https://www.mbari.org/blue-whale-foraging-ecology/; John P. Ryan, Kelly J. Benoit-Bird, William K. Oestreich, Paul Leary, Kevin B. Smith, Chad M. Waluk, David E. Cade, et al., "Oceanic Giants Dance to Atmospheric Rhythms: Ephemeral Wind-Driven Resource Tracking by Blue Whales," *Ecology Letters* 25, no. 11 (November 2022): 2435–2447, https://onlinelibrary.wiley.com/doi/full/10.1111/ele.14116.

30 Robert L. Pitman, John W. Durban, Trevor Joyce, Holly Fearnbach, Simone Panigada, and Giancarlo Lauriano, "Skin in the Game: Epidermal Molt as a Driver of Long-Distance Migration in Whales," *Marine Mammal Science* 36, no. 2 (2020): 565–594, https://onlinelibrary.wiley.com/doi/full/10.1111/mms.12661?af=R.

31 Robert L. Pitman, Volker B. Deecke, Christine M. Gabriele, Mridula Srinivasan, Nancy Black, Judith Denkinger, John W. Durban, et al., "Humpback Whales Interfering When Mammal-Eating Killer Whales Attack Other Species: Mobbing Behavior and Interspecific Altruism?," *Marine Mammal Science* 33, no. 1 (2017): 9, https://onlinelibrary.wiley.com/doi/full/10.1111/mms.12343.

32 See the introduction for discussion of the origins of Earth Day in 1970, following the Santa Barbara oil spill.

33 Brent B. Hughes, Kerstin Wasson, M. Tim Tinker, Susan L. Williams, Lilian P. Carswell, Katharyn E. Boyer, Michael W. Beck, et al., "Species Recovery and Recolonization of Past Habitats: Lessons for Science and Conservation from Sea Otters in Estuaries," *PeerJ* 7 (2019): e8100, https://doi.org/10.7717/peerj.8100.

34 Coco Ballantyne, "How Do Marine Mammals Avoid Freezing to Death?," *Scientific American*, May 13, 2009, https://www.scientificamerican.com/article/marine-mammals-cold-avoid-freezing-death/.

35 James A. Estes and John F. Palmisano, "Sea Otters: Their Role in Structuring Shore Communities," *Science* 185, no. 4156 (1974): 1058–1060, https://www.science.org/doi/10.1126/science.185.4156.1058; Byers, *View from Cascade Head*, 131.

36 Charles A. Simenstad, James A. Estes, and Karl W. Kenyon, "Aleuts, Sea Otters, and Alternate Stable-State Communities," *Science* 200, no. 4340 (1978): 403–411, https://www.jstor.org/stable/1746443.

37 Alastair Bland, "Kelp Forests Surge Back on Parts of the North Coast, with a Lesson about Environmental Stability," *Bay Nature*, September 13, 2021, https://baynature.org/2021/09/13/kelp-forests-surge-back-on-the-north-coast-with-a-lesson-about-stable-environments/; National Park Service, Channel Islands National Park, "Kelp Forests," updated June 10, 2019, https://www.nps.gov/chis/learn/nature/kelp-forests.htm.

38 Hughes et al., "Species Recovery and Recolonization"; Brent Hughes, "Sea Otter Conservation and Ecology in the 21st Century," American Cetacean Society, San Francisco Bay Chapter, webinar, November 17, 2020, https://www.acs-sfbay.org/events/2020/4/28/brent-hughes-sea-otter-conservation-and-ecology-in-the-21st-century.

39 Hughes et al., "Species Recovery and Recolonization."

40 US Fish and Wildlife Service, "Feasibility Assessment: Sea Otter Reintroduction to the Pacific Coast," 2022, https://www.fws.gov/sites/default/files/documents/SEA%20OTTER%20REINTRO%20REPORT%202022%20508%20compliant%20-%20FINAL%2007082022%20with%20cover.pdf.

41 Byers, *View from Cascade Head*, 39–52.

42 Jessica Morton, Ryan Freedman, Jeffrey D. Adams, Jono Wilson, Aliya Rubinstein, and Sean Hastings, "Evaluating Adherence with Voluntary Slow Speed Initiatives to Protect Endangered Whales," *Frontiers in Marine Science*, February 15, 2022, https://www.frontiersin.org/articles/10.3389/fmars.2022.833206/full.

43 Calambokidis et al., "Biologically Important Areas."

44 Morton et al., "Evaluating Adherence"; R. Cotton Rockwood, John Calambokidis, and Jaime Jahncke, "High Mortality of Blue, Humpback and Fin Whales from Modeling of Vessel Collisions on the U.S. West Coast Suggests Population Impacts and Insufficient Protection," *PLoS ONE* 13, no. 7 (2017): e0201080, https://journals.plos.org/plosone/article?id=10.1371/journal.pone.0183052.

45 Protecting Blue Whales and Blue Skies, accessed July 15, 2023, https://www.bluewhalesblueskies.org/.

46 Protecting Blue Whales and Blue Skies, *Report on the Vessel Speed Reduction Initiative Program in the Santa Barbara Channel and Bay Area Region*, 2022, https://nmschannelislands.blob.core.windows.net/channelislands-prod/media/archive/management/resource/pdf/brochure_vsr_71317.pdf.

47 NOAA National Marine Sanctuaries, "SanctSound," accessed July 15, 2023, https://sanctuaries.noaa.gov/science/monitoring/sound/.

48 Vanessa M. ZoBell, Kaitlin E. Frasier, Jessica A. Morten, Sean P. Hastings, Lindsey E. Peavey Reeves, Sean M. Wiggins, and John A. Hildebrand,

"Underwater Noise Mitigation in the Santa Barbara Channel through Incentive-Based Vessel Speed Reduction," *Nature Scientific Reports* 11 (2021): 18391, https://www.nature.com/articles/s41598-021-96506-1.

49 Megan F. McKenna, John Calambokidis, Erin M. Oleson, David W. Laist, and Jeremy A. Goldbogen, "Simultaneous Tracking of Blue Whales and Large Ships Demonstrates Limited Behavioral Responses for Avoiding Collision," *Endangered Species Research* 27 (2015): 219–232, https://doi.org/10.3354/esr00666.

50 Morton et al., "Evaluating Adherence."

51 Sean Hastings, personal communication to author, November 22, 2022.

10. The Chumash Channel and Its Islands

1 Adapted from "The Island Girls," a Chumash story told by María Solares of Santa Ynez to John P. Harrington, probably between 1914 and 1919, when Harrington worked most extensively with her, in Thomas C. Blackburn, ed., *December's Child: A Book of Chumash Oral Narratives* (Berkeley: University of California Press, 1975), 193–194.

2 Lynn H. Gamble, *The Chumash World at European Contact: Power, Trade, and Feasting among Complex Hunter-Gatherers* (Berkeley: University of California Press, 2008), 276.

3 Kristina M. Gill, Mikael Fauvelle, and Jon M. Erlandson, eds., *An Archaeology of Abundance: Reevaluating the Marginality of California's Islands* (Gainesville: University Press of Florida, 2019).

4 Kristin Hoppa and Matthew Vestuto, "Navigating Cultural Landscapes through Ethnographic Place Names" (video presentation), Western National Parks Association, April 23, 2020, https://drive.google.com/file/d/1SPX-XD5GlS5DWmBFwL9vylp5Z0SG-Yyl/view?ts=61a91eb4.

5 Robert F. Heizer and William C. Massey, "Aboriginal Navigation off the Coasts of Upper and Baja California," Smithsonian Institution, Bureau of American Ethnology Bulletin 151, Anthropological Papers, no. 39 (1942), map 5, p. 290, https://digitalcommons.csumb.edu/cgi/viewcontent.cgi?article=1006&context=hornbeck_ind_1; The Stanford Inn, "Sewn Plank Canoes from Southern California," 2022, https://catchacanoe.com/canoes-mendocinos-chumash-tomol/.

6 James Wiener, "Polynesians in California: Evidence for an Ancient Exchange?," World History.org, March 26, 2013, https://etc.worldhistory.org/interviews/polynesians-in-california-evidence-for-an-ancient-exchange/.

7 John R. Johnson, "The Trail to Fernando," *Journal of California and Great Basin Anthropology* 4, no. 1 (1982): 132–138, https://escholarship.org/uc/item/1j17p1td#main; National Park Service, Island of the Blue Dolphins, "Fernando Librado (Kitsepawit)," updated November 16, 2018, https://www.nps.gov/subjects/islandofthebluedolphins/fernando-librado.htm; Islapedia,

"Librado, Fernando," updated October 21, 2020, https://www.islapedia.com/index.php?title=LIBRADO,_Fernando.

8 Victor Golla, "A Harrington Chronology," updated March 17, 1997, https://web.archive.org/web/20080513230305/http://www.library.csi.cuny.edu/dept/history/lavender/389/golla.html; Daniel Golding, *Chasing Voices: The Story of John Peabody Harrington* (video), Hokan Media, 2020, https://www.humanarts.org/projects.php?s=chasing-voices-the-story-of-john-peabody-harrington.

9 Brian Fagan, *Before California: An Archaeologist Looks at Our Earliest Inhabitants* (Walnut Creek, CA: Altamira Press, 2003), 329.

10 Charles King, *Gods of the Upper Air: How a Circle of Renegade Anthropologists Reinvented Race, Sex, and Gender in the Twentieth Century* (New York: Doubleday, 2019).

11 Richard B. Applegate, "Chumash Placenames," *Journal of California Anthropology* 1, no. 2 (1974): 187, https://escholarship.org/uc/item/3s34f5ss.

12 National Park Service, Channel Islands National Park, "Chumash Tomol Crossing," updated April 7, 2022, https://www.nps.gov/chis/learn/historyculture/tomolcrossing.htm; Eva Pagaling, "Dark Water Journey," NOAA National Marine Sanctuaries, November 2018, https://sanctuaries.noaa.gov/news/nov18/dark-water-journey-chumash-tomol-crossing.html.

13 Alfred L. Kroeber, "The Chumash and Costanoan Languages," *University of California Publications in American Archaeology and Ethnology* 9, no. 2 (1910): 237–271, https://ia902607.us.archive.org/30/items/chumashcostanoan00kroerich/chumashcostanoan00kroerich_bw.pdf.

14 Terry L. Jones, quoted in Wiener, "Polynesians in California."

15 Here I refer to a "native speaker" as someone for whom the language was their first language, learned in the home and with at least a somewhat intact culture.

16 Braje, Erlandson, and Rick, *Islands through Time*, 39–40.

17 Ross Anderson, "The Search for America's Atlantis," *Atlantic*, September 7, 2021, https://www.theatlantic.com/magazine/archive/2021/10/prehistoric-america-atlantis/619819/; Erlandson and Braje, "From Asia to the Americas by Boat?"; Braje, Erlandson, and Rick, *Islands through Time*; Gill, Fauvelle, and Erlandson, *Archaeology of Abundance*.

18 Hoppa and Vestuto, "Navigating Cultural Landscapes."

19 Douglas J. Kennett, *The Island Chumash: Behavioral Ecology of a Maritime Society* (Berkeley: University of California Press, 2005), 5.

20 Amy E. Gusick, Jillian Maloney, Todd J. Braje, Gregory J. Retallack, Luke Johnson, Shannon Klotsko, Amira Ainis, and Jon M. Erlandson, "Soils and Terrestrial Sediments on the Seafloor: Refining Archaeological Paleoshoreline Estimates and Paleoenvironmental Reconstruction off the California Coast," *Frontiers in Earth Science: Quaternary Science, Geomorphology and Paleoenvironment* 10 (2022), https://www.frontiersin.org/articles/10.3389/feart.2022.941911/full.

21 Jon M. Erlandson, personal communication to author, July 13, 2023.

22 Jon M. Erlandson, Todd J. Braje, Kristina M. Gill, and Torben C. Rick, "Island of Hope: Archaeology, Historical Ecology, and Human Resilience on California's Tuqan Island," forthcoming in *Sustainability in Ancient Island Societies: An Archaeology of Human Resilience*, ed. Scott M. Fitzpatrick, Jon M. Erlandson, and Kristina M. Gill (Gainesville: University Press of Florida, 2024). The word "Tuqan" in the title is the Chumash name for San Miguel Island.

11. The View from Limuw

1 Wilderutopia, "Chumash Story: Seeds of Creation and the Rainbow Bridge," May 12, 2014, https://wilderutopia.com/traditions/myth/chumash-story-seeds-of-creation-and-the-rainbow-bridge/.

2 King, *Gods of the Upper Air*.

3 Jürgen Trabant, "How Relativistic Are Humboldt's 'Weltansichten'?," in *Explorations in Linguistic Relativity*, ed. Martin Pütz and Marjolyn Verspoor (Amsterdam: John Benjamins, 2000).

4 W. T. Jones, "World Views: Their Nature and Their Function," *Current Anthropology* 13, no. 1 (February 1972): 79–109, https://www.jstor.org/stable/2741076.

5 Matthew Masa Vestuto, Ventureño Chumash language scholar, video presentation for Santa Barbara Historical Museum exhibit "Sacred Art in the Age of Contact: Chumash and Latin American Traditions in Santa Barbara," 2017, https://www.youtube.com/watch?app=desktop&v=ukga7igNi7c.

6 Hoppa and Vestuto, "Navigating Cultural Landscapes."

7 Anchorage Park Foundation, "Indigenous Place Names Project," https://anchorageparkfoundation.org/programs/indigenous-placemaking/.

8 Dana Hedgpeth and Rachel Hatzipanagos, "We Are Still Here," *Washington Post*, November 19, 2021, https://www.washingtonpost.com/nation/interactive/2021/native-american-heritage-month-were-still-here/?itid=ap_danahedgpeth.

9 National Park Service, Channel Islands National Park, "Limuw: A Story of Place," excerpted from *The Chumash People: Materials for Teachers and Students* (Santa Barbara, CA: Santa Barbara Museum of Natural History, 1991), updated June 21, 2016, https://www.nps.gov/chis/learn/historyculture/limuw.htm.

10 Byers, *View from Cascade Head*.

11 Fagan, *Before California*, 329.

12 Thomas C. Blackburn, ed., *December's Child: A Book of Chumash Oral Narratives* (Berkeley: University of California Press, 1975).

13 Blackburn, *December's Child*, 63–64.

14 Blackburn, 66.

15 Blackburn, 68.

16 Blackburn, 69.

17 Blackburn, 71.

18 Blackburn, 72.

19 History.com editors, "California Missions," updated August 21, 2018, https://www.history.com/topics/religion/california-missions.

20 Erik Davis, *The Visionary State: A Journey through California's Spiritual Landscape* (San Francisco: Chronicle Books, 2006), 12, http://visionarystate.com/.

21 California Department of Parks and Recreation, "Chumash Painted Cave State Historic Park," 2023, https://www.parks.ca.gov/?page_id=602.

22 Davis, *Visionary State*, 16.

23 Vestuto, video presentation for Santa Barbara Historical Museum, 2017.

24 Leopold, *Sand County Almanac*; White, "Historical Roots"; Snyder, "Four Changes"; Eileen Crist, *Abundant Earth: Toward an Ecological Civilization* (Chicago: University of Chicago Press, 2019).

25 Bruce A. Byers, Robert M. Cunliffe, and Andrew T. Hudak, "Linking the Conservation of Culture and Nature: A Case Study of Sacred Forests in Zimbabwe," *Human Ecology* 29 (2001): 187–218. http://www.brucebyersconsulting.com/wp-content/uploads/2011/07/Zimbabwe-Sacred-Forests-Paper-in-Human-Ecology-2001.pdf.

26 Organización Indígena, Gonawindua Tayrona, *Jaba y jate: Espacios sagrados del territorio ancestral de la Sierra Nevada de Santa Marta*, October 2012, accessed September 13, 2023 (Spanish), https://gonawindwa.files.wordpress.com/2015/07/final-fjaba-y-jate1.pdf; quote translation by the author.

27 The Nature Conservancy, "The Jack and Laura Dangermond Preserve," updated November 28, 2022, https://www.nature.org/en-us/about-us/where-we-work/united-states/california/stories-in-california/dangermond-preserve/.

28 Blackburn, *December's Child*, 98.

29 Applegate, "Chumash Placenames," 200.

30 National Park Service, Channel Islands National Park, "Limuw: A Story of Place"; Julie Tumamait-Stenslie, *The Rainbow Bridge*, film by Channel Islands National Park and Community Access Partners of San Buenaventura, 2016, https://www.nps.gov/chis/learn/historyculture/limuw.htm; Wilderutopia, "Chumash Story."

31 The Santa Barbara Maritime Museum summarizes the story and attributes it to Russell A. Ruiz, a Santa Barbara historian and Chumash scholar; Jon Erlandson also attributes the story to Ruiz and wrote in a message, "It may not be as old as the stories Harrington recorded, but it's still a good and authentic story."

32 Greg Sarris, *How a Mountain Was Made: Stories* (Berkeley, CA: Heyday, 2017).

12. Coyote's Basket

1 Sarris, *How a Mountain Was Made*, 1.

2 Interpretive display information on the summit of Mount Umunhum, Sierra Azul Preserve, Midpeninsula Regional Open Space District.

3 "Sentinel of Silicon Valley: The Radar Tower at Mount Umunhum Is Saved," *Mobile Ranger* (blog), 2016, http://www.mobileranger.com/blog/sentinel-of-silicon-valley-the-radar-tower-at-mount-umunhum-is-saved/.

4 Midpeninsula Regional Open Space, "Sierra Azul Preserve," 2021, https://www.openspace.org/preserves/sierra-azul#tabs-preserve_tabs-middle-4.

5 Interpretive display information on summit of Mount Umunhum.

6 Fagan, *Before California*, 183.

7 Eleanor Castro, Amah Mutsun Tribal Band elder, "Return to Mt. Humunhum – Place of the Hummingbird," 2022, http://amahmutsun.org/land-trust-newsevents/return-to-mt-humunhum-place-of-the-hummingbird.

8 Fagan, *Before California*, 9.

9 Fagan, 131.

10 Doug Jones, "Ritual and Religion in the Ohlone Cultural Area of Central California" (master's thesis, San José State University, 2015), https://scholarworks.sjsu.edu/etd_theses/4642.

11 Fagan, *Before California*, 128.

12 Fagan, 141.

13 Fagan, 131–138.

14 Fagan, 147.

15 Fagan, 147.

16 Jones, "Ritual and Religion," 10; Fagan, *Before California*, 147.

17 Fagan, *Before California*, 147.

18 Jones, "Ritual and Religion," 12.

19 State of California Native American Heritage Commission, "Ohlone (Costanoan)-Affiliated Tribes," https://nahc.ca.gov/cp/p10ohlone/.

20 California Native American Heritage Commission, "Digital Atlas of California Native Americans," https://cnra.maps.arcgis.com/apps/View/index.html?appid=03512d83d12b4c3389281e3a0c25a78f.

21 Kent G. Lightfoot, *Indians, Missionaries, and Merchants: The Legacy of Colonial Encounters on the California Frontiers* (Berkeley: University of California Press, 2005).

22 Drew Penner, "Town's Efforts to Acknowledge Earliest Residents Fraught with Challenges," *Los Gatan*, August 10, 2022, https://losgatan.com/tribes-say-los-gatos-didnt-do-enough-to-consult-on-general-plan/; Quirina Geary, "Tamien Nation Deserves to Be Recognized as Historical Los Gatos Tribe," *Los Gatan*, December 15, 2022, https://losgatan.com/op-ed-tamien-nation-deserves-to-be-recognized-as-historical-los-gatos-tribe/.

23 Andrew Schelling, *Tracks along the Left Coast: Jaime de Angulo and Pacific Coast Culture*, (Berkeley, CA: Counterpoint, 2017); Syukhtun Editions, "Jaime de Angulo," https://www.angelfire.com/sk/syukhtun/Jaime.html.

24 Schelling, *Tracks along the Left Coast*, xxi.

25 Wendy Leeds-Hurwitz, *Rolling in Ditches with Shamans: Jaime de Angulo and the Professionalization of American Anthropology* (Lincoln: University of Nebraska Press, 2005).

26 California Revealed, Pacifica Radio Archives, "Indian Tales: Jaime de Angulo," https://californiarevealed.org/islandora/object/cavpp%3A114329.

27 Jaime de Angulo, *Indian Tales* (New York: Hill and Wang, 1953).

28 Samuel A. Barrett, "Pomo Indian Basketry," *University of California Publications in American Archaeology and Ethnology* 7, no. 3 (1905): 134, https://digitalassets.lib.berkeley.edu/anthpubs/ucb/text/ucp007-005.pdf.

29 Alfred L. Kroeber, "California Basketry and the Pomo," *American Anthropologist* 11 (1909): 234, https://anthrosource.onlinelibrary.wiley.com/doi/pdf/10.1525/aa.1909.11.2.02a00060.

30 Elizabeth Kornhauser and Shannon Vittoria, *Jules Tavernier and the Elem Pomo*, Metropolitan Museum of Art Bulletin 79, no. 1 (Summer 2021), exhibition catalog, https://www.metmuseum.org/art/metpublications/Jules_Tavernier_and_the_Elem_Pomo.

31 Jeannine Goreski, "The Ritual and Myth of Pomo Gift Baskets," Colorado State University (Fall 1988), 2, https://mountainscholar.org/bitstream/handle/10217/179382/STUF_1001_Goreski_Jeannine_Ritual.pdf.

32 Quotation from Clint McKay to accompany display of miniature baskets at the *Jules Tavernier and the Elem Pomo* exhibition; McKay speaking in video on "Pomo Basketry" for the exhibition, https://video.search.yahoo.com/search/video;_ylt=AwrErUYF3aJk8soBdDxXNyoA;_ylu=Y29sbwNiNiZjEEcG9zAzEEdnRpZAMEc2VjA3BpdnM-?p=pomo+basketry+the+met+2021+2022&fr2=piv-web&type=E210US0G91761&fr=705fxqfbjxi#id=1&vid=9e1ba3aa38bfb8a13fa20856191bfab7&action=view.

33 Sherri Smith-Ferri speaking in video on "Pomo Basketry" for the *Jules Tavernier and the Elem Pomo* exhibition.

34 Suzi Jones, ed., *Pacific Basket Makers: A Living Tradition* (Fairbanks: University of Alaska Museum, 1983), 29, quoted in Goreski, "Ritual and Myth of Pomo Gift Baskets," 4.

35 Heizer and Massey, "Aboriginal Navigation," map 5, p. 290.

36 Louis Choris, "Voyage pittoresque autour du monde," Wisconsin Historical Society, American Journeys, https://www.americanjourneys.org/aj-087/summary/; Louis Choris, *Ohlone Indians in a Tule Boat in the San Francisco Bay*, 1816, published 1822, Santa Clara University Digital Exhibits, https://dh.scu.edu/exhibits/exhibits/show/santa-clara-mission-fall-2022/item/3484#?c=0&m=0&s=0&cv=0&xywh=-3%2C0%2C4001%2C2640.

37 San Francisco Chronicle Documentaries, "Ohlone Community Members Build a Tule Boat to Mark Occupation of Alcatraz," 2019, https://www.facebook.com/SFChronicle/videos/ohlone-community-members-build-a-tule-boat-to-mark-occupation-of-alcatraz/2513740308913269/.

38 National Park Service, Golden Gate National Recreation Area, "Alcatraz

Occupation," 2017, https://www.nps.gov/goga/learn/historyculture/alcatraz-occupation.htm.

39 Monterey Bay Aquarium, "A Hand-Built Tule *Kónon*," 2022, https://www.montereybayaquarium.org/stories/boats-connect-monterey-history; Tracy Seipel, "Tule Magnificent," *Santa Clara Magazine*, November 26, 2019, https://magazine.scu.edu/magazines/winter-2019/tule-magnificent/.

40 Dino Labiste and Susan Labiste, "Tule Boat Project," Primitive Ways, 2016, http://www.primitiveways.com/Tule_boat3.html; East Bay Regional Park District, "Ohlone Youth Summit: Building a Tule Boat," 2018, https://video.search.yahoo.com/search/video?fr=mcafee&ei=UTF-8&p=East+Bay+Regional+Park+District.+%E2%80%9COhlone+Youth+Summit%3A+Building+a+Tule+Boat.%E2%80%9D&type=E211US0G0#id=1&vid=9d8f2f61d0221a1cb4635f902ac87f02&action=click.

41 Miwok Archeological Preserve of Marin, "Construct a Pomo-Style Tule Boat at MAPOM Fall 2006 Indian Skills Class," *MAPOM News*, Fall 2006, https://www.mapom.org/newsletters/Acorn_37_2.pdf; Point Reyes National Seashore Association, "Charles Kennard," 2019, https://ptreyes.org/people/charles-kennard/.

42 Malcolm Margolin, "Malcolm Margolin Discusses the Ohlone Way," https://www.youtube.com/watch?app=desktop&v=qRJK1nFQ8GA.

43 Malcolm Margolin, *The Ohlone Way: Indian Life in the San Francisco–Monterey Bay Area* (Berkeley, CA: Heyday Books, 1978), viii.

44 Margolin, *Ohlone Way*, 4.

45 Gary Snyder, *The Practice of the Wild* (San Francisco: North Point Press, 1990), 178.

46 Snyder, *Practice of the Wild*, 37, 40.

47 Snyder, 178.

48 Theodora Kroeber, *Ishi in Two Worlds: A Biography of the Last Wild Indian in North America* (Berkeley: University of California Press, 1961).

49 Ursula K. Le Guin, *Always Coming Home* (New York: Harper and Row, 1985), https://newxcommoners.files.wordpress.com/2015/07/ukl_alwayscominghome_mainreading.pdf.

50 Le Guin, *Always Coming Home*.

51 Story by the author with inspiration from María Solares, Richard Ruiz, Jaime de Angulo, and Greg Sarris.

13. Circling the Mountain

1 Snyder's translations of some of Han Shan's poems were first published in 1958 as "Cold Mountain Poems" by the *Evergreen Review*, no. 6, and republished in *Riprap and Cold Mountain Poems* in 1969 and 2009 by other publishers.

2 Gary Snyder, "The Circumambulation of Mt. Tamalpais," 17–20, and Philip Whalen, "Opening the Mountain, Tamalpais: 22:x:65," 21–22, in Matthew Davis and Michael Farrell Scott, *Opening the Mountain: Circumambulating*

Mount Tamalpais; a Ritual Walk (Emeryville, CA: Shoemaker and Hoard, 2006).

3   Davis and Scott, *Opening the Mountain*, 12.

4   Snyder, "Circumambulation of Mt. Tamalpais."

5   Robert F. Rhodes, "The *Kaihōgyō* Practice of Mt. Hiei," *Japanese Journal of Religious Studies* 14, nos. 2–3 (1987): 185–202, http://nirc.nanzan-u.ac.jp/nfile/2354.

6   Davis and Scott, *Opening the Mountain*, 10.

7   Gary Snyder, quoted in Fields, *How the Swans Came to the Lake*, 213.

8   Davis and Scott, *Opening the Mountain*, 12–14.

9   Alan Watts, *Cloud Hidden, Whereabouts Unknown: A Mountain Journal* (New York: Vintage/Random House, 1973), viii.

10 Alan Watts, *The Way of Zen* (New York: Vintage/Random House, 1957), 3.

11 Watts, *Way of Zen*, 4.

12 Watts, 5.

13 Watts, 9.

14 Watts, ix–x.

15 Mill Valley Oral History Program, "Tom Killion: An Oral History Interview Conducted by Debra Schwartz in 2016," 4, http://ppolinks.com/mvpl39241/2016.081.001_KillionTom_OralHistoryTranscript.pdf; see also Davis, *Visionary State*, 7–9.

16 Davis and Scott, *Opening the Mountain*, 129.

17 Davis and Scott, 125.

14. Wild Mind

1   Henry David Thoreau, *The Journal of Henry David Thoreau*, vol. 9, August 16, 1856–August 7, 1857, Walden Woods Project, 43, https://www.walden.org/wp-content/uploads/2016/02/Journal-9-Chapter-1.pdf.

2   Raymond Barnett, *Earth Wisdom: John Muir, Accidental Taoist, Charts Humanity's Only Future on a Changing Planet* (North Charleston, SC: CreateSpace, 2016), 14, https://www.raymondbarnett.com/earth_wisdom__john_muir__accidental_taoist__charts_humanity_s_only_future_on_a_ch_131327.htm.

3   Barnett, *Earth Wisdom*, 80.

4   John Muir, *My First Summer in the Sierra* (Boston: Houghton Mifflin, 1911), entry for September 7, 1869, https://vault.sierraclub.org/john_muir_exhibit/writings/my_first_summer_in_the_sierra/.

5   Donald Worster, *A Passion for Nature: The Life of John Muir* (Oxford: Oxford University Press, 2008).

6   Barnett, *Earth Wisdom*, xiii.

7   Muir, *My First Summer in the Sierra*, entry for September 7, 1869.

8   Bruce A. Byers, "Criticizing Muir and Misunderstanding the Foundation of American Nature Conservation," *Ecological Citizen* 5, no. 1 (2021): 65–73,

https://www.ecologicalcitizen.net/pdfs/epub-047.pdf.

9   Bruce A. Byers, "Alexander von Humboldt for Ecologists," *Ecotone: News and Views on Ecological Science* (Ecological Society of America), January 6, 2021, https://www.esa.org/esablog/2021/01/06/alexander-von-humboldt-for-ecologists/.

10 Andrea Wulf, *The Invention of Nature: Alexander von Humboldt's New World* (New York: Alfred A. Knopf, 2015), 25–38.

11 Horst Lange, "Goethe and Spinoza: A Reconsideration," *Goethe Yearbook* 18, no. 1 (2011), https://www.researchgate.net/publication/254943874_Goethe_and_Spinoza_A_Reconsideration.

12 Arne Naess, "The Shallow and the Deep, Long-Range Ecology Movement," *Inquiry* 16 (1973): 95–100, http://biophilosophy.ca/Teaching/2070papers/Naess%281973%29shallow-and-deep.pdf; Eccy de Jonge, *Spinoza and Deep Ecology: Challenging Traditional Approaches to Environmentalism* (New York: Routledge, 2004); Eccy de Jonge, "Thinking Ecologically: A Post-enlightenment Perspective," 2021, https://www.researchgate.net/publication/350789311_Thinking_Ecologically_a_post-Enlightenment_perspective.

13 Naess, "Shallow and the Deep," 95.

14 Byers, *View from Cascade Head*, 166.

15 Schelling, *Tracks along the Left Coast*, 76.

16 Schelling, 76.

17 Schelling, 287.

18 Claude Lévi-Strauss, *Wild Thought: A New Translation of* "La pensée sauvage," trans. Jeffrey Mehlman and John Leavitt (Chicago, University of Chicago Press, 2021).

19 Watts, *Way of Zen*, 11.

20 Watts, 10.

21 Watts, 3.

22 David Hinton, *China Root: Taoism, Ch'an, and Original Zen* (Boulder, CO: Shambala, 2020), 2–3.

23 Hinton, *China Root*, 1.

24 Shunryu Suzuki, *Zen Mind, Beginner's Mind* (New York: Weatherhill, 1970), 21.

25 Hinton, *China Root*, xii.

26 Gary Snyder, *Regarding Wave* (New York: New Directions, 1970), 39; note his use of essentially Maoist terms in this poem: "masses," "class," "party," "exploiter."

27 Barnett, *Earth Wisdom*, xii.

28 John Muir, *John of the Mountains: The Unpublished Journals of John Muir*, ed. Linnie Marsh Wolfe (Madison: University of Wisconsin Press, 1979), 439, https://vault.sierraclub.org/john_muir_exhibit/bibliographic_resources/book_jackets/john_of_the_mtns_wolfe_j.aspx.

29 Li Po, translated by Barnett, *Earth Wisdom*, 81.

30 John Muir, "Auroras," in *Travels in Alaska* (Boston: Houghton Mifflin, 1915),

https://vault.sierraclub.org/john_muir_exhibit/writings/travels_in_alaska/
chapter_19.aspx.

15. Reinhabiting Our Place on the Planet

1 Peter Berg and Raymond F. Dasmann, "Reinhabiting California," *Ecologist*
7, no. 10 (1977): 399–401, reprinted in Peter Berg, *The Biosphere and the
Bioregion: Essential Writings of Peter Berg*, ed. Cheryll Glotfelty and Eve
Quesnel, 35–40 (quote p. 36) (London: Routledge, 2015), http://ndl.
ethernet.edu.et/bitstream/123456789/57862/1/Cheryll%20Glotfelty%20
_2015.pdf.

2 Eric Noble, "San Francisco Diggers," FoundSF, https://www.foundsf.org/
index.php?title=San_Francisco_Diggers.

3 Elaine Woo, "Peter Berg Dies at 73: Advocate for Bioregionalism," *Los Angeles
Times*, August 21, 2011, https://www.latimes.com/local/obituaries/la-me-
peter-berg-20110821-story.html.

4 Berg and Dasmann, "Reinhabiting California," in Berg, *Biosphere and the
Bioregion*, 35–36. Jon Erlandson commented that "this is what the Island
Chumash did for millennia on the Northern Channel Islands."

5 Berg and Dasmann, "Reinhabiting California," in Berg, *Biosphere and the
Bioregion*, 40.

6 First sentence in publisher's introduction to Berg, *Biosphere and the Bioregion*.

7 World Health Organization, "Registered Vehicles Data by Country," 2022,
https://apps.who.int/gho/data/node.main.A995.

8 See definition in the Wilderness Act, 1964: "A wilderness, in contrast
with those areas where man and his works dominate the landscape, is
hereby recognized as an area where the earth and its community of life are
untrammeled by man."

9 Bruce A. Byers, "A Strategy to Stabilize the Agricultural Frontier and Conserve
Biodiversity in Malawi," 2013, http://www.brucebyersconsulting.com/a-
strategy-to-stabilize-the-agricultural-frontier-and-conserve-biodiversity-
in-malawi/; Bruce A. Byers, "Restoring Miombo Woodlands for Village
Development in Malawi," 2013, http://www.brucebyersconsulting.com/
restoring-miombo-woodlands-for-village-development-in-malawi/.

10 E. Dinerstein, C. Vynne, E. Sala, A. R. Joshi, S. Fernando, T. E. Lovejoy, J.
Mayorga, et al., "A Global Deal for Nature: Guiding Principles, Milestones,
and Targets," *Science Advances* 5, no. 4 (2019), https://www.science.org/
doi/10.1126/sciadv.aaw2869.

11 US Department of the Interior, *Conserving and Restoring America the Beautiful*,
2021, https://www.doi.gov/sites/doi.gov/files/report-conserving-and-
restoring-america-the-beautiful-2021.pdf.

12 California Natural Resources Agency, *30×30 California*, 2022, https://www.
californianature.ca.gov/pages/30x30.

13 Ian McHarg, a landscape architect from Scotland, used this phrase as the title of his 1969 book, *Design with Nature*. W. Fleming, F. Steiner, W. Whitaker, K. M'Closkey, and R. Weller, "How Ian McHarg Taught Generations to 'Design with Nature,'" June 10, 2019, Bloomberg, https://www.bloomberg.com/news/articles/2019-06-10/the-legacy-of-design-with-nature-50-years-later.

14 Crist, *Abundant Earth*, 74; in a note, Crist seems to attribute the term to Jerry Mander, https://centerforneweconomics.org/people/jerry-mander/.

15 Snyder, *Turtle Island*, 99.

16 See his poem "The Revolution in the Revolution in the Revolution," for example, in Snyder, *Regarding Wave*, 39.

17 Crist, *Abundant Earth*, 4.

18 Crist, 245.

19 *Ecological Citizen*, "About the Journal: Mission Statement," https://www.ecologicalcitizen.net/about.html.

16. Edging toward Ecotopia

1 Interview with Ernest Callenbach in Scott Timberg, "The Novel That Predicted Portland," *New York Times*, December 12, 2008, https://www.nytimes.com/2008/12/14/fashion/14ecotopia.html.

2 Rodolfo Dirzo, Gerardo Ceballos, and Paul R. Ehrlich, "Circling the Drain: The Extinction Crisis and the Future of Humanity," *Philosophical Transactions of the Royal Society B* 377 (2022): 20210378, https://doi.org/10.1098/rstb.2021.0378.

3 Daniel Ellsberg speaking to the Forty-Fifth Anniversary Gathering of the Rocky Flats Truth Force, April 29, 2023.

4 Peter Barnes, *Ours: The Case for Universal Property* (Cambridge, UK: Polity Press, 2021), https://peter-barnes.org/book/ours-the-case-for-universal-property/.

5 Robinson, *Ministry for the Future*, 41.

6 Thich Nhat Hanh, "Taking Refuge in Mother Earth," dharma talk, November 29, 2012, https://plumvillage.org/library/media/taking-refuge-in-mother-earth.

Selected Bibliography

Anderson, Ross. "The Search for America's Atlantis." *Atlantic*, September 7, 2021. https://www.theatlantic.com/magazine/archive/2021/10/prehistoric-america-atlantis/619819/.

Barnes, Peter. *Ours: The Case for Universal Property*. Cambridge, UK: Polity Press, 2021.

Barnett, Raymond. *Earth Wisdom: John Muir, Accidental Taoist, Charts Humanity's Only Future on a Changing Planet*. North Charleston, SC: CreateSpace, 2016.

Barrett, Samuel A. "Pomo Indian Basketry." *University of California Publications in American Archaeology and Ethnology* 7, no. 3 (1905): 133–163. https://digitalassets.lib.berkeley.edu/anthpubs/ucb/text/ucp007-005.pdf.

Berg, Peter. *The Biosphere and the Bioregion: Essential Writings of Peter Berg*. Edited by Cheryll Glotfelty and Eve Quesnel. London: Routledge, 2015.

Berg, Peter, and Raymond F. Dasmann. "Reinhabiting California." *Ecologist* 7, no. 10 (1977): 399–401.

Blackburn, Thomas C., ed. *December's Child: A Book of Chumash Oral Narratives*. Berkeley: University of California Press, 1975.

Boggs, Carol L., Ward B. Watt, and Paul R. Ehrlich, eds. *Butterflies: Ecology and Evolution Taking Flight*. Chicago: University of Chicago Press, 2003.

Byers, Bruce A. "Criticizing Muir and Misunderstanding the Foundation of American Nature Conservation." *Ecological Citizen* 5, no. 1 (2021): 65–73. https://www.ecologicalcitizen.net/pdfs/epub-047.pdf.

———. *The View from Cascade Head: Lessons for the Biosphere from the Oregon Coast*. Corvallis: Oregon State University Press, 2020.

Byers, Bruce A., Robert M. Cunliffe, and Andrew T. Hudak. "Linking the Conservation of Culture and Nature: A Case Study of Sacred Forests in Zimbabwe." *Human Ecology* 29 (2001): 187–218. http://www.brucebyersconsulting.com/wp-content/uploads/2011/07/Zimbabwe-Sacred-Forests-Paper-in-Human-Ecology-2001.pdf.

Callenbach, Ernest. *Ecotopia: The Notebooks and Reports of William Weston.* Berkeley, CA: Banyan Tree Books, 1975.

Cermeño, Sebastian Rodriguez, and Henry R. Wagner. "The Voyage to California of Sebastian Rodriguez Cermeño in 1595." *California Historical Society Quarterly* 3, no. 1 (1924): 3–24. https://www.jstor.org/stable/25613599?seq=1.

Chassé, Michael R. "San Francisco's Rare Endemic Manzanitas: Prospects for Recovery through Restoration." Master's thesis, San Francisco State University, 2013.

Cockerell, T. D. A. *Zoology of Colorado.* Boulder: University of Colorado, 1927.

Crist, Eileen. *Abundant Earth: Toward an Ecological Civilization.* Chicago: University of Chicago Press, 2019.

Dana, Richard Henry, Jr. *Two Years before the Mast: A Personal Narrative.* New York: Harper and Brothers, 1840.

Darwin, Charles. *The Voyage of the Beagle.* Annotated and with an introduction by Leonard Engel. Natural History Library Edition. Garden City, NY: Anchor Books, Doubleday, 1962.

Dasmann, Raymond F. *Called by the Wild: The Autobiography of a Conservationist.* With a foreword by Paul R. Ehrlich. Berkeley: University of California Press, 2002.

Davis, Erik. *The Visionary State: A Journey through California's Spiritual Landscape.* San Francisco: Chronicle Books, 2006.

Davis, Matthew, and Michael Farrell Scott. *Opening the Mountain: Circumambulating Mount Tamalpais; a Ritual Walk.* Emeryville, CA: Shoemaker and Hoard, 2006.

de Angulo, Jaime. *Indian Tales.* New York: Hill and Wang, 1953.

Diamond, Jared. *Guns, Germs, and Steel: The Fates of Human Societies.* New York: W. W. Norton, 1997.

Dirzo, Rodolfo, Gerardo Ceballos, and Paul R. Ehrlich. "Circling the Drain: The Extinction Crisis and the Future of Humanity." *Philosophical Transactions of the Royal Society B* 377 (2022): 20210378. doi:10.1098/rstb.2021.0378.

Egan, Timothy. *The Big Burn: Teddy Roosevelt and the Fire That Saved America.* Boston: Mariner Books, Houghton Mifflin Harcourt, 2010.

Ehrlich, Paul R. "The Population Biology of the Butterfly, *Euphydryas editha*. II. The Structure of the Jasper Ridge Colony." *Evolution* 19 (1965): 327–336. https://onlinelibrary.wiley.com/doi/10.1111/j.1558-5646.1965.tb01723.x.

Ehrlich, Paul R., and Peter H. Raven. "Butterflies and Plants: A Study in Coevolution." *Evolution* 18, no. 4 (1964): 586–608. https://onlinelibrary.wiley.com/doi/10.1111/j.1558-5646.1964.tb01674.x.

Erlandson, Jon M., and Todd J. Braje. "From Asia to the Americas by Boat? Paleogeography, Paleoecology, and Stemmed Points of the Northwest Pacific." *Quaternary International* 239 (2011): 28–37. https://www.sciencedirect.com/science/article/abs/pii/S104061821100125X.

Estes, James A., and John F. Palmisano. "Sea Otters: Their Role in Structuring Shore Communities." *Science* 185, no. 4156 (1974): 1058–1060. https://www.science.org/doi/10.1126/science.185.4156.1058.

Fagan, Brian. *Before California: An Archaeologist Looks at Our Earliest Inhabitants.* Walnut Creek, CA: Altamira Press, 2003.

Fields, Rick. *How the Swans Came to the Lake: A Narrative History of Buddhism in America.* Boston: Shambala, 1986.

Frost, Robert. *North of Boston.* London: David Nutt, 1914.

Gamble, Lynn H. *The Chumash World at European Contact: Power, Trade, and Feasting among Complex Hunter-Gatherers.* Berkeley: University of California Press, 2008.

Goerke, Betty. *Discovering Native People at Point Reyes.* Novato, CA: Museum of the American Indian, 2012.

Golley, Frank B. *A History of the Ecosystem Concept in Ecology: More Than the Sum of the Parts.* New Haven, CT: Yale University Press, 1993.

Griffin, L. Martin, Jr. *Saving the Marin-Sonoma Coast: The Battles for Audubon Canyon Ranch, Point Reyes, and California's Russian River.* Healdsburg, CA: Sweetwater Springs Press, 1998.

Gulliford, Andrew. "Pioneering Passion for Plants: Botanist Alice Eastwood Explored the Southwest." *Durango Herald*, March 14, 2020. https://www.durangoherald.com/articles/pioneering-passion-for-plants-botanist-alice-eastwood-explored-the-southwest/.

Gusick, Amy E., and Jon M. Erlandson. "Paleocoastal Landscapes, Marginality, and Early Human Settlement of the California Islands." In *An Archaeology of Abundance: Reevaluating the Marginality of California's Islands,* edited by Kristina M. Gill, Mikael Fauvelle, and Jon M. Erlandson, 59–97. Gainesville: University Press of Florida, 2019.

Harrison, Susan. "Long-Distance Dispersal and Colonization in the Bay Checkerspot Butterfly, *Euphydryas editha bayensis*." *Ecology* 70, no. 5

(1989): 1236–1243. https://esajournals.onlinelibrary.wiley.com/doi/abs/10.2307/1938181.

Harrison, Susan, and Brian D. Inouye. "High β Diversity in the Flora of Californian Serpentine 'Islands.'" *Biodiversity and Conservation* 11 (2002): 1869–1876. https://doi.org/10.1023/A:1020357904064.

Hart, John. *An Island in Time: 50 Years of Point Reyes National Seashore.* John Hart Books, 2012. https://johnhart.com/books/an-island-in-time/.

Hauer-Jensen, Miriam. "Analysis of Humpback Whale Songs: Applying the Traditional Method." MBARI. 2018. Accessed September 13, 2023. https://www.mbari.org/wp-content/uploads/2018/12/Hauer-Jensen.pdf.

Heizer, Robert F., and William C. Massey. "Aboriginal Navigation off the Coasts of Upper and Baja California." Smithsonian Institution, Bureau of American Ethnology Bulletin 151, Anthropological Papers no. 39 (1942). https://digitalcommons.csumb.edu/cgi/viewcontent.cgi?article=1006&context=hornbeck_ind_1.

Hinton, David. *China Root: Taoism, Ch'an, and Original Zen.* Boulder, CO: Shambala, 2020.

———. *Hunger Mountain: A Field Guide to Mind and Landscape.* Boulder, CO: Shambala, 2012.

Hoppa, Kristin, and Matthew Vestuto. "Navigating Cultural Landscapes through Ethnographic Place Names." Video presentation. Western National Parks Association, 2020. Accessed September 13, 2023. https://drive.google.com/file/d/1SPX-XD5GlS5DWmBFwL9vylp5Z0SG-Yyl/view?ts=61a91eb4.

Howard, Robert. *What Makes the Crops Rejoice: An Introduction to Gardening.* With Eric Skjei. Boston: Little, Brown, 1986.

Hughes, Brent B., Kerstin Wasson, M. Tim Tinker, Susan L. Williams, Lilian P. Carswell, Katharyn E. Boyer, Michael W. Beck, et al. "Species Recovery and Recolonization of Past Habitats: Lessons for Science and Conservation from Sea Otters in Estuaries." *PeerJ* 7 (2019): e8100. https://doi.org/10.7717/peerj.8100.

Johnson, John R. "The Trail to Fernando." *Journal of California and Great Basin Anthropology* 4, no. 1 (1982): 132–138. https://escholarship.org/uc/item/1j17p1td#main.

Johnson, Lizzie. *Paradise: One Town's Struggle to Survive an American Wildfire.* New York: Penguin Random House, 2021.

Jones, Doug. "Ritual and Religion in the Ohlone Cultural Area of Central

California." Master's thesis, San José State University, 2015. https://scholarworks.sjsu.edu/etd_theses/4642.

Jones, W. T. "World Views: Their Nature and Their Function." *Current Anthropology* 13, no. 1 (1972): 79–109. https://www.jstor.org/stable/2741076.

Kaufmann, Michael, Michael Vasey, and Tom Parker. *Field Guide to Manzanitas*. Humboldt County, CA: Backcountry Press, 2021.

Keeley, Jon E., V. Thomas Parker, and Michael C. Vasey. "Resprouting and Seeding Hypotheses: A Test of the Gap-Dependent Model Using Resprouting and Obligate Seeding Subspecies of *Arctostaphylos*." *Plant Ecology* 217, no. 6 (2016): 743–750. https://www.jstor.org/stable/24751072.

Keeley, Jon E., and Juli G. Pausas. "Evolutionary Ecology of Fire." *Annual Review of Ecology, Evolution, and Systematics* 53 (2022): 203–225. https://www.annualreviews.org/doi/abs/10.1146/annurev-ecolsys-102320-095612.

Keller, Zoe. *Limuw | Santa Cruz Island*. Graphite on paper. 2017. Accessed September 13, 2023. https://www.zoekeller.com/2017-limuw-santa-cruz-island.

Kennett, Douglas J. *The Island Chumash: Behavioral Ecology of a Maritime Society*. Berkeley: University of California Press, 2005.

Kerouac, Jack. *The Dharma Bums*. New York: Viking Press, 1958.

King, Charles. *Gods of the Upper Air: How a Circle of Renegade Anthropologists Reinvented Race, Sex, and Gender in the Twentieth Century*. New York: Doubleday, 2019.

Kornhauser, Elizabeth, and Shannon Vittoria. *Jules Tavernier and the Elem Pomo*. Metropolitan Museum of Art Bulletin 79, no. 1 (Summer 2021). Exhibition catalog. https://www.metmuseum.org/art/metpublications/Jules_Tavernier_and_the_Elem_Pomo?Tag=&title=Tavernier&author=&pt=0&tc=0&dept=0&fmt=0.

Kroeber, Alfred L. "California Basketry and the Pomo." *American Anthropologist* 11 (1909): 233–249. https://anthrosource.onlinelibrary.wiley.com/doi/pdf/10.1525/aa.1909.11.2.02a00060.

———. "The Chumash and Costanoan Languages." *University of California Publications in American Archaeology and Ethnology* 9, no. 2 (1910): 237–271. https://ia902607.us.archive.org/30/items/chumashcostanoan00kroerich/chumashcostanoan00kroerich_bw.pdf.

————. *Cultural and Natural Areas of Native North America.* Berkeley: University of California Press, 1947.

————. *Handbook of the Indians of California.* Washington, DC: Bureau of American Ethnography, 1925.

————. "The Nature of Land Holding Groups in Aboriginal California." In *Aboriginal California: Three Studies in Culture History,* ed. R. F. Heizer, 82–120. Berkeley: Archaeological Research Facility, University of California, 1966.

Kroeber, Theodora. *Ishi in Two Worlds: A Biography of the Last Wild Indian in North America.* Berkeley: University of California Press, 1961.

Langin, Kathryn M., T. Scott Sillett, W. Chris Funk, Scott A. Morrison, Michelle A. Desrosiers, and Cameron K. Ghalambor. "Islands within an Island: Repeated Adaptive Divergence in a Single Population." *Evolution* 69 (2015): 653–665. https://onlinelibrary.wiley.com/doi/10.1111/evo.12610.

Leeds-Hurwitz, Wendy. *Rolling in Ditches with Shamans: Jaime de Angulo and the Professionalization of American Anthropology.* Lincoln: University of Nebraska Press, 2005. https://www.nebraskapress.unl.edu/nebraska/9780803229549/.

Le Guin, Ursula K. *Always Coming Home.* New York: Harper and Row, 1985.

Leopold, Aldo. *The River of the Mother of God and Other Essays by Aldo Leopold.* Edited by Susan L. Flader and J. Baird Callicott. Madison: University of Wisconsin Press, 1991.

————. *A Sand County Almanac, with Essays on Conservation from Round River.* New York: Sierra Club/Ballantine Books, by arrangement with Oxford University Press, 1966.

Lévi-Strauss, Claude. *Wild Thought: A New Translation of* "La pensée sauvage." Translated by Jeffrey Mehlman and John Leavitt. Chicago: University of Chicago Press, 2021.

Margolin, Malcolm. *The Ohlone Way: Indian Life in the San Francisco–Monterey Bay Area.* Berkeley, CA: Heyday Books, 1978.

Markos, Staci E., Lena C. Hileman, Michael C. Vasey, and V. Thomas Parker. "Phylogeny of the *Arctostaphylos hookeri* Complex (Ericaceae) Based on nrDNA Data." *Madroño* 45, no. 3 (1998): 187–199.

McCullough, Dale R. *The Tule Elk: Its History, Behavior, and Ecology.* University of California Publications in Zoology 88. Berkeley: University of California Press, 1969.

McCullough, Dale R., Robert A. Garrott, Jay F. Kirkpatrick, Edward O. Plotka, Katherine O. Ralls, and E. Tom Thorne. "Report of the Scientific Advisory

Panel on Control of Tule Elk on Point Reyes National Seashore." National
   Park Service, Point Reyes National Seashore, 1993. https://www.nps.gov/
   pore/getinvolved/upload/planning_tule_elk_report_scientific_advisory_
   panel_1993.pdf.

McKenna, Megan F., John Calambokidis, Erin M. Oleson, David W. Laist, and
   Jeremy A. Goldbogen. "Simultaneous Tracking of Blue Whales and Large
   Ships Demonstrates Limited Behavioral Responses for Avoiding Collision."
   Endangered Species Research 27 (2015): 219–232. https://doi.org/10.3354/
   esr00666.

Meine, Curt. *Aldo Leopold: His Life and Work.* Madison: University of
   Wisconsin Press, 1988.

Millar, Constance I. "Bishop Pine (*Pinus muricata*) of Inland Marin County,
   California." *Madroño* 33, no. 2 (1986): 123–129. https://www.fs.usda.gov/
   research/treesearch/31878.

———. "The Californian Closed Cone Pines (Subsection *Oocarpae* Little and
   Critchfield): A Taxonomic History and Review." *Taxon* 15, no. 4 (1986):
   657–670. https://www.fs.usda.gov/research/treesearch/31879.

Millar, Constance I., Steven H. Strauss, M. Thompson Conkle, and Robert D.
   Westfall. "Allozyme Differentiation and Biosystematics of the Californian
   Closed-Cone Pines (*Pinus* subsect. *Oocarpae*)." *Systematic Botany* 13, no. 3
   (1988): 351–370. https://doi.org/10.2307/2419298.

Muhs, Daniel R. "T.D.A. Cockerell (1866–1948) of the University of
   Colorado: His Contributions to the Natural History of the California
   Islands and the Establishment of Channel Islands National Monument."
   Western North American Naturalist 78, no. 3 (2018): 247–270. https://
   bioone.org/journals/western-north-american-naturalist/volume-78/
   issue-3/064.078.0304/TDA-Cockerell-18661948-of-the-University-of-
   Colorado--His/10.3398/064.078.0304.short.

Muir, John. *John of the Mountains: The Unpublished Journals of John Muir.* Edited
   by Linnie Marsh Wolfe. 2nd ed. Madison: University of Wisconsin Press,
   1979. https://vault.sierraclub.org/john_muir_exhibit/bibliographic_
   resources/book_jackets/john_of_the_mtns_wolfe_j.aspx.

———. *My First Summer in the Sierra.* Boston: Houghton Mifflin, 1911.
   https://vault.sierraclub.org/john_muir_exhibit/writings/my_first_
   summer_in_the_sierra/.

———. "[Statement from John Muir.]" 1895. In *John Muir: A Reading
   Bibliography by Kimes, 1986 (Muir Articles 1866–1986),* entry 222. https://
   scholarlycommons.pacific.edu/jmb/222.

———. *Travels in Alaska*. Boston: Houghton Mifflin, 1915. https://vault.sierraclub.org/john_muir_exhibit/writings/travels_in_alaska/.

Naess, Arne. "The Shallow and the Deep, Long-Range Ecology Movement." *Inquiry* 16 (1973): 95–100. http://biophilosophy.ca/Teaching/2070papers/Naess%281973%29shallow-and-deep.pdf.

National Park Service, Golden Gate National Recreation Area. "Redwood Creek Watershed Assessment." 2011. Accessed September 13, 2023. http://npshistory.com/publications/goga/rcwa-2011.pdf.

New Day Films. *Rebels with A Cause: How a Battle over Land Changed the American Landscape Forever*. 2013. Video. Accessed September 13, 2023. https://www.pbs.org/video/rebels-with-a-cause-g718xi/.

O'Gallagher, Maritte J., Gregory A. Jones, Lorraine S. Parsons, Dave T. Press, Wende E. Rehlaender, Stephen Skartvedt, and Alison B. Forrestel. "2020 Woodward Fire Case Study: Examining the Role of Fire as an Ecological Process in a Coastal California Ecosystem. *Parks Stewardship Forum* 37, no. 2 (2021): 331–340. https://escholarship.org/uc/item/7hg7j88v.

Organización Indígena, Gonawindua Tayrona. *Jaba y Jate: Espacios sagrados del territorio ancestral Sierra Nevada de Santa Marta*. October 2012. Accessed September 13, 2023 (Spanish). https://gonawindwa.files.wordpress.com/2015/07/final-fjaba-y-jate1.pdf.

Parker, V. Thomas, Michael C. Vasey, and Jon E. Keeley. "Taxonomic Revisions in the Genus *Arctostaphylos* (Ericaceae)." *Madroño* 54, no. 2 (2007): 148–155. https://www.biodiversitylibrary.org/part/169007.

Pyle, Robert Michael. "Resurrection Ecology: Bring Back the Xerces Blue!" *Wild Earth* 10, no. 3 (Fall 2000): 30–34. https://www.environmentandsociety.org/mml/wild-earth-10-no-3.

Pyne, Stephen J. *Fire in America: A Cultural History of Wildland and Rural Fire*. Seattle: University of Washington Press, 1982.

Rhodes, Robert F. "The *Kaihōgyō* Practice of Mt. Hiei." *Japanese Journal of Religious Studies* 14, nos. 2–3 (1987): 185–202. http://nirc.nanzan-u.ac.jp/nfile/2354.

Rick, Torben C., Jon M. Erlandson, René L. Vellanoweth, Todd J. Braje, Paul W. Collins, Daniel A. Guthrie, and Thomas W. Stafford Jr. "Origins and Antiquity of the Island Fox (*Urocyon littoralis*) on California's Channel Islands." *Quaternary Research* 71 (2009): 93–98. https://repository.si.edu/bitstream/handle/10088/8210/Rick_et_al_2009_Origins_and_antiquity_of_the_island_fox_(Urocyon_l.pdf.

Rick, Torben C., T. Scott Sillett, Cameron K. Ghalambor, Courtney A. Hofman, Katherine Ralls, R. Scott Anderson, Christina L. Boser, et al. "Ecological Change on California's Channel Islands from the Pleistocene

to the Anthropocene." *BioScience* 64, no. 8 (2014): 680–692. https://
academic.oup.com/bioscience/article/64/8/680/2754245.

Robinson, Kim Stanley. *The Ministry for the Future: A Novel.* New York: Orbit,
2020.

Rockwood, R. Cotton, John Calambokidis, and Jaime Jahncke. "High Mortality
of Blue, Humpback and Fin Whales from Modeling of Vessel Collisions
on the U.S. West Coast Suggests Population Impacts and Insufficient
Protection." *PLoS ONE* 13, no. 7 (2017): e0201080. https://journals.plos.
org/plosone/article?id=10.1371/journal.pone.0183052.

Ryan, John P., Kelly J. Benoit-Bird, William K. Oestreich, Paul Leary, Kevin
B. Smith, Chad M. Waluk, David E. Cade, et al. "Oceanic Giants Dance to
Atmospheric Rhythms: Ephemeral Wind-Driven Resource Tracking by
Blue Whales." *Ecology Letters,* November 2022. https://onlinelibrary.wiley.
com/doi/full/10.1111/ele.14116.

Sarris, Greg. *How a Mountain Was Made: Stories.* Berkeley, CA: Heyday, 2017.

Schelling, Andrew. *Tracks along the Left Coast: Jaime de Angulo and Pacific Coast
Culture.* Berkeley, CA: Counterpoint, 2017.

Schoenherr, Alan A., C. Robert Feldmeth, and Michael J. Emerson. *Natural
History of the Islands of California.* Berkeley: University of California Press,
1999.

Sears, Paul B. "Ecology—a Subversive Subject." *BioScience* 14, no. 7
(1964): 11–13. https://academic.oup.com/bioscience/article-
abstract/14/7/11/237620.

Simenstad, Charles A., James A. Estes, and Karl W. Kenyon. "Aleuts, Sea
Otters, and Alternate Stable-State Communities." *Science* 200, no. 4340
(1978): 403–411. https://www.jstor.org/stable/1746443.

Snyder, Gary. *The Practice of the Wild.* San Francisco: North Point Press, 1990.

———. *Regarding Wave.* New York: New Directions, 1970.

———. *Turtle Island.* New York: New Directions, 1974.

Sochaczewski, Paul Spencer. *An Inordinate Fondness for Beetles: Campfire
Conversations with Alfred Russel Wallace on People and Nature Based on
Common Travel in the Malay Archipelago.* Singapore: Editions Didiet Millet,
2012.

Suzuki, Shunryu. *Zen Mind, Beginner's Mind.* New York: Weatherhill, 1970.

Thich Nhat Hanh. "New Heart Sutra Translation by Thich Nhat Hanh."
Plum Village, 2014. Accessed September 13, 2023. https://plumvillage.
org/about/thich-nhat-hanh/letters/thich-nhat-hanh-new-heart-sutra-
translation/.

————. *The Other Shore: A New Translation of the Heart Sutra with Commentaries*. Berkeley, CA: Parallax Press, 2017.

Thoreau, Henry David. *The Journal of Henry David Thoreau*. Vol. 9, August 16, 1856–August 7, 1857. Walden Woods Project. Accessed September 13, 2023. https://www.walden.org/wp-content/uploads/2016/02/Journal-9-Chapter-1.pdf.

Toogood, Anna Cox. "Historic Resource Study: A Civil History of the Golden Gate National Recreation Area and Point Reyes National Seashore." Vol. 1. National Park Service, 1980. Accessed September 13, 2023. http://npshistory.com/publications/goga/hrs-civil-history-v1.pdf.

UNESCO. *Statutory Framework of the World Network of Biosphere Reserves*. 2020. Accessed September 13, 2023. https://unesdoc.unesco.org/ark:/48223/pf0000373378.

————. *Use and Conservation of the Biosphere*. Proceedings of the 1968 Biosphere Conference, Paris, France. 1970. https://unesdoc.unesco.org/ark:/48223/pf0000067785.

Untold Stories. "Alice Eastwood: Pioneering Botanist, Explorer and Naturalist, Lifelong Lover of Flowers and Plants, California Academy of Sciences Curator of Botany." 2019. Accessed September 13, 2023. https://untoldstories.net/1879/01/plant-collector-extraordinaire-alice-eastwood/.

US Congress. *The Wilderness Act*. Public Law 88-577 (16 U.S.C. 1131–1136). 88th Cong., 2nd Sess. September 3, 1964. https://www.fs.usda.gov/Internet/FSE_DOCUMENTS/fseprd645666.pdf.

Wahlert, Gregory A., V. Thomas Parker, and Michael Vasey, "A Phylogeny of *Arctostaphylos* (Ericaceae) Inferred from Nuclear Ribosomal ITS Sequences," *Journal of the Botanical Research Institute of Texas* 3, no. 2 (2009): 674.

Watts, Alan. *Cloud Hidden, Whereabouts Unknown: A Mountain Journal*. New York: Vintage/Random House, 1973.

————. *The Way of Zen*. New York: Vintage/Random House, 1957.

White, Lynn. "The Historical Roots of Our Ecological Crisis." *Science* 155 (1967): 1203–1207. https://www.cmu.ca/faculty/gmatties/lynnwhiterootsofcrisis.pdf.

Whitehead, Kevin. *Why Jazz? A Concise Guide*. New York: Oxford University Press, 2011.

Wiener, James. "Polynesians in California: Evidence for an Ancient Exchange?" World History.org, March 26, 2013. https://etc.worldhistory.org/interviews/polynesians-in-california-evidence-for-an-ancient-exchange/.

Wildertopia. "Chumash Story: Seeds of Creation and the Rainbow Bridge."
    May 12, 2014. https://www.wilderutopia.com/traditions/myth/chumash-
    story-seeds-of-creation-and-the-rainbow-bridge/.

Worster, Donald. *A Passion for Nature: The Life of John Muir*. Oxford: Oxford
    University Press, 2008.

Wulf, Andrea. *The Invention of Nature: Alexander von Humboldt's New World*.
    New York: Alfred A. Knopf, 2015.

Zhang, Jing, Qian Cong, Jinhui Shen, Paul A. Opler, and Nick V. Grishin.
    "Genomics of a Complete Butterfly Continent." 2019. https://www.biorxiv.
    org/content/biorxiv/early/2019/11/04/829887.full.pdf.

Index